The J. Golden Kimball Stories

The
J. Golden Kimball
Stories

Eric A. Eliason

University of Illinois Press

Urbana and Chicago

Library of Congress Cataloging-in-Publication Data
Eliason, Eric A. (Eric Alden), 1967–
The J. Golden Kimball stories / Eric A. Eliason.
p.   cm.
Includes bibliographical references (p.) and index.
ISBN 978-0-252-03196-0 (cloth : alk. paper)
ISBN 978-0-252-07438-7 (pbk. : alk. paper)
  1. Kimball, Jonathan Golden, 1853–1938.
I. Title.
BX8695.K52E45   2007
289.3092—dc22   [B]   2007005068

Contents

Preface

This is a serious book about a humorous subject—the jokes, stories, and legends Mormons tell about their most beloved folk hero, the cowboy-preacher J. Golden Kimball (1853–1938). In addition to providing an as-complete-as-possible collection of J. Golden Kimball stories, the main purpose of this book is to take an in-depth look at the unlikely but enduringly appropriate combination of humor and religiosity present in the oral traditions about him and to place him and his stories in the historical and cultural contexts relevant to understanding his significance.

Some readers may feel that humor and religion suffer equally from close analysis in that the deeper one peers into their inner social and psychological mechanisms, the more the divine spark in both seems to recede. "I would rather enjoy what's on the movie screen than watch the projector run thank you very much," such a reader might suggest. Those who feel this way are more than welcome to skip right ahead past the Preface, Introduction, and chapter introductions to the collected stories themselves. But for those who feel that historical context and a deeper understanding of the workings of humor and religion only expand one's appreciation, read on! Even for those who choose to read the analytical part of this book it may be worthwhile to dabble some in the stories first to get a feel for what J. Golden Kimball's legacy is about.

Others may feel that in taking both religion and humor seriously, this book seeks a hopelessly divided audience. Common wisdom holds that those who consider religion to be important often discount humor, whereas those who take humor seriously discount religion. I hope my discussion of Elder Kimball's enduring popularity among devout Latter-day Saints and their neighbors as well as among professional folklorists will help put such notions to rest. Many coming to this book will do so knowing a lot about Mormonism and little of professional folklore scholarship and humor studies. Or, they might know much about folklore scholarship and little about Mormonism. With that in mind, two backgrounds for two different sets of readers need to be provided.

Folklore for the Student of Mormonism

J. Golden Kimball stories form a significant part of the larger system of Mormon folklore.[1] Because "folklore" has a popular meaning with a pejorative undertone, it is important to explain what academic folklorists mean when we employ the term. Folklore does not mean old-fashioned or spurious stories but rather traditional, meaningful, creative expression usually passed on orally in face-to-face situations within specific cultural groups.[2] The study of folklore can be broken into two parts based on the two parts of the word. The "folk" (or "folk group") part of folklore can be based on criteria as diverse as ethnicity, class, region, nationality, age group, occupation, or religion. People in today's complex world usually participate in several such overlapping folk communities simultaneously.

The "lore" part of folklore falls into several expressive categories. It can be *oral*, for example, legends, jokes, epics, sermons, rumors, folktales, proverbs, riddles, or occupational jargons. It can be *customary* and range in complexity from simple forms such as naming traditions, greeting and leave-taking formalities, children's counting-out rhymes, and workplace initiations to more complex, such as courtship patterns, wedding and burial practices, and community festivals. Or, lore can be *material* and take many forms, including quilts, engraved saddles and other folk art, grave-stone markings, and low-rider car customization and airbrushing. Usually these genres are interrelated. There are, for example, stories about customs, and folk art is often required for certain rituals.

In an overarching but sometimes more difficult to observe category, folklorists study the systems of *belief* held by a particular group. That aspect of folklore is particularly significant for religious folk groups such as Latter-day Saints. Although beliefs exist at one level in the heads and hearts of individual believers they also manifest in concrete social reality through other kinds of lore. This lore, in turn, instills and maintains the shape and substance of belief. Proverbs, for example, express notions of common-sense wisdom, and marriages are enactments of the belief that certain rituals must take place for relationships to be right in the eyes of God. Likewise, the emotions and drama of participation in such events can evoke and reinforce beliefs.

As is commonly the practice at married student housing complexes near Brigham Young University, swinging a wedding ring over a pregnant woman's wrist or belly suggests the participants believe, or at least have fun pretending to believe, that the ring will swing back and forth for a boy or in a circle for a girl.[3] Wearing a yarmulke, a rabbit's foot, a scapular, or, in the case of Mormon youth, a CTR (choose the right) ring all reference certain beliefs about how the world operates and who people want to be. In the case of the ring-swinging married students there is a shared community excitement about childbirth and motherhood in a culture where those are highly valued ideals. Likewise, seemingly trivial jokes and stories about J. Golden Kimball reveal, and in turn shape, the attitudes and beliefs of contemporary Mormons toward manners, wit, intimacy, faith, God, each other, and the larger world. All of which is far from trivial.

Whether or not something is folklore has more to do with the mode of its cultural transmission and its relationship to the particular groups in which it circulates than with the veracity, content, or composition of the item itself. Although many stories attributed to "Uncle Golden" in this collection are not traceable to him, others match his recorded words fairly well. Most seem in keeping with his style, personality, and personal history. Just because something is folklore does not mean it is not true, even in the narrow historical sense of truth. Conversely, as I often tell students at Brigham Young University, just because something is true or important does not mean it is not also folklore. People's deepest concerns, fears, hopes, aspirations, historical understandings, and beliefs are expressed through modes of folkloric transmission. This is the important stuff of life.

Despite the rise of literacy and other even more sophisticated communications technologies, the preponderance of human storytelling and communication is still oral and face-to-face. Even when it is not, media such as television, the Internet, and e-mail, each in its own way, try to simulate or depict aspects of face-to-face interaction. Such interaction seems to be an inherent need among humans. Unlike the images conjured by the popular usage of the term, folklore, properly understood, is not an idle pastime, and it is far from peripheral to human experience. Rather, folklore is the social glue that holds us together in defining cultural groups.

Because of this importance, folklorists cannot rely on slipshod methods for collecting folklore. Their most useful contributions come from ethnographic research based on long-term participant observation gathered by living in the community they study, participating in the rhythms of people's lives, and carefully observing and recording what people do and say. The essence of good ethnography is to analyze and present cultures in such a way that the ethnographer's description would be persuasive, enlightening, and perceived as accurate to most savvy cultural insiders as well as informed outsiders.[4] This is what I strive for in this book. As a Mormon by birth and conviction and a professional academic folklorist by vocation, I draw on a lifetime of experience with the J. Golden Kimball stories circulating around me and often through me.

Mormonism for the Student of Folklore

The religion of Elder J. Golden Kimball, and those who tell stories about him, has long been recognized by historians and folklorists as being an "American original" of peculiar interest. The particularly strong sense of coherent religious community, as well as the sense of being different from others, that Latter-day Saints share emerge from several factors.

The crux of Mormonism's religious claims and most of the revolutionary implications of its theology are encapsulated in Latter-day Saints' literal acceptance of the narrative reality of one event. Any treatment of the Mormon experience from a historical or theological point of view rightly begins with what Mormons call The First Vision.

In the spring of 1820 a spiritually yearning boy in rural western New York read in the Bible's Book of James, "If any of you lack wisdom, let him ask of God, that giveth to all [men] liberally, and upbraideth not; and it shall be given him" (James 1:5, KJV). Following that admonition, the boy went into the woods to pray for religious guidance. To his astonishment, the result of his personal appeal was for him to be thrust into the center stage of world religious history. God the Father and Jesus Christ appeared to him in the flesh in their actual form as two distinct physical persons. They appointed the boy as the prophet through whom religion by revelation would be restored to the earth for the first time since the death of Jesus' original apostles. Through him the world would be prepared for the second coming of Christ and the biblically promised "restoration of all things."[5]

That boy, Joseph Smith, who became the man whose name is synonymous with the beginnings of Mormonism, had many subsequent extraordinary experiences pertaining to his new understanding of his role in history. In 1830 he published the Book of Mormon as a companion book of scripture to the Bible. By Joseph's own account, he received the book in the form of Golden Plates from an angel named Moroni. During his life as a mortal man, Moroni had compiled the volume with his father, Mormon. Their book contained a sacred history of extinct pre-Colombian American Christian people to which Mormon and Moroni belonged. The young Joseph explained that he translated the inscriptions on the Golden Plates not through any special scholarly training but by the "gift and power of God." The book that bears the prophet Mormon's name was for many years much better known than the First Vision, and thus it became the attention-getting lightning rod that earned Joseph Smith's followers the nickname "Mormons." During the translation process the young prophet experienced ensuing visitations by an angelic John the Baptist and the apostles Peter, James, and John, who gave Smith and his associates the priesthood authority they needed to implement the promised restoration and to establish the Church of Jesus Christ of Latter-day Saints.

These accounts have come to be remembered by Mormons today as the foundational sacred episodes of their religious history. They also established the Mormon doctrinal ideas that most clearly set them apart from traditional Christianity—that humans, angels, and gods are of essentially the same class, or species, of physical beings but in different stages of development.

Whether one regards this explosion of other-worldly contact as concrete and factual occurrences (as believing Latter-day Saints do), as delusions or fabrications (as Mormonism's detractors do), or as complex subjective psychological experiences (as some middle-of-the-road scholars do), it remains that these accounts and Joseph Smith's further revelations form the doctrinal and organizational nucleus of what many historians consider the most innovative and successful religion to emerge during the spiritual ferment of antebellum America. Today, as the dominant religious culture of the Intermountain West, and with explosive growth that has pushed worldwide church membership past twelve million, the Church of Jesus Christ of Latter-day Saints is increasingly regarded by scholars as the first American-born world religion.[6]

Other identity-forming factors include adherence to strict moral and dietary laws; a common participation in a life-cycle–spanning set of covenantal religious rites, including temple worship; participation in the functioning of lay-run congregations (or "wards" in Mormon parlance) that require much of their time; the belief that their church literally constitutes the Kingdom of God on Earth; and a popular historical consciousness of systematic persecution, forced migration, isolated desert colonization in the American West, and ongoing and increasing world missionization. These factors have helped foster in Mormons a sense that the "Gentile" world eyes them with a mixture of bafflement, begrudging respect, and suspicion.[7] For many Mormons, a sense of identity and peoplehood can be so strong and historically rooted that some have argued that it is essentially an ethnic as well as a religious identity.[8]

The Mormon collective experience before and during Kimball's life would have had a profound influence on him and should influence how readers make sense of the stories about him. The constant threat of persecution forms an over-arching theme of Mormon history from the movement's inception to the mid-twentieth century. This "Mormon Conflict" was arguably the most protracted and intense persecution against a religious group in American history.[9]

Mormons' theological uniqueness, exclusive attempts at communitarian living, and friendliness toward free blacks in the South and Indians in the West incited hostility in areas into which Latter-day Saints moved en masse. Vigilantes destroyed and commandeered millions of dollars worth of Mormon property in Missouri and Illinois, where they beat and brutalized thousands of Latter-day Saints out of their homes in the 1830s and 1840s. While Mormons generally responded with disciplined nonviolence, some attempted occasional armed resistance that only increased brutality against them. On October 27, 1838, Missouri Governor Lilburn S. Boggs issued an extermination order urging the killing of Mormons slow to leave the state. Three days later the Missouri militia murdered eighteen unarmed men and a boy at the village of Haun's Mill.[10] In the summer of 1844, anti-Mormons murdered Joseph Smith near Nauvoo, Illinois, the city he established as a refuge from persecution.

Joseph Smith's successor, Brigham Young, led his people to the temporary safety of the Great Salt Lake Valley. There the church officially announced that some leaders emulated the polygamous family arrangements of biblical patriarchs. In 1856 the new Republican Party's first platform branded polygamy and slavery as "twin relics of barbarism."[11] Ironically, the same reformist zeal that emancipated the slaves would systematically strip away the civil rights of Mormon men and women. Sensationalistic literary "exposés" evoked popular support for an anti-Mormon crusade through outlandish fabrications portraying Mormon men as bloodthirsty, politically ruthless conspirators.[12] As with stereotypes of black men as sexual predators of white women or of Native Americans as "Indian givers," nineteenth-century anti-Mormon stereotypes inverted actual power relationships and attempted to obscure moral culpability.

In addition to Victorian public repugnance toward any sexual activity outside monogamous heterosexual marriage, historians recognize several motivations for late-nineteenth-century anti-Mormonism. Mormondom's centrally directed, cooperative economy clashed with the freewheeling capitalism of the Gilded Age. Any hint of theocratic government within their borders worried most Americans—even if, as in Utah, such a system protected others' religious freedom and was a clear expression of popular sovereignty. Nativists decried the immigration of thousands of yearly converts who were ostensibly never properly "Americanized" but "Mormonized" instead. Political attention paid to the "Mormon Question" distracted national attention from the more divisive slavery issue. Perhaps most significant, the expansive "Mormon Empire" of colonization extending from Utah well into the present-day boundaries of Idaho, Nevada, Arizona, Wyoming, New Mexico, and Colorado stood along with Indian nations as a geographic impediment to Manifest Destiny that needed to be swept aside or forcibly assimilated.

Suspecting Mormon reluctance to accept his Utah territorial appointees, President Buchanan dispatched a full third of the U.S. Army to quell a "Mormon rebellion" in 1857. The "Mormon War" that followed remained bloodless only due to Brigham Young's willingness to step down as governor and because of his insistence that his followers employ strictly nonlethal resistance to the invasion. In the one tragic breach of President Young's nonlethal resistance policy, an isolated and frightened group of Indians and Mormons wiped out an immigrant train whose rowdier members boasted of murdering Joseph Smith and threatened to raise another anti-Mormon army upon reaching California.

After the Civil War, the U.S. Army established three new garrisons in Utah to keep the Mormons in check. In 1879 the church managed to get the case of George Reynolds, a polygamist, before the Supreme Court to test the constitutionality of antipolygamy legislation. The Court made a distinction between religious belief and practice and ruled against polygamous families' right to live according to their convictions.

Tough legislation followed *Reynolds v. United States*, making "co-habitation" a felony and denying polygamists the right to vote, hold office, or sit on a jury. New laws provided for the disincorporation of the church and seizure of all its assets in excess of $50,000 dollars. (During this time of cooperative economic arrangements among Mormons, much "Church property" was the farms and buildings that constituted many families' livelihoods.)

The federally appointed "Utah Commission" sent marshals out across the territory, throwing 1,035 men in jail. While many plural families fled to Mexico and Canada, Utah became essentially a police state hostile to 70 percent of the territory's more than two hundred thousand inhabitants. Mormons resisted this onslaught with legal appeals and developed an elaborate "underground" for shuttling fugitives among various safe houses.

In early 1890 Congress neared certain passage of a bill disenfranchising all Latter-day Saints regardless of their marriage arrangements. On September 25, the Mormon prophet Wilford Woodruff felt inspired that the Lord no longer required this sacrifice from his people and publicly advised Latter-day Saints to cease "contracting any marriage forbidden by the laws of the land." In 1896, Utah finally achieved statehood.

While Mormon missionaries in the South were tarred and feathered and occasionally lynched until past the turn of the century, by World War II violent persecution had ceased and the Mormon Question disappeared from national political debates.

Today, few Mormons and fewer Americans remember the magnitude of Mormon's past social and geographic marginalization in American society, but those factors were central issues at the time the J. Golden Kimball story cycle emerged.[13] Vestiges of past traumas still live on in the Mormon psyche, not exactly in a cultural inferiority complex but in a sense that others see the religion Mormons regard as wholesome and good as somehow dangerous and threatening. Hints of an anxiety about public image show up in Kimball's stories in direct and indirect ways.

Mormons and J. Golden Kimball in Folklore Scholarship

Considering the singular character of Latter-day Saint culture, it should perhaps not be surprising that the study of Mormons as a folk group has played an important part in American folklore studies and that Mormon folklore and Mormon folklorists have significantly shaped the field of folklore.[14] That J. Golden Kimball stories represent an important part of the Mormon experience is evident in the fact that he appears in virtually every landmark work of Mormon folklore scholarship.

In 1942 the western literary great Wallace Stegner devoted considerable ink to Mormon folklore in general and half a chapter to J. Golden Kimball in particular in *Mormon Country*—his lyrical local-color book about what was then a little-visited American regional backwater. Stegner went on to win the Pulitzer Prize for his novel *Angle of Repose* in 1971, but his treatment of J. Golden Kimball inspired the founders of Mormon folklore, Austin and

Alta Fife, to include a chapter on Kimball in *Saints of Sage and Saddle* (1956). It was the first comprehensive book-length treatment of Mormon folklore. The Fifes call Elder Kimball "the most beloved preacher of the first four decades of our century."[15] Richard Dorson—the dean of midcentury folklore studies—discovered "Uncle Golden" by reading the Fifes and listening to recorded performances of Kimball's stories by folklorist Hector Lee. Dorson included the stories in the Mormon chapters of both his best-selling *American Folklore* (1959) and his collection of American regional folklore texts, *Buying the Wind* (1964). In the latter work he touted this "cowboy who became a revered Mormon preacher and elder" as "part of living Mormon tradition."[16]

In 1974 a Brigham Young University English professor, Thomas E. Cheney, published the first book about Kimball as a folkloric figure: *The Golden Legacy: A Folk History of J. Golden Kimball*. Unfortunately, Cheney did not always distinguish among transcriptions of orally circulating stories, his own tellings, and sermon and book excerpts. In the 1970s and 1980s, the work of William A. Wilson, a Mormon folklorist and Dorson protégé, occasionally touched on Kimball. In his often-reprinted essay "The Paradox of Mormon Folklore" Wilson observed that "Mormons still tell more anecdotes about him [Kimball] than about any other figure in Church history." Wilson was also the first to identify J. Golden Kimball as Mormondom's major trickster figure.[17]

In 1999 J. Golden Kimball's nephew, Stan Kimball, produced a locally published book sold in supermarkets, *Mormonism's Colorful Cowboy: J. Golden Kimball Stories*, consisting mostly of written versions of the stories Stan Kimball himself likes to tell. Several other popular books and tapes about J. Golden Kimball have appeared for Mormon audiences over the years and will be examined more fully in the Introduction. This volume, however, is the first work of folklore scholarship to focus on his oral narrative cycle as distinct from sermons he delivered.

I hope that scholars as well as a popular audience in search of a good laugh will find value in this work. Most stories collected here can be appreciated by anyone, on one level at least, as humorous insights into the universal problems inherent in the human condition. It is often helpful, however, and sometimes critical, to unpack the layers of thick insider context and terminology that make the stories uniquely Mormon. In this sense Mormon humor is akin to Ozarks humor as described by Vance Randolf: "The best Ozark humor, it seems to me, is of this esoteric type. Our finest stories depend for their effect upon intimate experience, local idiom, and certain fantastic traditions held in common."[18]

To assist readers with the more esoteric stories in the volume I have provided glosses and explanations as necessary in chapter introductions and endnotes. One gloss is already in order. "Elder" plus a last name is the way in which Mormons refer to male missionaries and to members of the presiding hierarchy of church leaders collectively known as "General Authorities" or "the brethren." J. Golden is often referred to as "Elder Kimball" because he was one of seven presidents of the First Quorum of the Seventy, the third-highest governing body of the Church of Jesus Christ of Latter-day Saints.[19]

So, on we go to meet Elder Kimball.

Acknowledgments

Thanks are due to the archivists, folklorists, and folklore students at Brigham Young University and Utah State University whose work in collecting J. Golden Kimball stories made this project possible. Thomas E. Cheney's collection proved an invaluable reference source, as did the William A. Wilson Folklore Archive at Brigham Young University and Austin and Alta Fife's Mormon Collection, edited by Alta Fife in 1989 and housed at the Utah State University Archive in Logan (FMC: 1: 245–54, 259, 284, 300, 314, 315, 335, 336, 386, 396–98, 401, 402, 425, 429, 436, 437, 456, 457, 526, 527, 578, 590, 632, 633, 636, 637, 668, 796, 943, 985, 986, 989). Brigham Young University's collection of J. Golden Kimball stories can be found in the William A. Wilson Folklore Archive under the index numbers L 4.11.2.1.1 through L 4.11.2.49.1 and in the student projects "J. Golden Kimball: Mormon Folk Hero" by Marguerite Sadler (focused field project index number BYUFA: Collection 621) and "J. Golden Kimball Folktales" by Rebecca Kent (focused field project index number BYUFA: Collection 1640). Cheney's J. Golden Kimball collections can be found in his *The Golden Legacy: A Folk History of J. Golden Kimball.*

The Joseph Fielding Smith Institute for Latter-day Saint History generously made it possible for the English department to give me time off from teaching to complete this project, and the Religious Studies Center at Brigham Young University also provided support.

Folklore archivists Kristi Bell, Randy Williams, and Mary Aldred were especially helpful in assembling this collection, as were J. Golden Kimball aficionados Kent Larsen, Dennis "C" Davis, and especially my father-in-law, David E. Smith. Jody Waits scanned and Rebecca Kent formatted most of the stories from their original written forms into something usable by the publisher. My extraordinarily diligent research assistant provided by the BYU Department of English, Angie Margetts, tracked down and checked sources and worked with archives finalizing permissions. Geneil Johnson of the BYU Humanities Publication Center expertly guided the manuscript through the prepublication editing process. Richard H. Cracroft, David Allred, Jill Terry Rudy, William A. Wilson, Dean Hughes, Doris Dant,

Steven C. Walker, and my wife, Stephanie Eliason, all provided invaluable critical readings and scholarly guidance.

I am thankful for the work of my editors at the University of Illinois Press, Judy McCulloh and Mary Giles, and the especially useful suggestions of this book's peer reviewers, Jim Leary and others who have remained anonymous. Of course, the responsibility for any faults or errors in this work is mine alone.

The J. Golden Kimball Stories

J. Golden Kimball was examining a hat in ZCMI [department store].
When a clerk approached him, he asked the price.

The clerk replied, "Ten dollars," whereupon Brother Kimball started
to look inside the hat, pulling back the band. The clerk, confused by the
close inspection, inquired, "What are you looking for?"

Without looking up, Brother Kimball responded, "Holes."

"Holes?" questioned the now confused clerk.

"Yes," said Kimball, "for the ears of the jackass who would pay $10 for
this hat."

—Recorded by a Brigham Young University folklore student from a
Mormon rancher, Coalville, Utah, 1977

Introduction

With his gaunt figure, magpie voice, and fiery vigor, Elder J. Golden Kimball embodied the down-to-earth humor he so un-self-consciously provided his people. He was loved by all Latter-day Saints; even religiously disinterested "jack-Mormon" farmers and wayward youths emptied fields and pool halls to gather around the radio to hear his sermons broadcast from Temple Square during the semiannual General Conferences of the Church of Jesus Christ of Latter-day Saints. As he toured the Mormon settlements of the West, "Uncle Golden," as people of no particular relation to him often called him, charmed congregations with frank talk and refreshing, if slightly irreverent, quips occasionally peppered with his famous salty language. In particular, his not-necessarily-theological evocations of the place where unrepentant souls go after death, and the spiritual condition that causes them to go there, made him an unlikely and unique sort of leader for a people who are today generally known for their conscientious efforts to avoid such improprieties.

J. Golden's probing insight into the human condition as well as his love of God and fellow human beings were rarely obscured by overzealous attention to decorum. That earned him a much-revered place in the collective memory of Mormons. On J. Golden's eightieth birthday the apostle John Henry Evans may have been the first—but certainly not the last—to call Elder Kimball "our Mark Twain and Will Rogers."[1] More than sixty years after Elder Kimball's death, a lively oral narrative cycle of legends, jokes, and folktales continues to revolve around the man and perpetuates the beloved preacher's place in the memory of contemporary Latter-day Saints. This book presents and analyzes a comprehensive selection of stories about Uncle Golden lovingly maintained in Mormon oral tradition. But to understand the stories, it helps to know a little more of the life of the man, his world, and the dynamics of folklore.

A Biographical Sketch

Jonathan Golden Kimball was born in Salt Lake City on June 26, 1853, to Christeen Golden and Heber C. Kimball, and was one of the first of a new generation of Mormons to be born in the Utah Territory after the great trek west from Nauvoo, Illinois.[2] (Being given his mother's maiden name for his middle name was and is common in Latter-day Saint naming ways, as is the use of first or middle initials for Mormons who rise to high church office.)[3] J. Golden's father, along with Brigham Young, was one of only two of the original apostles of the Church of Jesus Christ of Latter-day Saints to never waver from total loyalty to Joseph Smith, a fact surely impressed upon young Golden as he was growing up.

After Joseph Smith's martyrdom, Brigham Young selected the little-educated and unpolished but energetic and emotive Heber C. Kimball to be his first counselor in the First Presidency—the highest governing body of the church. J. Golden was one of sixty-five children born to this prominent man, who, with forty-three wives, may have been the most married Mormon polygamist in history.[4] According to tradition, J. Golden would say that "he was the son of Heber C. Kimball—one of seventeen—and not a bastard among them."[5]

When Heber C. Kimball died, his son was only fifteen and the eldest of his mother's three children. To earn money for the family, young Golden left home to take up work as a mule driver. His mother took in boarders and sewed for ZCMI, Zion's Cooperative Mercantile Institution, a legacy of Brigham Young's communitarian efforts and the nation's first department store.[6] These efforts, however, did not prevent the family from falling on hard times.[7]

J. Golden blamed the mule-skinner's work environment for his habit of cussing. Mules, he claimed, won't move if you speak to them in ordinary English. They understand only the most powerfully colorful language. "I assure you my cussing now is only the pitiful remnant of a far larger vocabulary," goes one version of the justification Elder Kimball is said to have used later in life. In 1876 J. Golden and his brother Elias began ranching in Rich County, Utah. Perhaps while ranching, if not before, J. Golden began another of his infamous bad habits, drinking coffee, the cowboy's ambrosia. During the winters he helped cut timber used to build the church's temple in Logan and eventually rose to be superintendent of a saw mill.

During the summer of 1881, J. Golden experienced a pivotal moment that would eventually veer him away from a life of manual labor and neglect of religion. The German-born Mormon convert and educator Karl G. Maeser came to Rich County to speak of the importance of learning and faith. Maeser's speech electrified J. Golden. Experiencing a spiritual and intellectual awakening, he left to attend Maeser's Brigham Young Academy (later Brigham Young University) in Provo, Utah.

In 1883 he received a religious calling that interrupted his education. In the Latter-day Saint tradition, prospective ministers do not take it upon themselves to seek an ordination to pastoral or missionary service because they sense a divine calling. Rather, an ordained priesthood officer, who acts, as Mormons believe, by divine authority and inspiration, informs the church member where the church wants that person to serve. Those so "called" are expected to respond voluntarily without pay. J. Golden did so, and despite being somewhat older than usual and fully engaged in his schooling he set off to be a missionary for two years in the Southern States Mission.

It was only eighteen years after the end of the Civil War, and the American South was a harsh place for Mormon missionaries. Beatings, tarring and feathering, and even murder were very real threats for what many southerners saw as meddlesome outsiders.[8] The Ku Klux Klan disrupted meetings and shot down Mormon missionaries and their converts.[9] Several of J. Golden Kimball's fellow missionaries lost their lives for their cause at the hands of lynch mobs. His frustrating experiences in the South are reflected in such still-told legends as "Destinations" (chapter 2); "The Priest," "Saving the South," and "the Fortunate Companion" (chapter 3); and "Missionary Prayers" and "Obnoxious Traveling Companions" (chapter 7).

J. Golden himself told stories about the sometimes harrowing nature of missionary service. On one occasion he and his companion retreated to what they thought was a private outdoor spot to practice their preaching and praying skills away from prying eyes. J. Golden felt his awkward, untrained companion could use a lesson or two. Closing their eyes and with their hands in the air—a customary prayer position that preceded the contemporary Mormon practice of folding one's arms—J. Golden's companion gave a long, loud, and enthusiastic prayer, which made for a strange sight in the middle of the woods. "I thought he would never get through," J. Golden remembered, "and when he said Amen, we looked back, and there were four men standing behind us with guns on their shoulders. I said to my companion, 'That is another lesson, from this time on in the South; I shall pray with one eye open.'"[10] "I know what it is like to smell powder, and am glad of it," he quipped to Saints in the Salt Lake Tabernacle on another occasion, "and I thank the Lord I did not run. I guess I would have done so, but I had no place to go."[11]

Compounded to his troubles with persecution, Elder Kimball was, on one occasion at least, laid low by jaundice and malaria.[12] After the Klan gunned down LDS missionaries and church members during a Kane Creek, Tennessee, worship service, Kimball took to sleeping behind a barricaded door and with a loaded pistol. Deathly ill and even more frighteningly emaciated-looking than usual, he gave this up after a few days, saying, "Well, by heck, if anyone can come here and look at me and then make an attack on me, I'll let him do it." That night he took down the barricade and put the pistol in a trunk under some books.[13]

Despite his illness and the threats Mormons faced in the South, J. Golden was a successful missionary. He was so successful that in 1892 the church called him again to serve, this time as president of the Southern States Mission. While still serving as mission president he was called to be one of the Seven Presidents of the First Council of the Seventy—a lifetime appointment to service in the church hierarchy. Again, this calling carried no salary. Viewing himself as too unpolished and not somber enough for such a life, he marveled all his days about what seemed to him to be an unlikely career path. Thomas Cheney records that J. Golden said of the inscrutability of his calling's wisdom: "A lot of people in the Church believe that men are called to leadership in the Church by revelation and some do not. But I'll tell you, when the Lord calls an old mule skinner like me to be a General Authority, there's got to be revelation."[14]

Between his two missions, J. Golden briefly returned to ranching in the Bear Lake Valley, where he married Jennie Knowlton in 1887. Together they raised three boys and three girls. Unlike his missionary successes, J. Golden's family life was marked by deep sadness and disappointment. His meager personal income and many days traveling on church business proved to be a constant source of friction in the marriage. Such friction may provide meaningful context for stories such as "Paint" and "The Singing Bride" (chapter 2) and "Falling in Love" and "Promise Keepers" (chapter 6), all of which allude to unsatisfactory gender divisions in spousal relationships.

Financial misfortune lay at the heart of much of Elder Kimball's personal and familial unhappiness. J. Golden entered the 1890s a successful rancher but left the century broke and on church assistance. As was the case with many Americans, the financial Panic of 1893 and the five-year depression that ensued, hit him hard.[15] Church finances—still reeling from the federal government's devastating campaign against polygamy in the 1880s—were only worsened by the nation's general economic downturn. J. Golden suffered further burns in bad business deals that he came to see as having exploited his trusting nature. Again, life may have influenced art in the financial motifs in stories such as "Real Estate Prophecy" (chapter 2), "A Word of Advice" and "Radio Broadcast" (chapter 5), "The United Order" (chapter 6), and "Bills" (chapter 11).

Issues of debt and money management frequently appeared in his sermons as well. He once jokingly explained how he could stay out of debt by his method of trying to borrow money: "[The banker] said, 'How do you expect me to take your endorsement?' I replied, 'On my looks and general character. That is all I have got.' And he turned me down; and I have been tickled to death ever since. That is how to stay out of debt."[16]

In stressing the importance of investing in eternal life he once contrasted salvation's security with the risks that can accompany temporal financial investments. He explained that only one of his many attempts at investing had been successful. As for the rest, "All I ever got out of it was experience; the other fellow got my money."[17]

Family difficulties exceeded even his financial problems. For a man so enthusiastic about his faith, which placed such a strong emphasis on family togetherness, it must have been painful to see only two of his six children remain actively involved with Mormonism. Two of the Kimballs' daughters had affairs with married men, and the third's husband was tried for murdering a man he claimed had alienated his wife's affections. The jury acquitted the son-in-law on account of his "protecting the sanctity of his home," as provided for by Utah law at the time. The daughter's adultery was never proven, but the damage to her reputation was sealed as the sordid drama of the trial played out publicly in the pages of the *Salt Lake Tribune* and the *Deseret Evening News* from June through October of 1917.[18] The event is probably the situation alluded to in the story "The Lord's Family" (chapter 2) and "Trouble with Kids" (chapter 11). In "How to Raise Kids" (chapter 9), J. Golden Kimball is remembered by someone who heard him speak to be deeply troubled by the issue of child-rearing.

Those who experience deep personal pain and embarrassment over family and financial tragedies know that successes in other areas can seem as much like cruel irony as balancing compensation. J. Golden Kimball was probably no different in this respect. Although he enjoyed public speaking, cheering hearts, and making people laugh, being the most popular celebrity in Mormondom may not have done much to counterweigh what he experienced as his wife's animosity and their children's' waywardness. Had

J. Golden's success as an entertainer come in a secular rather than sacred arena his remuneration may have been much more lucrative and more pleasing to Jennie Kimball. It is almost a cliché to observe that misfortune and profound personal tragedy often form the backdrop for comic genius, but J. Golden Kimball's life is evidence of that connection. As is often the case with successful professional men who have difficult family lives, he may have felt compelled to spend even more time and energy in public duties, which would have further driven a wedge between the couple.

Elder Kimball's satisfaction at work with peers in church leadership appears to have been higher than his satisfaction at home. His relationship with fellow Seventies President Brigham H. Roberts is particularly noteworthy as an example of an important ecclesiastical and personal friendship.[19] If J. Golden Kimball is remembered as the great humorist among General Authorities, B. H. Roberts's stature is equal as one of the great thinkers and theologians of twentieth-century Mormonism.[20] The two Seventies formed their friendship in the American South when J. Golden served as an assistant to Roberts, who served as president of the Southern States Mission.[21] The younger Elder Kimball accompanied President Roberts when the senior missionary disguised himself as a farmhand in order to recover the bodies of murdered missionaries from an area hot with anti-Mormonism.[22] J. Golden also served as Robert's lifelong confidant as the latter struggled deeply and painfully with debilitating diabetes and depression.[23] Elder Roberts would have known that in J. Golden he had a friend who understood the depths of personal pain, and J. Golden publicly described their relationship as "akin to that of David and Jonathan."[24] It endured despite differences of age, temperament, and personality.

Despite general good feeling and much mutual admiration, Elder Kimball's uniqueness in background and style among church leaders probably led to tensions with his generally more sober and dignified peers in Mormon leadership. This dynamic appears in oral tradition with stories such as "Sleepy" (chapter 2); "Elder Smoot's Calling," "Quorum Succession," "Assistants to the Twelve," "The Church Office Building," "The Fortunate Companion," "When You Die," and "Boring Speeches" (chapter 3); "Note Passing" (chapter 5); and "Too Popular" (chapter 9).

Along with B. H. Roberts, Elder Kimball sometimes felt that the apostles did not accord the First Quorum of the Seventy the equality in authority he regarded as proper according to Latter-day Saint scripture.[25] This concern is reflected in the creative venting in the story "Apostles" (chapter 3). Despite occasional concerns, his loyalty not only to B. H. Roberts but also to all the men his people sustained as prophets, seers, and revelators, as well as to all Mormon people, down to the lowliest, was deep and fierce: "I sustain and uphold with all my heart and soul president Heber J. Grant as Prophet of God. It was only two months ago that a young lawyer—I suppose he considered himself one of the brilliant young lawyers—undertook to criticize severely the President of the Church. I was somewhat disturbed. I said, 'I am going to take out my watch and give you five minutes to name a better man.' I haven't heard from him yet."[26]

Statements like these should give pause to those who would make J. Golden Kimball into some sort of hero for dissent from Mormon orthodoxy. There is no hint in the humor surrounding him of the handwringing or condescension that sometimes accompanies doubting about, or anger toward, religion. If such humor were to appear in the oral tradition it would be counter to his personality. J. Golden Kimball served for forty-six years as a General Authority, giving thousands of sermons and visiting nearly every Latter-day Saint settlement in the Intermountain West. To the end of his days, and despite severe life trials and failing health, his faith gave him comfort and direction that he attempted to impart to others.

On September 2, 1938, the elderly J. Golden Kimball was riding in the back seat of a car fifty miles east of Reno, Nevada, when it suddenly veered out of control and crashed into an embankment, throwing him a considerable distance off the road. The great Mormon humorist and defender of the faith was dead. Presaging his continuing life in the memory of his people, more mourners came to his funeral in the Salt Lake City tabernacle than to any other funeral of a Mormon leader since Brigham Young.

J. Golden Kimball Stories as Folklore Artifacts

In comprehending the J. Golden Kimball phenomenon it is useful to distinguish the Elder Kimball of history from the Uncle Golden of folklore. We can know Elder Kimball through reading his sermons, interviewing those who knew him, and consulting historical documents contemporary with his life. We know Uncle Golden through stories and jokes passed on in the LDS oral tradition. To be sure, the J. Golden Kimball of folklore is inspired by, and bears a certain similarity to, his historical relative. Nevertheless, the J. Golden of folklore is in many ways a different person, and the things he says may or may not relate to historically verifiable events or utterances.

Of course, even historians recognize a great deal of slippage between what is documented and what "really happened," and they occasionally acknowledge that oral tradition can sometimes preserve reasonably accurate accounts of past events that slipped by textual chroniclers altogether.[27] "Folklore" and "history" are not two competing ways of making sense of the past—the former being dubious and the latter more sure. Instead, the two methodologies, working together, illuminate how people in the present use and make sense of the past in daily life. Excerpts from Elder Kimball's historically documented sermons help in understanding the oral tradition:

> My brethren and sisters, I hope you have confidence in me, and that I can hold your attention for a few moments. I feel happy, just as happy as a man can feel with the rheumatism.[28]

> My brethren and sisters, I have been hanging on the hook so long during this conference that I am nearly exhausted. I have had some wonderful thoughts, but you waited so long they have nearly all oozed out of me.[29]

> I am not going to announce any blood and thunder doctrine to you today. I have not been radical for four long months, not since I had appendicitis. I came very nearly being operated upon. I thought I was going to die for a few hours. People said to me, "Why, brother Kimball, you needn't be afraid, you'll get Justice." "Well," I said, "that is what I am afraid of."[30]

> When it comes to self-sacrifice, fighting for the truth, [some people] are like the dying man who was asked by the minister, "Will you denounce the devil and all his workings?" the dying man looked up in a feeble and distressed way and said, "Please don't ask me to do that. I am going to a strange country, and I don't want to make any enemies."[31]

Entertaining and down-to-earth as these quotations may be, excerpts from Elder Kimball's recorded sermons have not usually become part of oral folklore in a direct way. For selections from his actual sermons see Mikal Lofgren's *Wheat: Humor and Wisdom of J. Golden Kimball*; Linda Ririe Gundry, Jay A. Parry, and Jack M. Lyon's edited volume *Best-Loved Humor of the LDS People*; and Claude Richard's *J. Golden Kimball: The Story of a Unique Personality*.[32]

This book, however, focuses on the orally circulated jokes and anecdotes that Mormons tell in homage to the man but not necessarily as accurate quotes from his sermons. It is about folklore and how folklore relates to the Mormon people. It is also not a biography designed to reveal the "true man."[33] Instead, this collection reveals more about the J. Golden Kimball of the Mormon imagination—the created Uncle Golden who is the way that Mormons *need* him to be.

Like all folklore, J. Golden lore tends to stereotype complex figures and follow patterns of expectation that often have more to do with the conventions of a narrative genre than with historical events. J. Golden Kimball, for example, undoubtedly cussed across the pulpit in real life but not nearly as frequently or as consistently as he does in the stories told about him. Many oral narratives ostensibly inspired by J. Golden's sermons and sayings include a "hell" or a "damn," apparently only because cussing has come to be an expected feature of a J. Golden Kimball story.

Many stories also include a straight man required to set up the humor; usually, LDS Church president Heber J. Grant plays Abbott to J. Golden's Costello. In the minds of many Latter-day Saints, Grant's reputation for having a businesslike demeanor suited him well to this role. In some joke versions, however, Grant's successor, George Albert Smith or the apostles Stephen L. Richards or Rutger Clawson, or fellow Seventies Orson F. Whitney or B. H. Roberts fulfill the same straight-man function. Unlike the straight man of American stand-up comedy who usually controls the routine's pacing, topic, and direction, straight men in the J. Golden Kimball oral tradition usually have explosions of his humor thrust upon them despite their attempts to contain it (e.g., "Conference Talk" and "Bridges" [chapter 5]).[34]

Folklore has a way of migrating from one place or from one culture to another and adapting itself to new local circumstances.[35] A few J. Golden Kimball stories are nearly identical—other than the details of main character and setting—to those told about colorful politicians and preachers elsewhere. Versions of the following anecdote are told in the legend cycle of many local heroes around the world.[36] Each one is shaped, as this version, by local personalities and geography:

> There was to be an impressive tour given to some dignitaries from other lands. J. Golden Kimball was assigned to the tour as a guide. They first took a bus trip to the important historical sites in and around Salt Lake City. Brother Kimball would constantly remind the visitors how fast the industrious Mormons put up buildings.
>
> Every time he would say so, one of the dignitaries on the tour would say, "Oh, is that right? In our country we could do it in half the time." J. Golden began to get madder and madder as the dignitary persisted to offer such com-

ments. The tour was to end by having the bus drive around Temple Square. Then this dignitary asked, "What is that building there?" as he pointed at the Temple.

"Damned if I know," said J. Golden. "It wasn't there yesterday."[37]

Even in specifically Mormon storytelling, J. Golden Kimball acts as a magnet, pulling in free-floating stories having to do with slightly subversive but basically benign humorous behavior. Fellow Church General Authority Henry Eyring underscored that observation, "Many times men of importance have attributed to them things they never said. I think that J. Golden Kimball, if he said all of the things he was said to have said, he'd have had to talk even more than he did."[38]

This story collection makes no effort to separate "things J. Golden Kimball really said" from "things J. Golden Kimball is said to have said." Such sorting is an impossible task—especially when a folk hero gains fame from his own storytelling and language skills. Moreover, stories along the wide range of being "very much like" to "not at all like" utterances that actually came out of Elder Kimball's mouth circulate and reflect the concerns of the Mormon people in similar ways. In reading the stories in this book, assume what playwright James Arrington assumes when he has his fictitious J. Golden Kimball say: "They [the Mormon people] put into my mouth what they would like to say if they were here."[39] This is exactly what Arrington does himself in his play.

It is difficult to determine to what degree the Mormons who circulate J. Golden Kimball stories accept them as accurate representations of what really happened or to what degree they understand the stories to be as generally fictitious as most jokes. In this sense J. Golden Kimball stories could be classified in folkloristic terminology as "anecdotes" that fall between "legends" that are generally told as true and "folktales" that are told as fiction. Anecdotes are short, humorous narratives "purporting to recount a true incident."[40] But the issue of whether the people involved with telling and hearing them believe them to be true is in practice not the paramount concern. Rather it is that they are informal, short, humorous, and about real or ostensibly real people. Although "anecdote" has a certain usefulness as a generic category and analytical term, in this book I follow the lead of Mormon storytellers who most frequently refer to J. Golden Kimball anecdotes as "stories," "legends," or "jokes."

Perhaps knowing their words were going to be recorded, some tellers represented in this collection acted more self-conscious about the veracity of their story than they otherwise might have been in informal face-to-face conversation. Storytellers sometimes prefaced their tellings with a comment such as, "I don't know if J. Golden Kimball really said this, but. . . ." Many familiar with the stories seem to approach their historicity with a certain bemused skepticism. At a university luncheon, the president of Brigham Young University asked what kind of project I was working on as a young scholar recently hired under his watch. I explained a little about folklore and how I was interested in J. Golden Kimball stories even if they were not historically verifiable. "You mean some of them are not true?!" he responded in mock surprise.

One variety of J. Golden Kimball story necessarily emerged after his death and cannot even be falsely attributed to him except by relying on supernatural contact, namely jokes about Kimball in heaven (e.g., "St. Peter" [chapter 2] and "Helping St. Peter" [chapter 6]). I suspect, however, that most often in the telling and hearing of J. Golden Kimball stories, evaluations of "historical truth" take a back seat to enjoying the humor. Entertaining the possibility that J. Golden Kimball may have actually done what he is said to have done in the folklore about him, however, makes his stories all the more appealing.

Either way, genuine and spurious "Goldenisms" would die out equally fast if they ever stopped resonating with the concerns of contemporary Mormons. Likewise, genuine and spurious Goldenisms will continue to thrive intermixed and indistinguishable as long as they mean something to those who tell them. These stories do not circulate because they are historically true but because they are culturally true in servicing the psychological, cultural, and religious needs of the people among whom they are found.

The stories in this collection are not all historically verifiable, but they are all real. By that I don't mean J. Golden necessarily actually said them or the events described actually took place. Rather, by *real* I mean that these stories can be found circulating among the Mormon people—at least among Mormons from, or in close contact with, the traditional Mormon culture region in the Intermountain West.

The stories are not compositions or confabulations of creative writers. They are all transcriptions of anecdotes that my students and I have personally heard other Mormons tell, or they are stories collected by other folklorists and folklore students and housed in the folklore archives of Brigham Young University and Utah State University since the 1940s. As is traditionally understood, authentic folklore does not arise from popular authors who compose stories on "folksy" themes. Folklorist Richard Dorson in *Folklore and Fakelore* called this variety of self-conscious manufacture "fakelore" and considered Paul Bunyan to be the epitome of this genre because he took shape and found primary expression as a pseudo folk hero in logging company advertisements, children's books, and animated cartoons rather than in the oral narrative tradition of actual working loggers in logging camps. Unlike Paul Bunyan, J. Golden Kimball is not only a real person; he is a real folk hero around whom a genuine and vibrant cycle of oral narratives has developed.

Because so many years have passed since his death and so few of those who actually heard him speak are still alive, one might assume that J. Golden Kimball lore is dying out. I found little evidence for this, however, and had no trouble collecting numerous stories from Mormon storytellers. Many in this book are apparently of recent origin and do not appear in older collections; some that are currently popular are "The Lantern" (chapter 1), "The Stolen Lawnmower" (chapter 3), and "The Splinter" (chapter 7). It may well be the case that the body and frequency of tellings of J. Golden Kimball lore has grown with the receding of the actual events of his life into the mists of the past and with the rapid growth of the Church of Jesus Christ of Latter-day Saints.

The Stories' Relations to Contexts and Tellers

When folklorists examine the lore of religious groups they have sometimes been drawn to cultural expressions easily depicted as backwoods or primitive. The supposed differences between these traditions and mainstream religion (i.e., religion more like the ethnographer's) are played up as alien and exotic. But the stereotyped—even condescending and offensive—assumptions that such an approach entails has led other folklorists to emphasize that all kinds of religious groups pass on folklore—from poor rural Baptists in Appalachia to the most prestigious Episcopal congregations in upscale eastern suburbs. Folk religion is not just the purview of particular folksy denominations in certain quaint parts of the country. It is a part of all religiosity everywhere.[41]

When dealing with religious groups today, most folklorists are interested in those parts of adherents' religious lives that are not part of the official texts, theology, programs, or organizational structure of any religion. Vernacular aspects such as spontaneous prayer styles, supernatural religious legends, jokes about pastors, and popular (but unofficial) doctrines are not necessarily unorthodox or antagonistic in any way to institutional religion, nor do they comprise trivial components of one's religious life. Rather, they occur traditionally outside, alongside, or in conjunction with the institutional, programmed aspects of religiosity within a particular group.[42]

J. Golden Kimball stories are such an aspect of Mormonism. There is nothing doctrinally necessary about them, and they circulate mostly outside official avenues of ecclesiastical communication. Although they may show up in informal discussions in Sunday school class, they are less frequently told over the pulpit (for the results of an exception to this rule see "Opening Line: 2" [chapter 2]). They have been somewhat scarce, but not entirely absent, in official church publications. Many LDS Church leaders such as Spencer W. Kimball and Franklin Richards, however, were fond of telling them and employed J. Golden Kimball stories as attention-getting devices to illustrate a point or introduce a discussion of a certain principle.[43]

J. Golden Kimball stories can circulate in almost any informal context where two or more Mormons are gathered. They are, for example, among the most common contributions to an Internet discussion list dedicated to Mormon humor.[44] They come up in water-cooler and car pool chit-chat as part of the flow of daily conversation. Often they serve as commentary on a topic of conversation. Such phrases as "that reminds me of a J. Golden Kimball story" and "that's like what J. Golden Kimball meant when he said" often link Uncle Golden with the conversational flow. Sometimes the interjection of a J. Golden Kimball story will shift the topic of discussion to Kimball himself, and interlocutors will take turns sharing stories before moving on to another topic.

Folklore archive materials attest to the fact that a wide variety of Mormons can and do spin J. Golden Kimball yarns. They seem to be more likely to be told by males and are a favorite of the LDS Church's mostly male missionary force, most of whom are nineteen or in their early twenties. The purpose of missionary service is primarily religious rather than cultural, but sociologists of Mormonism have described those two years as a rite of passage.[45] Missionaries come home at age twenty-one to find that they are entering the world of adult responsibilities and information access.

It is perhaps not surprising then that missionary service is the first time many Latter-day Saints hear J. Golden Kimball stories because they are often deemed unsuitable for, and kept from, children. One woman, for example, who was organizing a campout for her ward (congregation) called to ask if

I could be a special campfire speaker and talk about J. Golden Kimball and tell stories. I asked whether children would be present and how their bishop (lay pastor) and parents would feel if I did so. She reconsidered and decided that it was perhaps best to find a different topic for campfire stories. I am not sure every Mormon would come to the same decision, but many would. Such reluctance likely has less to do with parents worrying about J. Golden Kimball corrupting young morals than with a distinction between child and adult culture. Parents also recognize that few children are savvy about the historical context from which Kimball's stories emerged or the appropriate social contexts in which they can be shared without embarrassment. Such shielding, although understandable, sometimes leads to disbelief on first exposure. LDS young adults sometimes find a swearing General Authority hard to fit in to their mental categories.

One of the most unique types of J. Golden Kimball storytelling situations comes from Mormon folk performers who affect a Kimball-style squeaky voice when relating anecdotes about him. The affectation is more common among older tellers, but some have become such accomplished J. Golden Kimball impersonators that they have made professional productions of doing so. Although stories continue to circulate among Mormons in casual settings, J. Golden Kimball is no longer merely a figure of Mormon folklore. With numerous books, cassette tapes, CDs, video cassettes, and one-man plays portraying Brother Golden, he has become an icon of Mormon popular culture as well.[46]

The J. Golden Kimball phenomenon shows that Richard Dorson's folklore-fakelore distinction may draw too solid a line between folklore and popular culture to be of much use in making sense of the relationship between the media and oral storytelling in contemporary society. The J. Golden Kimball of LDS popular culture operates in symbiosis with the J. Golden Kimball of LDS folklore. Popular entertainers in theaters and on CDs, videocassettes, and television specials draw on the oral tradition and may speed and multiply a story's reentry into the informal stream of oral transmission, where Uncle Golden continues to enjoy his greatest vibrancy. Many of the same anecdotes that storyteller James Kimball (a nephew of J. Golden) performed for his much-rebroadcast December 3, 1998, special for Utah Public Television quickly began circulating on the Internet and in Brigham Young University hallways during the weeks following his show's initial airing. One of his stories, "The Splinter" (chapter 7), has become particularly popular and seems to have risen in popularity in the oral tradition. In few, if any, of the tellings I heard did the teller attribute Jim Kimball as their most immediate source, but neither does Kimball always attribute the most immediate source from which he gleaned his stories.

In considering the relationship between technological media and oral tradition, however, it is important to go beyond anecdotal evidence and consider more recent scholarly findings. Contrary to what is commonly assumed about the power of the media to influence and displace oral culture, the humor scholar Christie Davies has shown that joke cycles that circulate orally tend to be highly resistant to trends and taboos found in the media.[47] Alan Dundes may be mistaken in suggesting that Polish jokes may have emerged in the 1960s to "take the heat off of blacks" as denigrating jokes about African Americans became increasingly taboo in many settings, particularly public ones such as the mainstream media.[48] Davies, however, shows that jokes about blacks, as African Americans well know, have continued, alive and well, in many settings privately among friends despite disappearing from the popular media.[49]

The purpose in bringing up this research is not to justify or condemn any particular kind of joke but to underscore the importance of folklore's vibrancy in a rapidly developing society erroneously convinced that oral cultures are in constant retreat before the juggernaut of an ongoing communications technology revolution. On the contrary, traditional face-to-face oral communication patterns continue to be the broad base upon which rests the artifice of new communications media. In fact, folkloric modes of communication continue in traditional patterns and also thoroughly infuse newly emergent ones. The new media technology that has been the most successful are those that better emulate the immediacy of face-to-face communication. Consider television's popularity over radio, the telephone's over the telegraph, and e-mail's ongoing erosion of the postal service's market. These eclipses happen because the presence of faces, audible words, and speed make them more like traditional face-to-face conversation.

In this vein, the relationship of popular entertainers on television, stage, videotape, cassette, CD, or DVD to the people who carry on J. Golden Kimball's orally circulating legend cycle is akin to that of a boat to water. The boat may add a valuable new dimension to playing in water, but the water exists and supplies joy in and of itself. The boat's existence is purposeless and even inconceivable without water.

Just because a joke cycle is strong, lively, and resistant to media influences, however, does not mean it is pervasive within a culture. As is the case with even the most common oral traditions, many otherwise well-informed members of Latter-day Saint culture have never heard of J. Golden Kimball. In introducing the topic to my extraordinarily enculturated—yet perhaps not fully initiated into adult life—students at BYU, I get plenty of knowing smiles but also many blank stares. "Wasn't he that cussing apostle?" some say with nervous reservation, erring in giving the man an ecclesiastical promotion. I try to ease any insecurities by explaining that not knowing any J. Golden Kimball stories does not make them cultural illiterates and that by going out and "shaking the tree" a little they will find stories dropping all around them.

Student opinions about this uneven distribution of cultural knowledge vary. One came to my office to express a somewhat extreme point of view of Elder Kimball's cultural importance. "I can't believe some of my classmates had not heard of J. Golden Kimball!" she exclaimed. "If you know God and you know Jesus, you should know J. Golden Kimball!"

A Transitional Figure in a Transitional Time

Perhaps the student overstated J. Golden Kimball's significance a little, but it is true that many do not realize his importance in helping usher Latter-day Saints through a tough transition period in their history. Those Mormons from the mountain West whose parents and grandparents knew the living man remember Elder Kimball's struggles with swearing and with the coffee proscription in the Mormon health code known as the Word of Wisdom. (This principle is found in section 89 of the Doctrine and Covenants, a book of scripture composed mostly of revelations received by Joseph Smith.) J. Golden Kimball was much more than these aspects of his personality, but they are highlighted in the folklore about him featured in chapters 4 and 5.

Struggles with cussing and the Word of Wisdom reflect J. Golden's situation in a time of great change in LDS history. Elder Kimball's service as a General Authority from 1886 to 1938 encompasses the entire period from 1890 to 1930 that Thomas Alexander refers to in *Mormonism in Transition* as the most significant era of change in Mormonism since the days of its inception. Latter-day Saints, like many western Americans, were in the throes of metamorphosing from a pioneer to a modern society coping with changes in technology and the economy.[50] Mormons bore the added burden of self-transforming from a marginalized and persecuted religious group into respected members of the American religious and cultural mainstream.

Polygamy and theocracy were the chief irritants to other Americans and began to be abandoned before social and governmental pressure on Latter-day Saints started to ease. J. Golden Kimball folklore perpetuates the memory of this time in stories such as "Marriage Problems" (chapter 6) and "Forgiveness and Repentance" (chapter 9).

The abandonment of polygamy and theocracy were the most notable results of this period of transition, but changes at the core of Mormon society rippled throughout the system. Changing attitudes about swearing and the Word of Wisdom are just as illustrative of J. Golden Kimball's times because they, too, have to do with Mormons entering the respectable mainstream of America. Women and new technology were also problematic issues for J. Golden Kimball in his story cycle.

A Short History of Mormon Swearing

For faithful Mormons, concern about bridling the tongue has always existed, but what exactly that entails and the relative priority given to it has changed over the years. Joseph Smith taught "abstain from . . . swearing, and from all profane language."[51] Almost as if he could see J. Golden Kimball in the future, however, Joseph Smith also displayed a somewhat relaxed attitude about swearing when he proclaimed, "I love that man better who swears a stream . . . than the long, smooth-faced hypocrite."[52] Mid-nineteenth-century Mormons had a reputation among some Gentiles for using hard language incessantly, even over the pulpit. J. Golden's father and Brigham Young were also said to dip into colorful vocabulary from time to time.[53] One famous example concerns Heber C. Kimball's alleged response to suggestions that he pray for the enemies of the church: "Sure I'll pray for our enemies! I pray that they may all go to hell." During his visit to Utah in the 1860s, however, the British explorer Richard Burton failed to find much evidence that Mormon leaders swore and chalked up their reputation for doing so as one of a number of the unflattering exaggerations about Mormon lifestyle he was able to debunk while in Utah.[54]

Still, Burton did not say he found no evidence of Mormon swearing, and many Mormons today would probably be surprised at their ancestors' speech habits.[55] One pop etymologist of American English usage, Stuart Flexner, provides intriguing speculation on the evolution of Mormon swearing. Nineteenth-century Mormons, he suggests, invented and contributed to American English such exclamations as "by hell" and "oh my hell" as alternatives to similar language that used the Lord's name in vain.[56] Today, Utah's polite society considers even these mild substitutes too strong. Among Utah LDS teens in particular, the unique and even tamer regional expletive "oh my heck" holds sway as the preferred euphemism of a euphemism.[57]

In J. Golden Kimball's lifetime, scrutiny of language became part of the transformation of Mormonism. In 1901 church president Joseph F. Smith expressed concern over members' use of profanity: "We should stamp out profanity, and vulgarity, and everything of that character that exists among us; for all such things are incompatible with the gospel and inconsistent with the people of God."[58] Later, Stephen L. Richards, one of J. Golden Kimball's contemporaries in the Quorum of the Twelve, proclaimed, "I cannot pass this point without importuning some of my brethren to stop swearing. No man can love God and damn him any more than he can love his wife and damn her. Think again, please. Think of the utter futility of this vulgar habit. Think of its effect on youth. Men teach boys profanity. It is not congenital with the race. It is the nature of man to love God and not to damn him."[59]

Elder Richards was referring to a particular form of personal and God-directed cursing uncommon in the J. Golden Kimball cycle, but the scope of condemnations later expanded beyond that rather narrow prohibition. In 1965 a First Presidency member, Hugh B. Brown, taught that "the man or woman who is guilty of profanity, swearing, or crude slang unwittingly reveals a soiled mind and a limited vocabulary, and is pitied and shunned by all cultured people. Profaning the name of God is an affront to Him, and He has forbidden it." And in 1948 church president David O. McKay remarked, "Swearing is a vice that bespeaks a low standard of breeding. Profanity is a vice all too prevalent in America, and though we say it with embarrassment, all too frequently used in the Church."[60]

An increased attention to swearing ironically caused accounts of J. Golden Kimball's cussing to be multiplied and exaggerated as noteworthy in his legend cycle rather than be downplayed. No Mormon authority has provided a list of words to avoid, but the tendency among lay Mormons seems to be to increase the number that count for exclusion. A senior citizens' women's group helped explain this to me. I had been invited to discuss J. Golden Kimball and worried that the group might be offended. They explained, however, that although a younger audience might find hells and damns funny because of their shock value, such language was little more than incidental to the humor for them. The women remembered that swearing was not as much of an issue when they were young as it is now. It would cause a problem if used over the pulpit, but everyday conversation down on the farm—where more people worked in those days—was a different matter. One woman, a convert, maintained she never heard much swearing until she joined the church and left the East to move to Utah in the mid-twentieth century. Evidently, the transforming process was still working itself out. In the group's memory, swearing was more acceptable among devout Mormons in the past than it is now. By the late twentieth century the scope of acceptable Mormon cussing had shrunk to J. Golden Kimball jokes alone, and many otherwise well-spoken LDS people seemed free in abandoning those taboos when "quoting" him.

The J. Golden Kimball of history may have enjoyed more linguistic latitude than today's Mormons, but he still ran into problems because of his position and the contexts in which he would cuss. Golden's outdoor-loving, mule-skinner background sometimes chafed against the increasing domestication of the West and a Mormon culture—starting with its leadership—that was bent on achieving respectability. His heart was willing, but he was late in catching on that swearing over the pulpit, or anywhere else, was becoming increasingly unacceptable. He also resisted certain definitions of what was taboo and what was not. "Where I come from 'hell' and 'damn' are not swearing," he supposedly complained, "they are geography."

Providing a defense of his friend and expressing sentiments perhaps not shared by other Mormons, Elder Ben E. Rich, president of the Southern States Mission, said in the October 1905 General Conference: "I know I am looked upon as very radical. In fact, it is said that brother Golden Kimball and myself swear once in a while. I think that if Jesus would come here, He would express His opinion of some people in almost similar language to that used sometimes by Brother Golden Kimball."[61] Elder Rich went on to speak regularly at General Conferences for the rest of his life, but he offered no further defenses of swearing. The times were changing.

Word of Wisdom Transformations

According to stories told about him, J. Golden did not exactly charge ahead at the forefront of reformation efforts, as the church under Heber J. Grant's leadership began to regard the Word of Wisdom as a strict rule for Mormons rather than "not by commandment or constraint," as the original revelation states.[62] The significance of this increasing emphasis on the Word of Wisdom can be interpreted as a sociological marker in at least two ways. First, with the disappearance of polygamy, Mormonism needed a new boundary maintenance device to ensure continued distinctiveness. Second, emphasis on temperance and abstinence from filthy habits would help move Mormons more into the realm of respectability. These two interpretations can be combined by suggesting that although Mormons have always seen themselves as a people striving for obedience to God's commands, Mormon society was moving toward a preference for being seen as a people who now adhered to commands easier for outsiders to appreciate.

Efforts to eradicate bad behavior of all sorts—including drinking, smoking, gambling, and coarse language—were very much in vogue throughout America during J. Golden Kimball's time. As Mormon leaders struggled to stamp out such practices they did so arm in arm with other religious and social reformers of the prohibition era. Such efforts did not go unopposed. Bad habits had advocates in the media and corporations that benefited financially from Americans' consumption of vices.[63]

With such powerful forces marshaled both for and against vice, significant shifts in behavioral patterns were hard to achieve on both an individual and a societal scale. Although far from alone among members of the church at this time, Kimball, as one of the Seven Presidents of the Seventy, was expected to lead by example in abstaining from alcohol, tobacco, tea, and coffee. For J. Golden Kimball, coffee was the problem:

> When Heber J. Grant called for the church to live the Word of Wisdom more faithfully, J. Golden's wife would no longer allow him to fix his coffee at home. J. Golden would sneak to downtown Salt Lake to a couple of different restaurants and have a cup of coffee. One time while he was sitting in a back booth near the restrooms, a lady spied him and confronted him saying, "Is that you Elder Kimball drinking coffee?" J. Golden replied, "Ma'am, you are the third person today who has mistaken me for that old s.o.b.!"[64]

Make no mistake, J. Golden always displayed unwavering devotion to his church and was sincerely and openly repentant about any embarrassment his verbal and temperance slips sometimes caused. That humble aspect of his personality further endeared him to church members and kept him out of serious trouble with colleagues who always lovingly, but sometimes sharply, tried to get him to rein in his tongue and curb his coffee habit. Mormons took courage, however, in knowing that one of the Lord's anointed experienced struggles similar to their own and was nonetheless completely devoted to building the Kingdom.

J. Golden was not the rebel who is sometimes inferred from the quip attributed to him—"They can't cut me off from the Church. I repent too damn fast." As former LDS Church president Spencer W. Kimball—J. Golden Kimball's nephew by way of another of Heber C. Kimball's wives—suggested of this story, "Here is a great lesson, if it is correctly interpreted. There is never a day in any man's life when repentance is not essential to his well-being and eternal progress."[65] Spencer W. Kimball's recounting of this story does leave out one word however.

Other Social Changes—Women, Technology, and Humor

In addition to a new emphasis on language discipline and the Word of Wisdom, J. Golden Kimball stories also reflect other important social transitions that took place during the twentieth century that have less to do with the specific tenets of Mormonism. Many stories chronicle his always frustrating, sometimes near-death, encounters with the new technology of his time such as cars, telephones, and dangerous industrial machinery ("Indignation" and "Round and Round" [chapter 2] and "Telephone Trouble" [chapter 8]). These anecdotes express the mixed feelings of delight and fear that people have commonly experienced in coming to terms with the popular inventions that transform their lives. Considering this common motif in J. Golden Kimball lore, it is tragically ironic that he lost his life in an automobile accident.

A few Uncle Golden jokes exhibit what could be seen as a mean streak toward women, which some would find uncomfortably amusing at best and unfunny and demeaning at worst by today's standards of political correctness ("Falling in Love" and perhaps "Slippery Hazards" [chapter 2] and "Marriage Problems" and "Treating Women Right" [chapter 6]). But such humor was very common in the early-twentieth-century folk humor of American males, and it appears more frequently in archive collections of an earlier date. In contrast to the implication of some of these stories, "I'll Call for You" (chapter 6) demonstrates Kimball's kindness toward a scorned and verbally abused woman.

In her entry on humor in the *Encyclopedia of Mormonism*, Margaret Baker explains another important transition ostensibly demonstrated by the J. Golden Kimball legend cycle. Kimball, she maintains, was a transitional figure in the history of Mormon humor.[66] She proposes that until J. Golden's pioneering wordsmithing, most humor about Mormons was from Gentiles who ridiculed the beliefs that Mormons held sacred and delighted in the severe persecutions faced by the fledgling church.[67]

According to Baker, J. Golden Kimball's own humor, and the subsequent lore about him, were some of the first signs that sectarian strife had cooled enough, and LDS culture had matured enough, for Mormons to begin to laugh self-confidently in public forums at their own peculiarities. J. Golden represents—and by his words may have helped bring about—a coming of age in a maturing religious culture. Latter-day Saints familiar with the cycle often point out his important role in providing therapeutic humor that allows high-strung people to take themselves less seriously.

Jill Terry Rudy's research on Mormon folksongs, however, suggests that Mormons engaged in humor at their own expense long before the emergence of the J. Golden Kimball story cycle. Nineteenth-century Gentiles sang the following song highlighting the humorous potential of what were for Latter-day Saints the sacred institutions of plural marriage and the church presidency:

> Old Brigham Young was a stout man once
> > But now he is thin and old
> And I love to state, there's no hair upon his pate
> > Which once wore a covering of gold.
> For his youngest wives won't have white wool
> > And his old ones won't take red,
> So in tearing it out they have taken turn about,
> > 'Til they've pulled all the wool from his head.[68]

Mormons sang this song as well, and this version was collected from a seventy-seven-year-old Mormon man in 1946 who remembered learning the song sixty years earlier and being requested to sing it at Mormon gatherings in the 1880s during the height of the federal persecution of Mormons for polygamy. It is one of several folksongs that extends back to the earliest days of the colonization period in the 1850s.

Folklorists have noted that insiders can appreciate and roar with laughter about certain kinds of humor that would appear to be deeply offensive coming from outsiders who had not paid their dues in co-experience with, and participation in, a cultural group.[69] That is not a double standard but recognition that the same set of words emerging from a different context can mean something completely different. For insiders to sing a song like the one quoted indicates self-confidence more than sacrilege.

Rather than a humorless culture progressively opening to mirth, it seems more likely that at any given time streams of stuffed-shirt prickliness and open, self-depreciating humor have coexisted and intermixed among Mormons. J. Golden Kimball may not have introduced something totally new, but he probably did help shift Mormonism's cultural moorings toward acceptance and appreciation of its own homegrown humor.

Folklore and Historical Knowledge

The ability of the J. Golden Kimball legend cycle to faithfully maintain accurate information about the past should not be overstated. The idea that folklore only preserves archaic historical features from the evolutionary history of a society has been long abandoned as an antiquarian error.[70] In this vein, many contemporary folklorists hold that orally circulating narrative cycles reveal more about the present of their telling than about the past to which they refer.[71] Unlike written documents that can more stably preserve attitudes and concerns of the past without the intrusion of multiple human transmitters, oral narratives must stay current and relevant to the people who tell them. Stories that no longer resonate with potential tellers and audiences cease to be told and die forgotten. William A. Wilson calls the set of ideals, concerns, and beliefs that each culture holds its "value center."[72] The form, content, and message of stories stay true to their culture's value center or they do not get repeated. Hence, today's J. Golden Kimball stories can reasonably be said to reveal more about contemporary Mormon culture and values than about any previous period in Mormon history.

There are, however, some points to consider in valuing J. Golden Kimball stories as windows to the past as well. For example, many of his stories collected by Austin and Alta Fife in the 1940s and 1950s are virtually identical to ones still in circulation. The following two stories are remarkably similar although more than fifty years apart in their telling.

First Story. Brother Kimball was speaking before a group of Relief Society sisters. There was some discussion about latter-day prophecy and current-day revelations. The question was asked of Brother Kimball as to why we didn't hear very much about this doctrine in the Church lately. "Well," Brother Kimball said, "any man can receive revelations for himself and for his own family, but there is only one person authorized to receive revelations for the whole Church, and that is President Heber J. Grant, and I wish to hell he'd get on the job."[73]

Second Story. Once when Brother Kimball was conducting a discussion on modern-day revelation in an adult Sunday School class, a member asked why they didn't hear as much about this as in the early days of the Church. "Well," began Golden, "it's like this: any man can receive revelations for himself and for his own family. But there is only one person authorized to receive revelations for the whole body of the Church, and that is President Heber J. Grant. And I wish to hell he'd get on the job! He travels around so damn much that God can't catch up with him!"[74]

It is not too unreasonable to assume that these stories have been stable since their origin sometime around J. Golden Kimball's ministry as a General Authority and the time in which he emerged as a public figure. Such remarkable stability can only be demonstrated through a mature folklore archive and may suggest that the value center of Mormon culture has not shifted much in fifty years. Perhaps we shold not assume that each uncannily similar telling of a particular J. Golden Kimball story is a new creation around a particularly stable value center, but maybe stories and their details can proceed through time on their own inertia, remaining stable unless compelled to change in order to survive. The reliability of oral texts as historical artifacts is perhaps not as suspect as we may think. For some questions and in some cultures, oral tradition is all we have.[75]

The social historian Robert Darnton has shown that even much changed and adapted modern versions of tales such as "Little Red Riding Hood" and "Hansel and Gretel" still provide glimpses into the austere realities of life in early-modern Europe, where wolves had not been eraticated, peasants often starved, temptation toward child abandonment existed, and many blended families included stepmothers.[76] "Little Red Riding Hood's" popularity has survived the extinction of the wolf in Western Europe despite the centrality of a wolf in the story. "Hansel and Gretel" continues to be enjoyed despite the fact that few German children need fear their parents will send them into the woods to save themselves from starvation. So perhaps J. Golden Kimball stories likewise preserve cultural artifacts from an earlier time.

When stories emerge, they are by their newness hardly a window to the past. The times they reveal, if they reveal anything at all, are those of their emergence. Story themes, motifs, and features that are neutral in respect to value center can be expected to be stable. Although a story may adapt to keep current, not all of its details need to change for it to do so. The stories people pass on generally tend to stay the same unless there is a pressing reason for them to change. Useful cultural information about the past may well be preserved in oral tradition.[77]

The People's Champion in Cross-Cultural Perspective: J. Golden Kimball as Performer-Hero

Understanding the J. Golden Kimball phenomenon is not just a matter of understanding his place in LDS Church history. It is also a matter of grasping the vital roles that well-developed folk hero story cycles play within the cultural groups to which they belong.

Folklorists' theories about the significance of folk heroes have evolved and changed. As early as the fourth century, the Sicilian philosopher Euhemerus proposed that the denizens of Olympus were in fact historical figures about whom the ancient Greeks made much-embellished stories—gods and heroes in the image of real men and women. Later, the heroic-age theory of H. M. and N. K. Chadwick continued with this line of thinking by proposing that mythical heroes such as England's Beowulf, Germany's Siegfried, France's Roland, and Ireland's Cuchulain were orally preserved collective memories of actual warrior chieftains of prehistoric Europe.[78]

During the 1930s the English scholar Lord Raglan proposed exactly the opposite idea in his myth-ritual theory. Raglan suggested in *The Hero* that a pattern of twenty-two motifs is so common in all hero stories throughout the world that it is impossible to think of heroes as historical characters. The high correspondences of motifs suggest all hero tales sprang from a common source rather than arose independently. According to Raglan, hero legends in their various versions are survivals of sacred stories (or one original story) originally dramatized as part of ancient religious rituals.

Raglan's motifs include ones that could be stretched to encompass J. Golden Kimball. These include being the son of a king (or important leader) but reared in humble circumstances, gaining victory over wild beasts (anti-Mormons), meeting death under unusual circumstances, and not being succeeded by his children. But it would be foolish to argue that J. Golden Kimball did not exist based on his story cycle's adherence to some of Raglan's criteria. Raglan's proposal that commonalities in the deeds of heroes necessarily argue against their historical reality has not been particularly useful to American folklorists. That is perhaps because they have realized that almost any story can be made to fit a template if one squeezes it enough and Raglan's proposal does not work well when applied to the American experience. In America, folk heroes have demonstrably emerged very much out of real historical figures. Richard M. Dorson applied Raglan's template to the American frontier to show Davy Crockett as a heroic-age figure, not only to demonstrate that America had developed its own folklore and heroic-age folk heroes but also that not all heroes are mythic only.[79]

Searching for common themes in what makes a hero cross-culturally may still be informative, but much of the momentum of scholarship in recent decades has been away from cultural universals and toward particulars. The Mexican American folklorist Américo Paredes has shown quite persuasively how who is considered a hero (and who is not) is most definitely tied to specific community determination.[80] Particular heroes are by no means heroes to everyone. The Texas Rangers painted a heroic image of themselves as they reported their pacification of the Rio Grande Valley to superiors in Austin. Generations of white Texans memorialized the Rangers' deeds as emblematic of universal heroic virtues of honor and bravery. But that folk memory does not square well with what Mexican American folk memory holds to be the treachery and racism of violent Rangers who aided in lynchings and the theft of Tejano land by whites. The point here is not to determine which version of folk historical memory better matches the historical record but to show that in the world of folk heroes, one people's hero can very well be another's villain.

If who is a folk hero is not easy to determine except by reference to the collective memory of given societies, the characteristics of a folk hero are likewise tricky to nail down. Attempts to describe features of a hero almost always encounter immediate contradictions and problems. Grimm's fairy tales are not the same as American heroic anecdotes and legends, but they bear comparison because heroes are a prominent concept in both. Maria M. Tatar examined the heroes of Grimm's tale collection and found that not only do dichotomies emerge in the behavior of heroes such as active/passive, seeker/victim, and naïve/cunning but also that it is often hard to determine when a hero is acting on which side of the dichotomy.[81] Does he seek adventure or endure trials? Do the hero's quips display sharp cunning or guileless innocence in penetrating social conventions? In the case of J. Golden Kimball, the latter distinction is not always clear, as the stories in chapters 2 and 7 in particular demonstrate.

Failing a solid definition, one is left with the somewhat circular definition that a person is a hero because he or she has performed deeds that someone considers heroic. Dubbing a person a hero in this way makes the most sense when a living community does the consideration and sustains a person's reputation. Individual scholars' assessments of who may or may not be a hero to a particular community do not amount to much, but collection of a large and thriving legend cycle about a person constitutes evidence that a particular community holds that person to be a hero. Such is the case with J. Golden Kimball.

This study does not attempt to propose or modify any ur-plot for heroic actions in traditional oral narratives. Examining the J. Golden Kimball legend cycle for specific plot motifs that might align him with an ostensibly universal hero type would probably not demonstrate much of anything. Using him and other Mormon and western American folk heroes as examples, however, allows for some general observations about what heroes do to merit their sustaining vote as such. As the case of J. Golden Kimball demonstrates, sometimes words speak louder than actions in the folk-hero stakes.

As Paredes shows, who is a folk hero and who is a villain is relative to the group that does the remembering. A hero becomes a hero by performing extraordinary deeds that benefit and unify those who remember the individual as a hero.[82] In the realm of storytelling, if not in actuality, American folk heroes break free from physical and societal constraints and vanquish foes, claim needed resources, and ensure safety for their people.[83] Mormon heroes check enemies of the church, bring peace to the community, and ease the trials of life with healing humor. Folk heroes articulate and reaffirm values and aspirations as well as provide vicarious psychological release from powerlessness and frustration.

Folk heroes embody and proclaim the values embraced by the culture whose interests they serve. Folk heroes powerfully go about doing what regular people wish they themselves could do but don't dare. As one of Wilson's informants said of Mormon hero figures, "You would always like to do something like that yourself, and you kinda admire someone who has the guts to do it."[84] Having risen to the high office of president of the First Quorum of the Seventy from the genteel poverty of being the son of the widow of a much-married man, he was, in today's parlance, a "regular guy who made it" and the last of the frontier demi-gods of Mormon folk history.

To Latter-day Saints today, stories of Joseph Smith, Brigham Young, Eliza R. Snow, Parley P. Pratt, and other founders of Mormonism are now sacred history of near-mythic proportions. In nineteenth-century Utah, legends of the gun-slinging "Avenging Angels" Porter Rockwell and Bill Hickman warmed the vengeful side of Mormons tired of being persecuted and powerless in their relations with other Americans. Bill Hickman dropped out of the Mormon folk hero pantheon, and out of Mormon popular memory, when he turned against Brigham Young and the church by writing a sensationalistic and highly embellished exposé of his deeds as a marauding "Danite."[85] Porter Rockwell—with his unwavering loyalty to the Kingdom, invincibility endowing, Samson-like locks, and itchy trigger finger—lives on in yarns told at Mormon Boy Scout camps and in a theme restaurant in Lehi, Utah.[86] Rockwell's long hair, hard drinking, and adherence to God's law over man's, however, have dampened his official celebration in the wake of the transformation of Mormonism.

As yin to Rockwell's yang, southern Utah's Jacob Hamblin, under the direction of the Holy Spirit, made a Christian pacifist's vow never to take the life of a Native American as the result of a promise from God that Indians would never kill him. Hamblin's fearless negotiation and hair-width escapes from death make him, in Mormon lore and popular drama at least, almost single-handedly responsible for the relatively peaceful Native American–Mormon relations of the nineteenth century.[87] It was indeed a time when giants walked the earth—the Mormon heroic age one might be tempted to say.

Despite J. Golden Kimball's place in the Mormon folk hero pantheon as a transitional figure between the pioneer and the contemporary Mormon worlds, he is, in one significant way, more like two of his Gentile Western folk hero counterparts in the Mountain West: the tall-tale-spinning mountain man Jim Bridger (1804–81) and the worker's hymn-writing radical labor martyr Joe Hill (1879–1915).[88] He also bears noteworthy resemblance to the medieval Muslim, Imam Nasraddin Hodja, whose outrageous stories are a dominant feature of Turkish oral culture to this day.

Jim Bridger's prowess as an early explorer of the Rocky Mountain West is evidenced in a plethora of place names, such as the Bridger Mountains, Bridger Pass, the town of Fort Bridger, and the Bridger National Forest. He roamed a vast territory from New Mexico to the Canadian border in pursuit of beaver pelts to feed the fashion for top hats in the East. Bridger was the first white man to see the Great Salt Lake and was among the first to report the natural wonders of what is today called Yellowstone National Park. Such experience made it easy for him to find gullible audiences to serve as marks for his many tall tales. He told of a petrified forest where petrified birds sat in petrified trees and sang songs that could not be heard because of being petrified. He told of a mountain of quartz so pure that the skeletons and corpses of woodland creatures lay in a line along its base—killed instantly from the impact of running, hopping, or flying into something solid yet invisible. He told of his favorite fishing spot, a spring cool at the bottom and boiling at the top where one could catch a fish and reel it up slowly to have it cooked and ready to eat before even removing the hook. Visitors to Arizona's Petrified Forest, southern Utah's Big Rock Candy Mountain, and Wyoming's Yellowstone will be able to detect the kernel of truth at the core of such prime examples of the American tall-tale genre. Like Kimball, long after Bridger's death tales attributed to him have continued to persist, evolve, and multiply far beyond what the man himself is likely to have said.[89]

The Swedish immigrant Joe Hill (Hägglund) wandered as widely in the West as Jim Bridger did more than seventy years before, but like J. Golden Kimball, Hill's fervor was evangelical and ideological rather than adventuresome and economic. Although they were contemporaries, the men appealed to, and are remembered by, very different constituencies. While the mostly agricultural Mormons in the valleys turned their ears to Kimball, the Gentile miners pulling ore from the mountains were Hill's main audience. As a leader of the radical Industrial Workers of the World (IWW), Hill organized public street-singing events and composed songs to recruit workers for the union's cause. "Casey Jones Was a Union Scab," Hill proclaimed in his parody of the popular folksong. According to Hill's parody, the ill-fated engineer should have stood up for his right to have safe working conditions and got what was coming to him for failing to organize and affiliate. Coining a phrase in his song "The Preacher and the Slave," Hill urged the workers who gathered to hear him sing not to pine for some afterlife "pie in the sky" delayed reward but to focus on establishing a workers' paradise right now. Hill sealed his immortality as a martyr in the memory of worldwide working-class union culture when he was executed in 1915 for the murder of a Salt Lake City merchant. He refused to say a word in his defense, and debate rages to this day about the merits of the case against him and who may have conspired to frame him. Joe Hill's last words linger as well, often quoted in folksongs and nostalgic gatherings of the class-conscious: "Don't waste any time in mourning—unionize!"[90] As with Bridger, Hill's greatest deeds as a hero were wrought with words. His songs and rhetoric galvanized and inspired workers before the Jazz Age and gave the IWW influence in the larger union movement far out of proportion to what its meager membership roles might suggest. Like J. Golden Kimball and Jim Bridger, Hill is remembered as a hero for his skills in moving people and creating with words.

Perhaps the figure in world history who most resembles J. Golden Kimball is the Turkish cleric Nasraddin Hodja. Persian (Mulla Nasreddin), Afghan (Mullah Nasruddin), and other central Asian variants of the Hodja cycle also exist.[91] In each country, locals insist that Hodja is in fact their own country's unique cultural hero.[92] Turkish legend, however, has it that more than 750 years ago, in western Anatolia, a man—in what even locals considered an outrageously large turban—rode backward on a donkey out of the small village of Hortu and into a permanent place in the hearts of the Turkish people.[93] The quick-witted but down-to-earth Muslim imam continues to be Turkey's most important cultural hero.

Exact details about the historical figure are hard to come by, but stories in the voluminous oral narrative cycle that arose around him suggest that Nasraddin was not only an imam but also a renowned scholar. According to tradition, he studied at the *medresses* (theological colleges) at Konya and later taught at Sivrihisar and Akshehir, earning the title *hodja* (master or teacher). Nasraddin Hodja's stature in Turkey can still be measured by the fact that any Turk will know who is being discussed by the remark "Hodja said." Although none of Hodja's many tales have even close variants in J. Golden Kimball's cycle and there is no evidence of the two traditions influencing each other, it is easy to imagine Uncle Golden appreciating the following Hodja stories:

On being asked his age, Nasraddin Hodja said, "Forty."
"But Hodja, that's what you said last year!"
"That's right. I'm a man of my word. I always stick to what I say."

The communal Friday prayer was about to start. Someone behind Nasraddin Hodja, thinking Hodja's shirt was rather short for the prayer pulled it lower. Nasraddin Hodja immediately pulled on the shirt of the man in front of him.
The man in front turned back and asked, "What are you doing?"
"I don't know," answered Hodja. "Ask the man behind me. He started it."

On a hot summer day Nasraddin Hodja was resting under a big walnut tree. He noticed that there were some enormous pumpkins growing in the field close by, and then looking up he saw walnuts on the tree.
"Oh, my God," he said silently. "Thou has made both of these—the huge pumpkins and the tiny walnuts. But aren't those walnuts up there too small

for the tree they grow on? A tree whose trunk cannot be encircled by two men stretching out their arms. Those branches spread out like a tent almost fifty yards. Would it not have been better for those big pumpkins to grow on the walnut tree and those walnuts on the pumpkin plant?"

No sooner had he said these words than a walnut fell and hit him right on his forehead. It caused him to see stars and he gave a cry of pain as he held his head in his hands.

A feeling of awe came over him, the fear of God entered his heart and he repented for what he had said. "Oh, my God!" he cried. I have sinned. Please forgive me. Never again will I presume to question the wisdom of thy Providence. Thou movest in mysterious ways! Ah, have mercy on me! What would have happened to my head if this tree had pumpkins on it and one of them had fallen on my head!"[94]

Hodja stories wrestle with issues of significance to the devout of any faith—the importance of honesty, appropriate dignity, and the proper modes of prayer as well as the wonder of God's wisdom. That a scholar-imam—who according to convention should be a model of pious decorum—handles these issues so playfully is one of many parallels between J. Golden Kimball and Nassradin Hodja. Both had titles of religious respect, elder and hodja, yet both were poor. Both were the sons of men of high religious office and called upon to judge and settle difficult issues. Both are remembered for their unaffected modesty and wit—often at the expense of the proud, powerful, and self-righteous. That modesty allows regular people to accept and even enjoy their rebukes. J. Golden Kimball's stories recount the frequent disapproval of other Mormons, and Hodja stories were banned for a time as subversive in the late 1800s' twilight of the Ottoman Empire by the unappreciative Sultan Abdul Hamid.[95]

Hodja, Bridger, and Hill, like J. Golden, became subjects of folklore in large part because of being extraordinary producers and performers of verbal art. "Stories by" and "stories about" blurred and became indistinguishable for all three over the years. The great deeds these heroes did were in many cases deeds of words, and it is their words as much as their deeds that are remembered. They could be called performer-heroes.

The particular nature of these performer-heroes reveals and helps bridge a gulf between two eras in the development of folklore scholarship.[96] Folklore scholars formerly approached their subject as if it were a static survival of the past maintained by communities in which individuals did not play overly important roles except perhaps collectively as "tradition bearers," preserving and perpetuating the old and anachronistic.[97] Folklorists thought in terms of stable tradition and long continuities. In the late 1970s a group of scholars aptly called "performance-centered theorists" pulled the carpet from under these old verities. Folklore was not timeless, they maintained, but in a constant state of change, reinventing and overturning itself through the work of creative performers. As cultures experienced inner turmoil and bumped and ground into each other, swapping influences, the notion that traditions tended to be ancient, monolithic, and uncontested was examined and found wanting.

What folklorists studied shifted from narratives themselves to the social and cultural contexts from which such materials emerged and the aesthetic and societal rules that generated them. Perhaps most important, performance-centered theorists insisted that individuals steeped in the aesthetic standards of their own societies were skillful at performing before audiences in specific settings and at molding and shaping stories and artifacts as expressive art in contexts of constant evaluation and modification.[98]

Folklore scholarship shifted from making broad theorizations about traditional societies to making thick descriptions of individual artistic performers and performances. Rather than presenting a collection of analyzed West Indian folktales with no attribution to authors or discussion of context, for example, Roger Abrahams writes of the "man-of-words," focusing on how individuals practice and perform, either successfully or not, gaining status or losing it, according to local understandings of eloquence and the workings of language.[99] Charles Briggs's work provides examples of the folktales, legends, jokes, and snippets of the banter of New Mexico's Mexicanos, whose ancestors have inhabited Northern New Mexico since before the Mexican War. His purpose is not to examine the texts or narratives for their own sake, however, but to use them as examples of how specific individuals exhibit "competence in performance" according to a culturally maintained Mexicano poetic aesthetic.[100] Both authors focus on the "nowness" of folklore's production and pay much less heed to the idea of tradition and perpetuation of art through time collectively by a community.

To some, such re-imaginings of the field have seemed irreconcilable with traditional understandings of folklore. But J. Golden, Hodja, Bridger, and Hill show one way in which old and new understandings of folklore can best be conceived, not as an eclipse of one perspective by another but as the expanding and refinement of methodological tools to more fully understand the operations of complex folkloric processes. To make sense of J. Golden Kimball it is necessary to understand how stories become part of a relatively stable and continuing tradition, most of which is passed on by people who place little of their own stamp on stories, and how one individual can be a skilled performer within a culture's system of recognized verbal arts.

Only with the new and old folkloristic approaches together can one understand J. Golden Kimball as an example of what might be called a performer-hero. He was a man of words, and his verbal achievements were so great that his stories have escaped the obscurity of undocumented history into which most first-person narratives plunge. They continue as part of a community-owned oral narrative cycle.

The performer-hero is a special case, however. Not all heroes are oral wordsmiths, and not all oral performers rise to hero status. The Mormon hero Porter Rockwell, for example, left no known written records and was not considered to be a talker or storyteller. His skill at keeping his mouth shut, not open, made him valuable as a bodyguard and law-enforcement officer. Many performers such as James Kimball and James Arrington have told great J. Golden Kimball stories and even received a measure of acclaim for doing so. Still, they have not become the subjects of an oral narrative cycle. J. Golden Kimball as performer-hero is more than a competent bearer of tradition. He is borne by tradition himself.

What makes a person skilled in language into a performer-hero rather than a culture-perpetuating bearer of tradition? A partial answer might lie in making use of work done by ballad scholar Eleanor R. Long. In a comprehensive ethnographic examination of a story cycle a scholar will look at the text, context, and storyteller.[101] Long's key insights focus not on texts or structure of the ballads or on the aesthetics of the culture in which they circulate. These are important to her, but not so much as the singer's personality and style.[102] She proposes four ballad performer types that can also describe performers of any genre. The first, perservators, pass on texts just as they hear them, even if parts of the text are unintelligible. The second, rationalizers, feel free to shape narratives only to the extent necessary to put them into conformity with their own religious, philosophical, or ideological stance. The third, integrators, are aware of traditional expectations but feel free to go beyond and create new narratives that use familiar themes. The fourth ballad performer type, confabulators, feel no particular loyalty to tradition and spin entirely new material.[103]

In their approaches to passing along folklore of a certain genre, these types can be arranged along a continuum, from conservative traditionalists (preservators) to innovative creators (confabulators). The innovators are less

34 / INTRODUCTION

likely to tell a story perpetuated by others. Without injections of innovation and adaptation, however, stories cycles ossify and begin slow deaths of irrelevance. Long does not state so, but her research implies a source for new ideas or "mutations" that can cause new traditions to emerge and reinvigorate ossified ones—extraordinary examples of performers toward the integrating center of her spectrum. These people are so conversant with the subtleties and nuances of a given culture that they know all its "sweet spots" that invite the greatest results from an audience, but they are bold and innovative enough to find novel ways to achieve a respected effect. Passed into the stream of oral tradition, new stories by such people are more likely to survive than those proposed by others less adept. J. Golden Kimball was such a contributing integrator in relation to Mormon audiences.[104]

Even this does not fully explain the J. Golden Kimball performer-hero phenomenon. As excerpts from his public addresses show, J. Golden did tell stories—personal narratives after the pattern of preacher's anecdotes and chroniclings of minor personal adventures. Narrative plotting, however, was not his great skill or his main goal in speaking. His genius lay in even more elementary knacks of language use—turns of phrase, dramatic pause, dispensing sudden and audacious truths, and concise insight provided in clear, humorous language. It took the Mormon people to fashion those non-narrative achievements by J. Golden Kimball into narratives about J. Golden Kimball that highlight his abilities.

Because of the profound effect of J. Golden's language on listeners, there are no J. Golden Kimball stories in which he says nothing. They all involve him speaking. J. Golden Kimball humor originates with the man, but his stories are perhaps more the Mormon people's creation than his. This creation owes its origin to J. Golden Kimball's integrative genius, not so much in handling genre conventions as in understanding many elements of Mormon cultural psychology. Mormons have expanded that genius in his legend cycle.

J. Golden Kimball and Mormon Cultural Psychology

Seeing J. Golden Kimball in cross-cultural perspective as a performer-hero figure helps explain some of his continuing appeal in Mormon folklore. But there are further reasons having to do with Mormon cultural psychology that contribute to his popularity and help explain the genius of his humor. Although Sigmund Freud's theories about the psychological function of jokes are not as widely hailed as they once were, his observation that "jokes have not received nearly as much philosophical consideration as they deserve in view of the part they play in our mental life" has encouraged considerable subsequent scholarship into the social and psychological function of humor.[105]

One does not have to be Sigmund Freud to recognize that every culture places behavioral demands on its members that inhibit individual desires and innate biological drives. One of the central insights of psychological and cultural studies of humor is that it can help release the tension that results from social, religious, cultural, and biological demands and constraints.

The temptation exists to attempt to resolve such tensions through abandoning cultural constraints or by adopting fanatic devotion to particular dogma. For Latter-day Saints, President James E. Faust, second counselor in the First Presidency, warns against such loss of balance. In response to these tendencies, he observes that "an important part of the gospel message is that we not be too rigid: that we open our minds, develop some tolerance. . . . For many years . . . I have blessed [children] with a sense of humor. I do this with the hope that it will help guard them against being too rigid, that they will have balance in their lives."[106] Through the medium of J. Golden Kimball stories, the particular set of tensions that Mormons experience come into focus, are exposed, and at least temporarily are resolved with appropriate creativity. Many are present in other cultures, but some are peculiarly configured to Mormons.

The humor that emerges within a certain society and is particular to it will often express features of the society that become more clear when compared to the jokes told in other cultures.[107] Comparing Hodja jokes with J. Golden Kimball jokes reveals underlying cultural differences. Despite the two cycles' similarity in dealing with religious humor, Hodja's stories, such as "The Pumpkin and the Acorn Tree," highlight an Islamic conception of an absolute qualitative gulf between God and man and the futility of man's reason and action. J. Golden Kimball jokes such as the following express more optimism, albeit tongue in cheek, about humankind's creative abilities. The stories are a better fit with Mormonism's theological views of humans as agents with divine potential:

> After delivering a powerful address to a local stake, Brother Golden was being congratulated by the Saints afterwards. Outside the chapel he was met by a woman glowering with apparent indignation and asked Brother Golden for a moment of his time. She said, "Brother Golden I resent you church authorities a little. You come down here and act like you are the Lord himself. Look at this beautiful tree here and the green grass as well as the

flowing stream there, you church authorities can't make these things possible only the Lord can do them." Pausing to think on this Brother Golden said, "Well sister you may be right, I couldn't make that tree grow and I couldn't create the grass, but I'll take you up on the water."[108]

Underlying theological differences between Islam and Mormonism, along with geographical distance and ethnic and language barriers, are perhaps the reasons there are no cognate stories between the J. Golden Kimball and Hodja story cycles despite their similar role in each society. Running through the J. Golden Kimball story cycle is concern with pride and dignity despite the acknowledgment of a lack of sophistication and refinement. Through honesty, directness, and wit, J. Golden Kimball bests the worldly and wise.[109]

During Mormonism's turn-of-the-century transition, such concerns would have resonated with many Mormons. They have diminished somewhat today but were still present in the 1940s, as demonstrated by a popular song of the period, "I Am a Mormon Boy." The song was written by Evan Stephens, the conductor of the Mormon Tabernacle Choir from 1890 until 1916; George Albert Smith (the president of the church from 1945 until 1951) said he remembered singing it in Sunday school as a boy.[110] The song captures to a certain extent J. Golden Kimball's attitude:

I AM A MORMON BOY

Kind friends, as here I stand to sing, so very queer I feel,
That now I've made my bow, I fear I don't look quite genteel;
But never mind, for I'm a boy that's always full of joy—
A rough and ready sort of chap—an honest "Mormon" boy.

Chorus: A "Mormon" boy, a "Mormon" boy, I am a "Mormon" boy;
I might be envied by a king, for I am a "Mormon" boy.

I'm proud to know that I was born among these mountains high,
Where I've been taught to love the truth, and scorn to tell a lie;
Yet I'll confess that I am wild, and often do annoy
My dearest friends, but that's a fault of many a "Mormon" boy.

Chorus

The attitudes and manners depicted in the J. Golden Kimball legend cycle, however, should not necessarily all be viewed as straightforward representations of Mormon values. As Charles Briggs observes, although jokes "closely reflect values that constitute central components of collective identity, this relationship is frequently indirect taking the form of comments on deviations from social norms."[111] If an anthropologist from Mars were to descend to earth in a million years and be able to find only the J. Golden Kimball stories in a folklore archive as the sole window into Mormon culture, her view of Mormon manners would be skewed. In many ways the personality of the J. Golden Kimball of folklore was as different from often-observed Mormon cultural traits as one might imagine. Beyond the cussing and coffee drinking, Uncle Golden was impatient with those who placed demands on his time; had terse and even withering things to say to people; and was combative with annoying outsiders. These motifs are so prevalent as to characterize virtually all the stories in his legend cycle.

Contrast the behavior depicted in the stories with what many note as contemporary Mormons' tendency to be hyper-friendly and patient with strangers—and their penchant for avoiding public interpersonal conflict, even if doing so requires silence or using a euphemism. Of course, every culture contains a wide variety of personalities, many of which do not lend themselves to easy generalizations, but these features of Utah Mormonism are well known to insiders and outsiders alike.

The experience of a friend from New Jersey who sometimes visits Utah illustrates how quickly one senses that "Mormonland" is different from other places in the United States. The friend became lost while looking for the Utah Arts Council office in downtown Salt Lake City and asked a construction worker near the railyard where to find it. The worker gave my friend undivided attention, smiling as he politely used many personal cell phone minutes to call directory assistance and track down the needed number and address. Construction workers by the New Jersey railyard, the friend assures me, do not behave that way.

A French journalist, Jean Sebastian Stehl, who was sent to write specifically on Utah Mormon culture for *L'Express*'s 2002 Winter Olympics coverage, remarked during a radio interview that he was surprised to find that Utahans were not the austere and secretive cultists imagined in the sarcastic French media. They were, he found, almost over the top in their friendliness and patience with his intrusions and questions.[112] Stehl also described being apprehensive about approaching a Salt Lake City librarian for help with an article that touched on a host of Utah's sensitive and controversial topics—liquor laws, church influence in politics, and the like. Instead of being surly and uncooperative, he found her to be "very generous with her time" and "not offended." Stehl repeatedly mentioned the friendliness and eager-to-please generosity of Mormons. "I was very impressed by the generosity of people everywhere," he said. "People would drive us for two hours to take us to a to a place. Families would open their homes to us, you know, even though we were reporters. I'm not sure I would let any reporter into my home!"

These are not isolated impressions. So many travelers through Mormon country have reported similar experiences that public politeness and friendly willingness to help strangers have become defining features of the state. It is common for some Utahans, both men and women, to take this tendency to a saccharine extreme of sweetness.[113]

Adapting to such expectations can sometimes be difficult. The same New Jersey friend expressed how familiarity with Utah's "niceness culture" inhibited him when he considered telling the attentive waiter who served us lunch to leave us alone so we could talk. In the urban East, such requests are common. In Utah, he feared, and not without reason, that the waiter might be hurt by such a request, even if delivered smoothly. Mormons in general—Utah Mormons in particular—will go to great lengths to avoid public expression of social friction. When incidents of friction do happen they are perhaps opportunities for scrutiny and self-reflection more than would be the case elsewhere.[114]

The history of Mormon persecution and the 1890 to 1930 transformation of Mormonism again helps explain these traits. Mormons' pioneer past and long history of being perceived as backward religious deviants have produced a kind of hyper-politeness, anxiety about being civil.[115] Coupled with the strong desire to serve, which comes from religious commitments, devout Mormons often approach encounters with strangers who may not be LDS as if the church's reputation and success were on the line. The world conjured in stories about J. Golden Kimball allows Mormons vicariously to unharness that load and imagine what it might be like to treat troublesome outsiders as he did in a story obtained from a Springville, Utah, college professor in 1998:

> J. Golden Kimball took a cross-country train on business. The people who shared his cabin began bad-mouthing Mormons. "I'm going north to escape the Mormons!" one said. "I'm going east to escape the Mormons!" said another. "I'm going south to escape the Mormons" said the last one. After an angry pause J. Golden bellowed, "Why don't you all go to hell! There aren't no Mormons there!"

Most of the chapter titles of this book are themed on values and behaviors as antithetical as one might imagine to Latter-day Saints' goal of a godly, cooperative society. If, as Wilson suggests, folklore is a mirror for truth, then like the image in a mirror, much of the J. Golden Kimball legend cycle presents an inverted image of Mormon cultural values. Even more than tweaking authority, Kimball's shocking outbursts run counter to the Mormon ethos of polite reticence and are the central theme of his cycle. J. Golden Kimball breaks free of bonds that hold other Mormons.

The Mormon Trickster Figure

Although J. Golden Kimball lore undoubtedly fulfills some folk hero–like psychological functions, particularly in his clever tirades against anti-Mormons and pests, J. Golden does not exactly fit the standard concept of a folk hero. He was his own man, an original, and thus the closest thing Mormon folklore has to a trickster figure who triumphs through his naive innocence as well as his quick wit. When the trickster is acting up, it is not always clear whether innocence or cunning is operative. Such ambiguity forms a large part of the humor of trickster tales.[116]

> A woman with two brothers came to see J. Golden Kimball. One of the brothers, who was a good and loving man with a young family, had just died. The other brother, who was a scoundrel at best, was still very healthy.
> The sister asked J. Golden why this could happen. Why couldn't the Lord take the other brother, the scoundrel, and leave the good brother here?
> J. Golden thought for a moment and said: "Well, I reckon the Lord didn't want that jackass of a brother any more than you do!"[117]

Tricksters appear in oral narrative traditions all over the world and seem to fulfill a universal human need. Among the most renowned are Coyote, a pan-Native American figure especially common in the Southwest and Plains; Anansi the Spider in West Africa and the Caribbean; and Brer Rabbit and the slavemaster-fooling "John" among antebellum African Americans.[118] Trickster figures appear as well among other American ethnic and religious minorities. Ed Cray has identified an American Jewish joke cycle featuring a rabbi trickster who tweaks Jewish and mainstream American convention while besting priests and ministers in contests of quick wit and theological acumen:

> This rabbi and a priest were discussing the merits of their religions and arguing which was the best. The priest was trying to convince the rabbi of the holiness of the Church. The rabbi wasn't very impressed, you know?
> So the priest started right from the beginning. "First you start out as an

altar boy, and then if you are very good and if you want to, you can study for the ministry. And if you study very hard and are very good, you are ordained a priest."

And the rabbi shrugs, "So what?"

"Then if you have the right qualities of leadership and you are very good, you can become a bishop."

And the rabbi says, "What's so good about that?"

"Well if you are a good bishop, then you can become an archbishop."

"So what?"

The priest is a little angry now. "If you are especially meritorious, they can make you a Prince of the Church. Think of that. A cardinal!"

"Big deal."

The Catholic priest is very angry now. "And one cardinal will be elected Pope, the highest office in the church."

"So what?" the rabbi says.

Finally the priest loses his temper. "Well, what do you want? Jesus Christ or something?"

"Vell, one of our boys made it."[119]

Trickster figures among American religious groups are not limited to Jews and Mormons. Larry Danielson has assembled and analyzed a collection of stories about the Reverend Alfred Bergin in Kansas. Bergin stories are a special variety of a common sort of dialect tale because they are applied to a particular performer-hero rather than a generic "Peter Peterson" or "Ole Olson," the everyman butts of humor about Scandinavian Americans. Bergin was an ethnic Swedish Lutheran pastor and college professor who despite being highly educated struggled mightily with English. Among his gems that are still told is the following: "One morning one of the English teachers up at the college . . . he was horrified because he had been to the church in the morning and there had been flowers on the altar, you know, and Dr. Bergin had said that 'Flowers on the altar today are placed there by the Lindquist family in thankfulness for their parents' death.'"[120] The humor comes in part from the hearer's suspicion that the pastor may have inadvertently stumbled onto truth highly inappropriate to express at a funeral.

Despite a paucity of close cognates between religious trickster tales, cross-cultural affinities of style and theme between the Jewish rabbi trickster, the Swedish Reverend Bergin, and the religious and regional hero J. Golden Kimball are easy to see. Even in their more mundane forms, tricksters are powerful mythic figures that impulsively violate the norms of society in spectacular and outlandish ways. In the usually short narratives told about them they sometimes attempt self-serving schemes that invariably go terribly wrong.

Folklorists once thought cultures circulated trickster tales for their ribald entertainment value alone.[121] More recently, tricksters' importance as religious figures and reaffirmers of cultural values have been more fully appreciated by anthropologists and folklorists.[122] Tricksters articulate a culture's deepest beliefs about appropriate moral behavior by violating them spectacularly. In folklore, the tricksters' violations are rarely allowed to stand. They are usually caught and must reap the consequences of their actions. For the Native American Coyote in particular, repeated, gruesome death is the result of violating the principles that lead to harmonious living with other humans and with nature.[123] In the J. Golden Kimball legend cycle a story has emerged that illustrates this principle:

> [J. Golden's swearing] became a problem and the story says that President David O. McKay, the prophet at the time, went to him before a General Conference and told him that he shouldn't swear in the upcoming conference and that if he did, he would not live to see the next conference. He did swear during the following conference, and he died before the next General Conference, just as President McKay had said.[124]

There is no historical evidence that President McKay made such a pronouncement (he was not even president at the time) or that Mormons at the time interpreted J. Golden Kimball's death as the punishment of an angry God. That some would perpetuate such a story is nonetheless evidence of Kimball's legend cycle taking on some of the features of a trickster cycle.

That cultures recognize the value of such stories in teaching the young is evident in their prominence in the ceremonies that elders and cultural guardians use to preserve and perpetuate healthy traditional culture. Through trickster tales, a moral universe in which humans must operate is literally talked into being; through these stories, mortals are taught how to live. Suzanne Lundquist maintains that Western teachers of culture and morals would do well to employ Native American cultures' recognition of the medicinal and pedagogical value of trickster tales.[125] To a certain extent, Mormons who tell J. Golden Kimball stories understand that as well, because young Mormons are initiated into adulthood in some small part through their introduction to the J. Golden Kimball story cycle.

Because tricksters are often important deities (or close thereto), it is not surprising that a Mormon trickster is a General Authority—one of God's anointed representatives. Were he not, he would not be as well remembered or as potent as an ironic figure. The notion of a cussing and slightly undignified church leader is an example of what the humor theorist Elliot Oring calls the element of "appropriate incongruity" at the core of all successful humor.[126]

Trickster tales have significant structural and functional differences among various cultures, but the J. Golden Kimball cycle is perhaps a special case in that he is not self-serving, nor especially ribald, nor very spectacular in his violation of Mormon standards. The J. Golden of folklore steers far clear of harming others and mocking sacred topics. He usually uses only the mildest swear-words—those that to some are more quaint relics than potent profanities.[127] The Antti Aarne Stith Thompson Index includes a section entitled "Jokes about Parsons and Religious Orders." Chief among the attributes of these folkloric ministers are laziness and a penchant for sexual dalliance, attributes completely absent in the J. Golden Kimball legend cycle.[128]

Unlike other tricksters, the J. Golden of folklore is, if not exactly kind in his manner, at least most often selfless in his motives and message and oriented correctly to his culture's central values, although he sometimes forgets himself in the minor details. He transgresses the values of the church he holds so dear out of fierce loyalty rather than insensitivity. Like other tricksters, the J. Golden Kimball of Mormon lore is sometimes impulsive, often punished, and usually reaps the consequences of untoward behavior. In contrast to the others, however, he at least attempts contrition when chastised by his leaders (chapter 8, "A Principle of Repentance" and "Thoughts on Southern Utah").

In a manner uncommon among Native American tricksters but common in the tales of enslaved African Americans, J. Golden often comes out on top.[129] In these jokes and stories he sometimes seems more like an antebellum, American-almanac folk hero such as adventurer Davy Crockett or river boatman Mike Fink.[130] Not with boastful taunts or physical bravado but a quick mind and a clever tongue, J. Golden bests the fools, bullies, pests, and prudes who annoy him (chapter 2). Among his quips is the following story:

> Pest: "Elder Kimball, do you believe that Jonah was really swallowed by a whale?"
> J. Golden: "I don't know. When I get to Heaven I'll ask him."
> Pest: "Suppose he didn't make it there?"
> J. Golden: "Then you can ask him."[131]

In such stories, J. Golden Kimball is the trickster champion of simple rural wit and wisdom against a sophisticated, intolerant world of genteels and Gentiles. He often plays tricks on his audience but always to its instruction, never its detriment.[132] Uncle Golden's tricks illustrate a principle or encourage righteous behavior, as a Springville, Utah, college professor recounted in 1998: "'How many in this congregation would give their lives for Jesus Christ?' All hands go up. 'All right, how many of you would give $5 to the Church welfare fund?' Suckered and shamed, the audience coughs up dough."

Rather than being a danger to Mormon standards, J. Golden Kimball stories reaffirm the necessity—perhaps on an even deeper level than straight-forward morality tales—for Mormons to get right with their God and obey church teachings. The stories and jokes in this book do not lend themselves as an excuse to violate LDS standards concerning polite language. It would be a mistake to interpret J. Golden Kimball stories as giving Mormons license to flippantly break the religion's rules. In the alternate reality created by the verbal renderings in sharing folklore, Uncle Golden swears and violates the Word of Wisdom. When he slips, he is also punished for doing so.[133]

J. Golden Kimball stories help relieve Mormons of the pressure of some-times facing situations in which they might want to curse but know they should not. His stories provide a release valve for frustration. Tricksters such as J. Golden Kimball are, in the words of Roger Abrahams, "a projection of desires generally thwarted by society. His celebrated deeds function as an approved steam-valve for the group."[134] J. Golden stories thereby encour-age the kind of behavior valued by a community striving for harmonious relationships with God and other humans.

Folklore scholarship recognizes the deep human importance of such matters, things other scholars sometimes regard as trivial or undignified. The tools of historians and theologians are insufficient to explain fully why J. Golden Kimball's funeral attracted more mourners than any other in Utah history except Brigham Young's. J. Golden was no revelator of new doctrine like Joseph Smith and no great colonizer like Brigham Young. Indeed, it can be safely assumed that the course of LDS Church history would have gone forward with little significant change had J. Golden Kimball never been born. The study of folklore can help us understand the need to show public respect and love for such a human folk hero.

The State of the Cycle: A Statistical Analysis

In my folklore and Mormon literature classes at Brigham Young University I always require students to collect folklore from its naturally occurring contexts in the flow of everyday life and transcribe their collections to be housed in the William A. Wilson Folklore Archives (WAWFA) at Brigham Young University. This tradition, begun by Wilson, has been on-going since 1969 and has resulted in an extensive collection of folklore at BYU.[135] In the fall semester of 1999 I gave all the students a special assignment: find at least one J. Golden Kimball story for their folklore collection assignment. I was curious about what statistical patterns such a snapshot of the contemporary state of the oral tradition might reveal. Because the purpose of the project was to get an impression of the state of the legend cycle at the turn of the twenty-first century, no stories collected before this class project are included in the statistical analysis.

Of course, such a snapshot is taken from a certain angle and displays only certain aspects of the overall tradition of J. Golden Kimball's storytelling. BYU is in many ways the intellectual and cultural center of Mormondom. To be allowed to come and stay at Mormon BYU, students must adhere to an honor code. They come from all over the United States and many parts of the world. Entrance requirements at BYU are academically rigorous and only "the best and brightest" get in. The collectors for this project, then, were disproportionately high-achieving and academically minded. Although perhaps fewer than half of the worldwide church membership would consider themselves devout (in Mormon parlance, "active"), all of the student collectors were active by definition.[136] Although fewer than 15 percent of Mormons live in Utah, and fewer than 50 percent live in the United States, the collectors were largely from the western United States.[137]

I gave no directions about whom students should ask to tell them J. Golden Kimball stories if they did not run across stories in the normal flow of daily conversation. I only stipulated that they could not use their memories but had to obtain stories from someone else. If, as was the case with a few students, they did not know who J. Golden Kimball was, finding out became part of the assignment. None had difficulty completing the assignment, and many came back with several stories, which indicates a vibrant living oral tradition. Geography limited collections to what was circulating locally in Utah, although some contacted friends and relatives elsewhere. In addition to friends and relatives, the collectors asked other students and professors, especially those in the religious education department.

Forty-one different story types appeared in the ninety-four items collected, suggesting a story cycle that is rich and varied. A version of the most common story appears in this volume as "A Principle of Repentance" (chapter 8). Versions of this brief, succinct, easy-to-remember tale accounted for 11 percent of all stories collected. Versions of "Obnoxious Traveling Companions" (chapter 7) accounted for 10 percent; versions of "Sustaining Leaders" (chapter 1) accounted for 9 percent; and versions of "Troublesome Tourists" (chapter 2) accounted for 6 percent. Most of the rest of the forty-one stories collected with multiple versions had only one variant; four had two, four had three, and four had four.

Although 65 percent of the collectors were female, reflecting the demographics of students taking classes in English departments across the country, 66 percent of informants were male. That probably indicates the disproportionate popularity of J. Golden Kimball stories among male Mormons, but it could also reflect BYU's disproportionately male faculty.

As one might expect on a college campus, 77 percent of the informants were under thirty, only 5 percent were between thirty-one and fifty, and 17 percent were fifty-one and older—the likely age of parents and grandparents. Even accounting for the truncated age demographics of the university context, the numbers indicate successful transmission of the tradition to a younger generation.

A full 74 percent of stories contained at least one cussword of some sort. "Hell" appeared in 51 percent, and "damn" in 36 percent; "S.O.B." or its uneuphemized form appeared in only 3 percent. Stronger language of various sorts only appears in 4 percent of the stories. Cussing was commented on or referred to in only 13 percent, figures that suggest ubiquitous but mild cussing as a central defining feature of the J. Golden Kimball oral narrative cycle.

In the stories, when J. Golden Kimball encounters opposition of some sort he comes out clearly on top 71 percent of the time. The outcome of conflict is left unresolved or unmentioned 26 percent of the time, and he is caught in the act or thwarted only 3 percent of the time. Anecdotal evidence suggests that in earlier decades J. Golden was less successful; the cycle has become more triumphalist in tone. In only 21 percent of the stories, however, is J. Golden Kimball actually angered or does he rebuke people. When his opponent is an anti-Mormon antagonist (which occurs in 26 percent of the stories) he always triumphs, but when he clashes with a fellow General Authority his success rate falls to 91 percent. His failure usually has to do with being caught violating the Word of Wisdom.

In 27 percent, nearly a third, of the stories, a fellow General Authority serves as straight man to J. Golden Kimball's humor. Seven of these twenty-five stories identify only "the brethren"; four identify President Heber J. Grant; and two President David O. McKay, who did not serve as head of the church until after Elder Kimball's death. Brigham Young (who died before J. Golden became a General Authority) is mentioned once, as are Francis M. Lyman and B. H. Roberts.

The stories contain several more historical anachronisms. In a full twenty-seven of the ninety-four, J. Golden Kimball is identified as an apostle even though his highest office in the church was one of the Seven Presidents of the Seventy. The folk historical tendency to "promote" Elder Kimball perhaps indicates the level of respect in which he continues to be held.[138]

Transcription and Attribution Considerations

Although I have tried to be as comprehensive as possible in my collecting, it would be a mistake to regard *The J. Golden Kimball Stories* as an authoritative guide to his story cycle. Books like this volume can only dip into the stream to catch a few fish for display. The stream flows on and the fish continue to swim about, reproduce, and evolve. The real authorities on J. Golden Kimball lore are Mormon storytellers; these tradition-bearers are the ones who shape and perpetuate the J. Golden Kimball of folklore. For convenience, I have titled the stories for reference, but the titles should not be viewed as "the" title of a story.

In reproducing stories in this book I have standardized spelling and punctuation and in a few cases slightly edited apparent faults in the original transcribed documents for ease of reading. A few stories include bracketed contextual information. For the most part, I have closely followed how the stories were told to me and the students or how they have been transcribed in folklore archives.

Because some storytellers consulted in this project are anonymous for various reasons or their stories are not in folklore archives, some items reproduced here do not have a citation. In order to highlight the fact that tellers are not authors, no storyteller's name is attached to the stories reproduced in this collection. The remarkable similarity in versions of particular J. Golden Kimball stories across time and among tellers underscores the community nature of transmission. Some archived stories show little variation for more than forty years.

It is perhaps not surprising then that the tellers from whom the students and I collected were often embarrassed about taking credit for stories. They were eager to pass them on but pushed ownership to the person from whom they had heard the stories. In a few cases I traced this reluctance back several generations—each eager to tell the story but insisting that credit for its authoritative telling lay one generation back from them. As one might imagine, this tendency was most pronounced when a story's learning lineage could be traced to a cultural authority figure such as a bishop, religion professor, actor portraying J. Golden Kimball, or General Authority.

This tendency sometimes made it hard to convince tellers that I was interested in their version of a story rather than that of the person from whom they heard it. There seemed to be a sense of humility and debt to the previous teller and the tradition itself, but the reluctance may also have to do with a desire for distance from whatever moral culpability that repeating swearwords may entail. The wish to avoid personal responsibility for cussing may also encourage tellers to hope their story actually did originate with J. Golden Kimball ("Hey, don't blame me! I'm just quoting a General Authority"). The tendency to push back credit may have led to some stories in this collection being credited not to the informant but to the person who told it to the informant, who then passed it on to the transcriber.

To ground stories in the particular contexts of at least one of their tellings, the occupation and gender of the informant and the location and date of the telling, where such information is available, are given in the notes. Stories collected before the 1980s do not always have much contextual information about tellers because folklorists and archivists had not yet become as attuned to gathering such information as they are now. People in university folklore courses gathered many of the stories for this collection, so a disproportionate number of the informants are college students and professors.

Some of the stories collected here come from the Internet, which presents opportunities for data collection as well as difficulties in doing so. Internet technology simulates in many ways the face-to-face interaction that folklorists have traditionally regarded as their communicative purview. It obscures, however, the identity of storytellers, and although no one would think of copyrighting an orally transmitted joke or legend some have tried to establish some sort of proprietary rights over similar material circulating on the Internet. Most e-mailed discourse, however, is widely recognized as circulating in the public domain.

In reproducing the J. Golden Kimball stories e-mailed to me, I have done my best to ask permission to publish and get contextual data from the people who first posted the items. In most cases I was able to do so, but in others it was unclear where exactly the e-mail had originated, and no one on the list of addresses on the e-mail's header responded to inquiries about the story. Such cases are identified in this collection as "Internet post, 199–." Many J. Golden Kimball stories circulating among friends, whether privately or publicly in discussion groups and mailing lists, have passed at one time or another through the mormon-humor or aml-mag (Association for Mormon Letters Magazine) mailing lists.[139]

Representing in print the cussing of J. Golden Kimball presents a special case that requires careful consideration. As I hope I have made clear, for contemporary Mormons circumspection in speech and avoidance of certain words is more than just a marker of good manners or a throwback to Victorian prudishness. It is part of a genuine religious commitment. American Mormons recognize a spectrum of words to avoid that is similar to the general American public's notions of what constitutes "bad" or "rude" language, but active Mormons tend to be more rigorous about observing these notions. Even those in good standing differ in their opinions as to where to draw the line in the swearing spectrum and what contexts, if any, justify moving the line one way or another to exclude or include more words and expressions.

Students from rural areas tell me that among older Mormons in their hometowns the line is drawn further back, allowing for hells, damns, and the occasional barnyard word in a barnyard context, but the line is drawn clearly nonetheless to exclude other words. Conscientious LDS people generally try to keep their language G-rated and feel guilty when they fail. Language taboos are, of course, structured differently according to country and local custom. One difference between the general American word taboo spectrum and Mormons' is that LDS people are much less likely to use common expressions that invoke God or any of God's names in a casual way as a graver transgression than speaking even the most foul curse words of a sexual or scatological nature. Near the mildest end of the Mormon swearing is the common hell and damn of J. Golden Kimball.

The incongruity of even such low-level cussing with high church office is central to the humor of these stories, but the swearing occurs in a specialized circumstance. For many LDS people, J. Golden Kimball stories are the only context in which they are comfortable with such language. Initial exposure to the tradition can be traumatic for some Mormons unfamiliar with the story cycle. When I was a novice nineteen-year-old LDS missionary in the Netherlands, a colleague played actor James Arrington's *J. Golden* cassette for me—to my great shock. I suspected it was a fake, surely part of some nefarious plot to undermine the true church of God. The world of swearing and the world of General Authorities simply had no overlap in my fresh, young, rigidly structured Mormon mind. I like to think, however, that I have matured in my understanding of the faith.

Even in the context of J. Golden Kimball stories, Mormons today have a range of opinion about how much sliding across the word-taboo spectrum is tolerable. A book such as this is bound to ruffle feathers no matter what I do. If I present these stories using their coarsest, but sometimes authentic, versions, I could be accused of perpetuating needlessly rude material in a manner unbecoming of a Latter-day Saint and in a way that needlessly offends the people whose culture I am representing. If I euphemize too severely, which also occurs occasionally among Mormon storytellers, I could be accused by Mormons and folklorists alike of fatally warping the nature of the stories and misrepresenting the commonest type of manifestations of the tradition.

I have pondered this issue with as much sensitivity to all possible views as I know how. The course I have chosen to follow is similar to that of the Varsity Theater at Brigham Young University, which used to show edited versions of recent popular cinematic releases.[140] Potentially offensive words were deleted from the sound track, but anyone so inclined could discern what was being said from lip-reading and context. Because the words *hell* and *damn* are such defining features of the J. Golden Kimball legend cycle and have been used in every book about Kimball, I have left them unaltered in the stories that follow. In a very few cases I use acronyms or have blanked out parts of words, a method similar to how the words would be euphemized in print during J. Golden Kimball's lifetime. In a few cases, the ¡%#@! of Sunday comic strips seemed the best option.[141]

Folklorists' attitudes about the ethics of representing taboos in the stories they collect have evolved. For many years they subjected potentially offensive material to latinization, elision, or some other form of alteration—often without informing the reader. In the 1960s, following many liberalizing cultural trends of the time, some began to cavalierly suggest full disclosure of totally uncensored offensive or sensitive material, with little regard to the special cultural context of the telling or the feelings of informants.[142] In more recent years the sensitivities of individuals and cultures from whom the stories come, as well as the importance of context, have guided how folklorists represent potentially controversial material.[143] For story collections such as this, most would now pay close attention to the wishes and feelings of the people from whom they collect stories. That is what I have tried to do.

Many will wonder why I have belabored an issue with which Mormons seem mostly comfortable and, by and large, take less seriously than I have here. In my view, however, this collection should not only be about this unique facet of the Mormon experience but also should be from the Mormon experience in a way that resonates with the cultural center of Mormondom and communicates that center. That can only be done by giving careful consideration to the wide variety of possible Mormon reactions to J. Golden Kimball stories and taking them all into account.

Chapter Organization

The first eight chapters of this book thematically categorize the J. Golden Kimball cycle into stories about such stereotypical activities as tricking, quipping, teasing, partaking (as in forbidden substances), cussing, ministering, chastising, and repenting. Even though these categories emerged easily and organically upon looking at the data, such categorizations can lead to a great possibility for overlap. In each case I have tried to identify the operative principle of the story and which category more closely characterized the central workings of the narrative.

Some chapters include multiple versions of the same story (if significant variation is present), but I have mostly chosen one version of the several available for representation. My aesthetic preferences tended to favor transcriptions that were concise and to the point. Many versions, however, were almost identical, even when collected thousands of miles and many decades apart. One of the more common kinds of variation was what folklorists call "regional oikotypes."[144] As stories pass between people they tend to take on features peculiar to the culture or region to which they migrate. The mountain mentioned in the story "Sustaining Leaders: 1 and 2" (chapter 1) tends to be Nebo for residents of Juab County and Timpanogos for those in Utah County, Utah.

The last three chapters are organized differently from the first eight. "Remembering" features personal-experience narratives that are reminiscences of the teller's interaction with J. Golden Kimball rather than a fully formed part of the folk tradition. They shape a sort of intermediary zone of oral history between the historical documentation of J. Golden Kimball's life and the much-passed-on stories of the folkloric tradition. "Resembling" presents a sampling of stories that are not about J. Golden Kimball but are Mormon folk humor in a similar vein. "Repeating" includes Kimball's stories told by his peers and subsequent officeholders in LDS Church general leadership positions.

Each chapter has a short introduction explaining the chapter's theme. Most of the stories and their broader significance are addressed in the analysis of this introduction or the chapter introduction. Many, however, are annotated to give cultural and theological context for details that may be unfamiliar or discuss the significance of differences between versions of the story. Often an allusion to a piece of esoteric Mormon knowledge occurs in several stories. In such cases, only the first story to allude to the issue will be annotated. Still other annotations analyze the humor of the stories, pointing out the appropriate incongruities and juxtapositions.

In a few cases, a J. Golden Kimball story is an adapted Mormon variant of a story circulating in another oral tradition or one that another tradition has borrowed from the Kimball legend cycle. In these cases, the annotation will present examples of story variants from other traditions. Most J. Golden Kimball stories do not have recorded variants outside of Mormon folklore and seem to be creations of Mormons.

The Worth of Story

If, as Wilson suggests, Mormon folklore is a mirror for the beliefs, values, concerns, and frustrations of Latter-day Saints, what do J. Golden Kimball stories reveal about Mormons?[145] They seem to suggest that Latter-day Saints are committed to doing good but aren't always successful. They are a people who, at their best, laugh at their failures and foibles, not to justify them but to gain courage and strength to move on and overcome. The following sentiments by Elder Kimball certainly reflect the sentiments of many who value his words and continue to enjoy the folklore about him. Displaying perhaps a deeper, more hopeful sentiment lying behind his joking fear of justice expressed at other times, this General Conference excerpt provides a fitting summation of Uncle Golden's life-affirming witness:

> Have I not been frank and honest and clear in my statements . . . ? I may not have a perfect and true conception of God, but I love God; I love him for his perfection; I love him for his mercy; I love him for his justice; and

notwithstanding my many weaknesses I am not afraid to meet him. For I know that he will deal justly by me; and the great joy I will have is that he will understand me and that is more than some of you have been able to do.

I believe with the same love and faith that Jesus is the Christ, the Redeemer of the world. I believe that Joseph Smith is a prophet of God, and there is no man living who reads the things that God has revealed through the Prophet, and the sayings of the Prophet with more joy and more satisfaction and more happiness than I have.[146]

These sentiments, so powerfully expressed in his life and teachings, go a long way toward explaining the enduring popularity of stories about him. Considering the literary value of J. Golden Kimball stories, there are several reasons one might want to discount or marginalize them. All the reasons I believe untenable.

Some Latter-day Saints might wish to be rid of or downplay the cycle because of the sometimes embarrassing lack of polish or decorum in them. J. Golden Kimball stories can stir up Mormon society's still simmering brew of civility anxiety concerning public image and the possibility of persecution. There are, however, important reasons why Mormon culture has seen fit to generate and maintain the cycle. Moreover, insiders are often not the best judges of what will endear outsiders to them. Consider, for example, the millions of goyim whose respect and understanding for Judaism have grown through the fiction of Chaim Potok, whose Orthodox family was concerned about negative reaction when he exposed tensions within their community.

To those who might wish to see the cycle vanish or lose its edge, it is perhaps worth remembering a principle the Mormon pioneers would have understood: Never throw anything away, even when it seems obsolete. You never know when it might come in handy. Cultural resources are like household resources in that respect, but the proportional costs involved in hanging on to cultural resources are considerably less than storage unit rental fees.[147] Another line of reasoning has kept all folklore in general, J. Golden Kimball in particular, largely outside the serious consideration of cultural commentators. Some scholars might be tempted to denigrate Kimball lore's significance to Mormon culture as epiphenomenal—a by-product of, or at best a commentary on, one society's character and achievements. Those people might claim that the J. Golden Kimball legend cycle is not a significant achievement in and of itself.

It would be foolish to stack a joke or legend against any serious work of fiction in the American or world literary canon. But as Wilson points out, that would not be the right or fair comparison to make.[148] Individually, each J. Golden Kimball story might seem trivial, a small, bright, shining star of worth at best. The complete cycle of his stories, however, constitutes a remarkable, interconnected, community-produced cultural artifact. It is a constellation, a starry sky. Taken as a living whole, the J. Golden Kimball cycle constitutes the most significant trove of Mormon humor and one of the great works of Mormon and western American literature. Like a multiauthored oral novel or epic poem, the cycle is a multifaceted exploration and amelioration of the human condition that elucidates life, death, God, marriage, children, irony, loss, love, pain, and happiness.

ONE

Tricking

J. Golden Kimball lore reveals a man willing to deceive, manipulate, and scold his audience—and they loved him for it. In the following stories, Elder Kimball's tricks are designed to bring out the best religious attributes in people—generosity, obedience, volunteerism, reverent attention, honesty, humility. Unless the story has to do with the Word of Wisdom, Kimball usually revealed his own tricks and thereby showed their higher purpose. Mormons find this sort of deception not only forgivable but also endearing because it is not self-serving but rather designed to help others improve.

In the stories in this chapter, the J. Golden Kimball of folklore most approaches the trickster figure type common in many cultures around the world. The methods employed in these stories may draw inspiration from an idea expressed in Mormon scripture. In Doctrine and Covenants (19:10), the Lord explains to Joseph Smith that the phrase "endless torment" in the Bible should not be interpreted to mean that suffering will never end for those found on the left hand of God after final judgment. Rather the torment is "endless" because it comes from God and "endless" is one of God's names. The Lord explains to Joseph Smith that this potentially misconstruable wording was intentional because "it is more express than other scriptures, that it might work upon the hearts of the children of men" (19:7). So if concealment and surprise were in J. Golden Kimball's persuasive tool kit, he was in good company as far as scripture is concerned.

Giving Your All

On one occasion Brother Golden had been sent to a community to raise funds. He started his appeal with the question to the audience in church: "How many of you would be willing to lay down your lives for the gospel?" Every hand was raised. "How many of you would give fifty cents to the Mutual Improvement Association fund?"[1] It took a little time, but hands went up one by one, and as the audience left every one of them gave fifty cents or an IOU to the bishop.[2]

Mark: Chapter 17

J. Golden Kimball began one of his stake conference addresses supposedly, by saying, "Brothers and sisters, how many of you have read the Seventeenth Chapter of Mark in the New Testament?"

Many hands went up, and he said, "Well, you're the people I want to talk to today! There are only sixteen chapters in Mark and my sermon for today is on liars and hypocrites!"[3]

Opening Line: 1

Once J. Golden Kimball was supposed to give a speech to a group of Mormons. The audience was really noisy—everyone was talking and seemed to be unaware that J. Golden Kimball was standing at the pulpit, waiting for them to settle down. He stood up there for quite a while and everyone ignored him and kept on talking. He got madder and madder and finally shouted, "GO TO HELL!" At once everyone's attention was on him, and they were really shocked. Then J. Golden Kimball continued ". . . and there you will find people who didn't take advantage of their opportunities."[4]

Opening Line: 2

I recall an opening line in a sacrament meeting talk in 1978, at, of all places BYU, in which the speaker pointed to the back row at some boys who were talking and screeched in his best J. Golden impersonation: "Young men in the back row, GO TO HELL."[5] Quiet pause. "And I'll tell ya something, when ya get there, you'll find people . . . who aren't satisfied." This was an attention-getter. The first counselor in our bishopric even woke up.[6] The speaker then went on to explicate what Brother Golden had to say on a topic I've forgotten since the only part I remember was about the satisfaction levels of inhabitants of outer darkness.[7]

Sustaining Leaders: 1

In the old days, General Authorities used to read the names of church officers that needed to be sustained by raising hands at the stake conference. [J. Golden Kimball] went through all the names of General Authorities.[8] After naming all these officers, the people were quite tired by then. Most of them were nodding their heads and were just prior to falling sleep. So finally Brother Kimball said, "All of those in favor of moving mount of Timpanogos down to St. George, please manifest by the raise of your hands." And everybody raised their hands. He said, "OK, we expect all men to be here tomorrow morning with your shovels."[9]

Sustaining Leaders: 2

It seems that Brother J. Golden Kimball was the visiting authority at a stake conference in a small rural stake in an area just south of Provo. The weather was warm and sunny. The afternoon session of conference began at that calm, lazy time of the early afternoon, resulting in a calm, lazy atmosphere among the congregation. After the opening formalities of song and prayer the congregation settled back in their seats to begin the tedious business of sustaining the authorities of the church.

It was the custom in this stake to read each name and office rather than just asking for a vote on the presently constituted board. Needless to say the reading of each name stretched into a lengthy affair. Brother Kimball noted the apathy of the audience, tapped the clerk on the shoulder, and took over the reading. The change of voices revived the gathering for a few minutes. Soon, however, the high-pitched, squeaky voice of Brother Kimball had the same effect the previous reader had had, and again the group settled back in their seats and listened with only partial attention.

Brother Kimball, noting the lack of attention he was receiving, became somewhat perturbed. He continued to read on in his high-pitched, squeaky voice for a time, then without a pause or a change in voice he said, "It is proposed that Mount Nebo be moved into Utah Lake, all in favor manifest by the usual sign." Surprisingly, a majority of the people raised their hands.

Disgusted by the obvious lack of attention the congregation had paid, he stopped, looked at the sleepy faces below him for a moment, then yelled into the microphone. "Just how in the hell do you people propose we get Mount Nebo into Utah Lake!"

After the uproar had died down and the lecture was completed, the meeting continued. In spite of the weather and the time of day, the attention for the rest of the meeting was considered excellent.[10]

Tithing

J. Golden Kimball was addressing an assembly of BYU students on the subject of tithing.[11] He asked the young people how many paid a *full* tithing, and only a fourth raised their hands. Brother Kimball then put this question to them, "How many of you would die for the Gospel?" Everybody shot up their hands. "That's what I thought," he said, "you'd rather die than pay your tithing."[12]

The Book of Mormon

President Kimball was giving a conference address during the April session of General Conference. He began by asking the audience in his high, squeaky voice whether any of them were interested in reading the sealed section of the Book of Mormon.[13] A raising of hands indicated that the congregation unanimously agreed they would like to do this. Brother Kimball continued: "Then why in the hell don't you read the parts that aren't sealed?"[14]

The Lantern

Uncle Golden was a visiting speaker at a stake conference near Bear Lake. The stake president, in his introductory remarks, got carried away bragging about how wonderful his stake was statistically. "Elder Kimball, we have more tithe payers and our youth program has the best attendance of any stake in northern Utah. We have more missionaries in the field, more temple marriages, and a larger percentage attendance at sacrament meeting than any stake in the church.[15] Ninety-five percent we have, yes we do. We just thought you'd like to know that Elder Kimball before we turn the time over to you."

Elder Kimball got up and said, "It is nice to be back here in this stake. As you may remember I was up here about a year ago for a welfare meeting.[16] I got a call from an old friend asking me to go fishing. I told him I couldn't go because I had a welfare meeting to go to. But he persuaded me and I went. We lit a lantern to attract the fish and were soon reeling them in like there was no tomorrow. But a wind come up on the lake and we had to head for shore. Fifty feet from shore the boat sank to the bottom and had to swim for it.

"Well, this year I am up here again and yesterday I went fishing again with my friend. (He promised me he had a better boat this time.) Wouldn't you know we saw last year's boat right by the shore twenty feet down. And wouldn't you know the fish and the tackle were still there! And that lantern was still burning away one year later!"

J. Golden called the stake president up to the stand and put his arm around him and said, "Now president do you believe that story?"

"No, Elder Kimball I don't. There is no way that a lantern can burn for a year under water."

J. Golden then said, "Well president, if you take 15 percent off of your attendance figures, I'll douse that lantern."[17]

Walking on Water

The pope, an atheist, and J. Golden Kimball went fishing one day. As they were sitting in the middle of the lake, the pope realized that he forgot his fishing pole on the shore, so he stepped out and walked across the water, returning promptly with it. Soon after, J. Golden Kimball realized that he forgot his fish bait, so he stepped out of the boat and walked across the water, returning promptly with the bait. The atheist was amazed but thought that if they could walk across the water, why couldn't he? So he stepped into the water and sank. While the pope and Kimball were helping him out of the water, the pope looked at Kimball and said, "I guess we should have told him about the rocks, huh?" Kimball's reply was, "What rocks?"[18]

TWO

Quipping

J. Golden Kimball, when asked how he decided what to talk about in his sermons, replied, "I feed them like you do your sick cows. I give them two or three apples and then throw in an onion. That gets their attention!"

Uncle Golden is a Mormon folk hero precisely because he was a man of words. In the following stories, and with a few short jabs, he turned the tables on adversaries, hostile Gentiles and bothersome Mormons alike. Responses to the pesky questioning of ignorant and self-righteous Mormons who accosted him after church meetings as well as replies to menacing Gentiles who tried to thwart his service to the Lord constitute the two most prominent story types. If the oral tradition accurately reflects his personality, he was nimble on his feet and quick with his tongue, ready to respond with a snappy comeback or smart one-liner to get himself off the hook and put his interlocutor on it. J. Golden's wit was not always acerbic, however. In "Slippery Hazards" his quip eased the tension of an awkward situation for Kimball and his interlocutor. Occasionally it is the interlocutor who gets in a quip at J. Golden's expense, as in "The Suit."

Words have the power to create and change. In this chapter they create a situation in which J. Golden Kimball has the upper hand and change the world to his advantage. Such power, enacted through means other than brute force, is a hallmark of the trickster type in folklore around the world. The Stith Thompson *Motif-Index of Folk Literature* devotes a large subsection to "Clever Practical Retorts" (J1500–J1649).[1] These stories would fit into it nicely.

Often the same story that can be regarded as word proficiency can also come across as a gaff of gross ineptitude, depending on how one interprets Golden's ability. This ambiguity highlights a key feature of how humor works that is virtually universal in story cycles of humorous figures worldwide. At the core of virtually all such humor lies an example of extraordinary intelligence or extraordinary density. The Turkish imam Nasreddin Hodja's legend cycle displays this feature as well. Sometimes he seems to be a verbal master, able to best any sophisticated adversary with a few well-chosen words. At other times he appears the epitome of oafish simplicity. In the story "Funeral Metaphor," for example, the humor works whether the pun was intentional or not.

Laying on of Hands

J. Golden Kimball was walking by his neighbor's house, and his neighbor, who was watering his garden, turned his hose on him, drenching him, and said, "You're a Mormon right? Don't you Mormons believe in baptism by immersion?" And then J. Golden Kimball, while jumping the fence and running at the man said, "Yes, and we also believe in the laying on of hands."[2]

Opinion of Gila Valley, Arizona

J. Golden came to visit the Saints in Gila Valley, Arizona. As the local stake president showed him around, he noticed that Elder Kimball did not seem terribly impressed with what he saw.[3]

"Why, Elder Kimball, Gila Valley isn't so bad. All we need is more water, cooler weather, and some more good people and we'd have a right fine place indeed.

J. Golden replied, "Sure. More water, cooler weather, and some more good people is all that hell would need to be a fine place too!"[4]

Jonah

Pest: "Elder Kimball, do you believe that Jonah was really swallowed by a whale?"[5]

    J. Golden: "I don't know. When I get to heaven I'll ask him."

    Pest: "Suppose he didn't make it there?"

    J. Golden: "Then you can ask him."[6]

Noah

J. Golden once owned two donkeys that constantly refused to work together. Instead, they would run off in different directions. Once when reflecting on these donkeys, J. Golden said, "It makes you wonder how Noah got two of the SOB's on the ark."[7]

Ten-Dollar Hat

J. Golden Kimball was examining a hat in ZCMI. When a clerk approached him he asked the price. The clerk replied, "Ten dollars," whereupon Brother Kimball started to look inside the hat pulling back the band. The clerk, confused by his close inspection, inquired, "What are you looking for?" Without looking up, Brother Kimball responded, "Holes."

    "Holes?" questioned the now utterly confused clerk. "Yes," said Kimball, "for the ears of the jack-ass who would pay ten dollars for this hat."[8]

Slippery Hazards

One snowy, cold winter day, J. Golden Kimball was walking north of the temple in Salt Lake City. A very large lady bumped into him, knocking him to the ground. The lady also fell, landing on top of J. Golden. They began sliding down the hill on the ice and snow, J. Golden acting as a sled for the large lady. After going about a block, they bumped into a curb and stopped. The lady wasn't quite sure what to do, so she just lay there on top of J. Golden. He finally told her, "Sorry lady, you'll have to get off now, this is as far as I go."[9]

St. Peter: 1

J. Golden was killed in an auto accident. It is rumored that arriving at the gates of heaven, he was greeted by the master receptionist, Saint Peter: "Well, Brother Golden, at last we got you here!"

"Yeah, but by hell, you had to kill me to do it!"[10]

St. Peter: 2

It is told posthumously of J. Golden Kimball that when he died and went to heaven he was met at the gates by St. Peter, who greeted him with, "Well, Golden, at last we got you up here!" Kimball is supposed to have replied, "Yeah, but you had to kill me to do it!"[11]

Indignation

After delivering a powerful address to a local stake, Brother Golden was being congratulated by the Saints afterwards. Outside the chapel he was met by a woman glowering with apparent indignation and [she] asked Brother Golden for a moment of his time. She said, "Brother Golden I resent you church authorities a little. You come down here and act like you are the Lord himself. Look at this beautiful tree here and the green grass as well as the flowing stream there, you church authorities can't make these things possible, only the lord can do them." Pausing to think on this, Brother Golden said, "Well sister, you may be right, I couldn't make that tree grow and I couldn't create the grass, but I'll take you up on the water." [12]

Round and Round: 1

Brother Golden was entering Hotel Utah in a revolving door, and Brother Grant was going through the other way.[13] Brother Grant made it through the other side, but Brother Golden in his lanky way stumbled around the revolving door once or twice and spilled into the hotel lobby. Brother Grant, seeing him thus, ran to his side and asked the former to speak to him, to which Brother Golden replied, "Hell, Heber, I passed you twice and you didn't greet me—why the hell do you expect me to speak to you now?"[14]

Round and Round: 2

This event took place at the church-owned woolen mills which Brother Kimball had been instructed to visit, representing the First Presidency of the church. Part of his gentleman's attire was a long frock coat which he always wore. As he was walking along discussing plant operations with his guide, his coat was accidentally caught on one of the machines, which began to pull him around so fast that he had to run as it pulled him around in circles. After being drug around for about twelve revolutions he was thrown to the floor. The young man who was showing him around the mill came running over and said, "Brother Kimball, speak to me! Speak to me!" He looked at him straight in the eye. "I don't know why the hell I should, I passed you twelve times just now, and not once did you speak to me!"[15]

Sleepy

This happened in St. George. J. Golden was down there with an apostle for stake conference. J. Golden fell asleep while the apostle was talking and fell off his chair right at the feet of the apostle.[16] The apostle looked rather strongly at Brother Kimball, who responded, "Well, you shouldn't be so damn boring."[17]

The Singing Bride

J. Golden Kimball once told the following story: "I knew a man who fell in love with a woman who had a beautiful voice. He loved to hear her sing. She could sing like a meadow lark. Well, he was so in love with her he couldn't wait to get married. After the preacher had hitched them up, they went off on their honeymoon that night. As they were settling in for bed, that good woman first of all took off her wig and put it on the bedpost. That startled the man a bit. Then next she took out her false teeth and put them in a jar on the bed stand. That shook him up a might also. And then when he thought he had seen about everything, she popped out her glass eyeball and put it on the bed stand. And that man took a long look at her and said, 'Well sing woman, for hell's sake. Sing!'"[18]

Paint

J. Golden was once asked his opinion of women wearing cosmetics, which some General Authorities in the early part of the 1900s frowned upon.

J. Golden said, "Well, a little paint never hurt any old barn."[19]

Troublesome Tourists

There was to be an impressive tour given to some dignitaries from other lands. J. Golden Kimball was assigned to the tour as a guide. They first took a bus trip to the important historical sites in and around Salt Lake City. Brother Kimball would constantly remind the visitors how fast the industrious Mormons put up buildings. Every time he would say so, one of the dignitaries on the tour would say, "Oh, is that right? In our country we could do it in half the time." J. Golden began to get madder and madder as the dignitary persisted to offer such comments.

The tour was to end by having the bus drive around Temple Square. Then this dignitary asked, "What is that building there?" as he pointed at the Temple. "Damned if I know," said J. Golden. "It wasn't there yesterday."[20]

Family Ties

J. Golden Kimball would always say proudly that he was the son of Heber C. Kimball, one of seventeen and not a bastard among them.[21]

Parentage

When J. Golden Kimball was being set apart as a General Authority, the apostle ordaining said in an apparent attempt to make J. Golden feel confident, "Brother Kimball, you are truly your father's son."

J. Golden turned around and said, "Well I'm certainly glad to hear that!"[22]

Ignoramus

Uncle Golden used to say, "Before I went on my mission I was such an ignoramus I thought 'epistles' were the wives of apostles. The gospel must
be true or ignoramus missionaries like me would have ruined it a long
time ago."[23]

Convention Prayer

At one point the church was all voting democratic. They were accused of
political bias due to religion, so the president of the church commanded
that when a congregation was seated, the bishop was to divide the right
and left side of the chapel into Democrats and Republicans.[24] The president of the church did the same with the General Authorities. J. Golden
was placed on the Democrat side. He did not want to be a Democrat, but
relented because he wanted to be obedient.

However, when he went to the Democrat National Convention it was
announced that he would give the opening prayer. He didn't get up. The
announcer called his name again, but he still didn't say the prayer. Finally,
after a third call, J. Golden stood up and said, "Look, I don't mind if you
all know I'm here, but I sure as hell don't want God to know I am."[25]

Dog Attack

Brother Kimball, while working up at Bear Lake as a young man, is supposed to have been attacked by the farmer's dog. (Perhaps since Uncle
Golden was so skinny, the dog smelled a bone.) Brother Kimball had
a pitchfork in his hand, and to protect himself he shoved it at the dog,
burying a tine in his throat and killing him. The farmer came at Kimball
in a rage and asked why in heaven's name he had shoved the pitchfork
down the dog's throat, and J. Golden Kimball answered, "Because that's
the end he came at me with!"[26]

Real Estate Prophecy

One day J. Golden Kimball spent $3,500 on a real estate deal, and the
man with whom he did the business said, "Golden, I am going to proph-
esy. Ten years from now you will be worth a million dollars!" Golden

said, "Now I am going to prophecy. If, in ten years from now I am worth a million dollars, I'll go to hell!"[27]

False Attribution

One day a nephew of Golden Kimball met him on the street and said, "Uncle Golden, I've got a brand new Golden Kimball story."

"I'll bet the damn thing ain't genuine. Every new story that gets started these days is hooked either on to me or Mae West!"[28]

The Lord's Family

They tell one about his [J. Golden Kimball] being brought on to the carpet because his family was going astray, not doing just what they ought to do. And they told him a church official ought to have a more exemplary family. He sat and listened, and then he said, "Well, I guess according to your idea of an exemplary family, I don't think that God Almighty made such a hell of a success."[29]

Baptism

One day he said, "I believe in being honest, true, chaste, benevolent, and virtuous, and in doing good at all times. What can you do with a man that is a cheat and a liar? You can baptize him every ten minutes, but it won't do him any good unless you hold him under."[30]

Destinations

[J. Golden Kimball once said] I had a chance to meet Reverend Weatherby. He got up and he spoke one night with me. And he went on and on about how all the Mormons are going to go to hell if they don't change their ways. "They don't have the truth. They're going to go to hell, straight to hell. This is a good man," he pointed to me, "but in the next life he'll go straight to hell." He spoke for forty-two minutes. Finally, it was my turn to speak and I got up and I said, "I only have one thing to say. I'd rather be a Mormon going to hell than not be a Mormon and not know where the hell I'm going."[31]

A New Suit

J. Golden Kimball walked into the big Salt Lake City department store ZCMI and told the clerk in the men's department, "I'd like to see a suit that would fit me."

The clerk eyed his tall, thin frame and said, "Hell, so would I!"[32]

Funeral Metaphor

In his most solemn and somber voice J. Golden Kimball spoke at a funeral, saying, "Brothers and sisters, what you see before you in this casket is just a shell. The nut has gone on."[33]

Reading Glasses

Well, J. Golden Kimball was giving a talk at church, and his eyes were going just like the rest of us. He probably needed bifocals, but I don't know if they had them much back then. He was reading from his notes, and he had to hold them out like this (at arm's length). He said, "It's not that I can't see, it's just that my arms are too damn short."[34]

Go to Hell

One night there were these teenagers out after dark, and they were making a lot of noise so he [J. Golden Kimball] couldn't sleep. So he opened the window and yelled out to them, "You all go to hell! It's obviously where you're going anyway, so why don't you just go now so those of us with morals can get some sleep."[35]

A Full 10 Percent

The prophet once asked J. Golden Kimball if he paid a full 10 percent tithing.

J. Golden replied, "Hell no! I don't even make 10 percent!"[36]

THREE

Teasing

Teasing can serve two very different social functions. It can be used to remind someone that they are disliked or not accepted. In other cases teasing happens when people are comfortable in the security of their bonds of fellowship. In such cases, teasing demonstrates not the absence of the ties that bind but their vigor. Similar observations could be made about the expressions of doubt that also come up in some of the stories in this chapter. For those insecure in faith, jokes about disbelief can be uncomfortable. For those who are secure, such jokes highlight that security.

In the framed and bracketed world of in-group joking where few things mean what they literally suggest and where doubts and acerbity are harmlessly vented, J. Golden Kimball says very surprising things about his religion and his fellow religious leaders. Mormons might find such comments highly offensive coming from outsiders—or even LDS people who are not General Authorities. But when recognized as the kind of teasing that occurs among other believers who are secure and belong to a special community, such stories must be interpreted very differently. Folklorist Roger L. Welsh points out that a relationship of trust and shared experience must preexist between individuals before such humor is interpreted as representing mutual friendly feelings rather than antagonism.[1]

In "The Bible," J. Golden shares a frustration common among Christians about the impenetrability of some sections of the Old Testament; in "Reading Choices" he acknowledges that many Mormons are slightly discomforted at preferring the Gentile-owned *Salt Lake Tribune* to the church-owned *Deseret News*. Interpreted at face value, it would seem that J. Golden's sharpest, most disturbing sentiments are directed at fellow Quorum of the Seventy president B. H Roberts ("Quorum Succession"), known to be among Golden's best friends in church leadership. To understand "Revelation" and "Elder Smoot's Calling" requires knowledge of a peculiar aspect of LDS Church governance—"being called," in Mormon parlance, by divine inspiration. A call is issued by those already in the hierarchy when a vacancy opens or an expanding church requires additional offices. Sometimes church members will speculate about whether political or personal considerations have also played a role in who receives a call to high office in the church.

Curiosity

In his last years, he [J. Golden] met a friend in the street who said to him, "How are you, Golden? How are you getting along?" "Well, to tell the truth, I'm not doing so good. Getting old and tired. You know, Seth, I've been preaching this gospel nigh onto sixty years now, and I think it's time for me to get over on the other side to find out how much of what I've been saying is true."[2]

The Selection Process

Brother Golden once said of the [mate] selection process, "I've been told you need to pray to find out which wife to marry. Well, while I was praying one day, another fellow up and married my gal."[3]

Visions

J. Golden was approached by a church member one time who said, "Elder Kimball, you are a General Authority; you're supposed to have revelations. Have you had any visions lately?"

"Hell no! But I've had some damn good nightmares."[4]

A Good Joke: 1

Elder Kimball had been chastised by President Heber J. Grant for telling so many jokes in General Conference. President Grant told him to be more dignified and requested that he tell no more jokes in Conference.

When Elder Kimball next spoke in Conference, he really tried to abide by President Grant's wishes, but he just couldn't get his talk moving. Finally, he gave up and started telling jokes right and left. President Grant leaned forward, tugged Elder Kimball on the coat, and began to scold him for telling jokes again. Elder Kimball merely motioned toward the congregation and said something like, "Well, hell President, the Lord must enjoy a joke, else he wouldn't have made half them people out there."[5]

A Good Joke: 2

J. Golden Kimball once said in a conference, "The Lord Himself must like a joke or he wouldn't have made some of you people."[6]

The Worth of a Soul

At a conference in Wyoming he angrily told the people that they were not as good as manure because at least you could use manure for something.[7]

Revelation

Uncle Golden used to say that there are three "shuns" to getting called to high position in this church—"inspiration," "revelation," and "relation." "And if I were not the son of Heber C. Kimball, I wouldn't have amounted to a darn thing in this church!"[8]

Elder Smoot's Calling

When Reed Smoot was called as a apostle, J. Golden Kimball came into his office to speak with him. "Brother Smoot," he said, "I just wanted you to know that I really and truly believe that your calling was inspired by

God. It must have been a genuine revelation from the Lord because sure as hell nobody else would have ever thought of you."[9]

Saving the South

[As a missionary in the American South, J. Golden Kimball had a lot of trouble with Baptist ministers and the KKK. So he would often say,] "The only way to convert the South is to burn it all and baptize for the dead.[10]

The Bible

During a General Conference of the church it was reported that J. Golden Kimball stood up and, motioning to the other general authorities behind him, said, "The brethren asked me if I had read the Old Testament. I said I had and if the Lord'll forgive me I never will again!!"[11]

Reading Choices: 1

Once while J. Golden was preaching a funeral sermon in Idaho he was listing all the good qualities of the person who had died. While doing this he said, "I know he was a good man. He always read the *Deseret News*, and it takes a damn good man to do that!"[12]

Reading Choices: 2

He was in San Francisco one day preaching a funeral sermon, and he was describing the great virtues and talents of the man who had died, and he concluded, "I know he was a good man. He paid his tithing regularly. He sent his sons on a mission for the church. He lived the gospel. And what's more, brothers and sisters, I know he was a good man. He always read the *Deseret News*, and it takes a damn good man to do that."[13]

Modern-Day Revelation

Once when Brother Kimball was conducting a discussion on modern-day revelation in an adult Sunday school, a member asked why they didn't hear as much about this as in the early days of the church. Brother Kimball replied, "Well, it's like this, any man can receive revelations for himself and for his own family. But there is only one person authorized to receive revelations for the whole church, and that's the president. And I wish to hell he'd get on the job. He travels around so damn much God can't catch up with him!"[14]

Advice to Senator Smoot

Senator Smoot was contemplating a second marriage, but before he undertook that step he thought it would be well to consult with his brethren, and he forthwith proceeded to call on Brother Heber J. Grant to ask him his opinion. Brother Grant was enthusiastic. He said, "Sister Sheets is a very fine woman, Brother Smoot, and the marriage has my hearty approval and what's more, I add my blessing." As Brother Smoot left the president's office he ran into Golden Kimball. He said, "Golden, I've just been talking with Heber about my forthcoming marriage, and he approves it heartily and what's more, he adds his blessing. What do you think about it?"

"Oh, I don't know so much about that, Reed. I don't know about that. She's a young woman, you know—now wait a minute—you're an old man you know, or fast getting that way, and she's a young woman, and she'll expect more from you than just the laying on of hands."[15]

The Fortunate Companion

To keep J. Golden Kimball out of trouble they used to send apostle Rudger Clawson with him on speaking tours to keep him in line. Elder Clawson would always go first, and he was fond of telling the story about how he and his missionary companion were attacked by an anti-Mormon mob many years ago. Evidently it was quite violent, and the mobbers killed Elder Clawson's companion. As the speaking tour progressed, J. Golden Kimball noticed that Elder Clawson's story got longer and longer and more and more embellished with gory details. Pretty soon Elder Kimball's time was squeezed out entirely, and he was relegated to giving only the closing prayer.

After one such church meeting in Richfield, a man came up to J. Golden and said, "Brother Kimball, I brought my son all the way up from St. George just to hear you speak. Aren't you angry and upset that you didn't get any time to give your talk?"

J. Golden replied, "Well, I'm not mad really but some times I wonder if those mobbers got the wrong missionary."[16]

Boring Speeches

One time President Francis M. Lyman complained to J. Golden that he upset the general authorities too much. Golden Answered: "Well, you see, Brother Lyman, you talk and send them to sleep, and I have to talk and wake them up!"[17]

A Word on Snoring

J. Golden Kimball and Apostle Francis M. Lyman often went together to visit conferences in various stakes. They always slept at the homes of the people in the stake. Apostle Lyman was known to be a humorless and rather dull speaker. He put people to sleep, and J. Golden woke them up. One night as the two brethren went to bed, sleeping in the same room, Apostle Lyman complained to J. Golden about his snoring. "Now," he said, "if you would keep your mouth shut while you sleep, you wouldn't snore." "I'll make a deal with you Brother Lyman," J. Golden said. "I'll keep my mouth shut while I am asleep, if you will keep yours shut while you are awake."[18]

Quorum Succession

B. H. Roberts, president of the Seventies, and J. Golden Kimball, his second counselor, were both speakers at a stake conference. Roberts of course preceded Kimball to the rostrum and in his heavy manner spoke for an hour and a half. Then he turned to Kimball and said, "Brother Kimball, do you have anything to say to these brothers and sisters?" "Only this," replied Kimball, "when you die I will be president of the Seventies."[19]

The Stolen Lawnmower

Supposedly, one Saturday morning, J. Golden Kimball came down the street and knocked on President Grant's door and when President Grant answered he says, "Heber, some SOB stole my lawn mower and I just came down here to see if you had it."[20]

The Priest

One morning while Elder Kimball was walking with his companion in the Southeast States mission they found themselves confronting a priest. As they approached the priest, he greeted the two missionaries by saying, "Good morning, you sons of the devil." Elder Kimball replied with a smile, "Why, good morning . . . father!"[21]

Separate Beds

The Presidency of the Church had decided that from that date on when they, or the apostles or other general officers of the church, went out to speak in the various communities, they would insist upon sleeping in separate beds.

Apostle McKay and J. Golden Kimball were on a trip together, and the issue came up when the family who was going to entertain them suggested that they would use such-and-such a room. President McKay explained to them that they were happy to eat together and pray together but that they didn't like to sleep together. "Yes," J. Golden remarked. "I would sooner sleep with an old yaller dog than with any one of these brethren."[22]

Assistants to the Twelve

At the time that the custom was instituted to have assistants to the Quorum of the Twelve, Elder Kimball was asked what he thought of having these additional members assist to the Quorum. He said, "I don't think it is a bad idea at all to have a few spares. There are plenty of flats!"[23]

Church Office Building

One time Brother Kimball was asked by a friend how many people work in the Church Office Building. Brother Kimball replied, "How many people work in the Church Office Building? Oh, I would say about one-third of them."[24]

Apostles

J. Golden Kimball got notified at the last minute that two members of the Council of the Twelve Apostles couldn't go as assigned to preside over a stake conference in St. George, and so he had the assignment. He was met at the station by the first counselor in the stake presidency, who exclaimed, "Well, Brother Kimball! Welcome to our stake. It's a real honor to have you with us, but where are the apostles?"

After the necessary explanations, the counselor took Brother Golden to the chapel, where the rest of the stake presidency was waiting: "What a pleasant surprise to see you, Brother Kimball! So where are the apostles?"

After the Saturday meetings, Golden went home with the stake president, whose wife met them at the door with a big smile: "Brother Kimball! What an honor to have you in our home! Tell me, where are the apostles?"

The next morning, he spoke in his customary shrill voice to the assembled stake membership: "Brothers and sisters! I had a dream last night. I dreamed I died and went to the Pearly Gates. Peter shook my hand, looked me in the eye, and said, 'Brother Kimball, what a treat to see you! Where are the apostles?'"[25]

J. Golden's Coffin

J. Golden Kimball once said in General Conference that if people say nice falsehoods at his funeral, he was going to kick the hell out of the coffin.[26]

When You Die

One of the brethren said to J. Golden Kimball, "When you die there will never be another like you in the church.

Uncle Golden replied, "Yes, and I am sure this is a great comfort to you."[27]

FOUR

Partaking

The following stories have to do with J. Golden Kimball's breaches of the Mormon health code called the Word of Wisdom. This code is described in section 89 of the LDS book of scripture, the Doctrine and Covenants. In the decades of the early twentieth century church leaders increasingly emphasized the code—originally revealed to Joseph Smith to be sent "not by commandment or constraint"—and formalized it to mean complete abstinence from narcotics, tobacco, alcohol, coffee, and tea. Today, adherence to the Word of Wisdom is required for good standing in the LDS Church. It is one of the defining practices that sets Mormons apart from many of their neighbors.

J. Golden Kimball struggled as many Mormons did during this time of increased emphasis on the Word of Wisdom. According to humor scholar Christie Davies, jokes about alcohol, and by extension any proscribed substance, "are most common under circumstances of moral uncertainty and disagreement about whether and how alcohol should be consumed."[1] Latter-day Saint society during Kimball's lifetime was in just such a situation. Coffee in particular posed a problem for Golden, perhaps because its evils were less pronounced than alcohol's and tobacco's and perhaps because it was such an integral part of the cowboy lifestyle of his youth. Although some stories emphasize J. Golden's personal struggles with the Word of Wisdom, others highlight his commitment to preaching it and living by it. The stories seem to indicate a hierarchy of sin. Smoking, in which J. Golden never seemed to indulge, was deemed more severe than drinking coffee, something with which he did struggle (e.g., "Stake President Selection Process").

In classic trickster form, stories such as "Caught in the Act" recount failed attempts at covering his transgression and thereby reaffirm the importance of the Word of Wisdom to LDS people. Speaking perhaps of his struggles with the Word of Wisdom, Kimball supposedly said, "I may not have walked the straight and narrow, but I tried to cross it as often as I could."[2]

The Influence

Supposedly, J. Golden Kimball stood in General Conference and said, "I would never have the courage to stand before this great congregation in this historic building without being under the influence . . . of the Holy Ghost of course!"[3]

What to Drink

He always liked to eat his lunches downtown in Salt Lake City at the Rotisserie. He liked to eat with a group of lawyers. And on this particular day he was seated at the end of the table, and the lawyers were seated around the table. The waiter came to his end to take Brother Golden's order first, and the waiter wrote the order down and then said, "What will you drink?" Now a good member of the church was not supposed to drink tea or coffee, and so Brother Golden said, "Water."

Someone next to him said to the waiter, "Oh, he likes coffee. Bring him coffee." So the waiter put down coffee, and Brother Golden watched him and didn't say a word until the waiter got to the other end of the table, and then he said, "The Lord heard me say water!"[4]

Caught in the Act

Well, first you need to understand that years ago the Word of Wisdom was not a commandment but rather a suggestion, and a lot of good church members would drink alcohol and coffee, and some would use tobacco. I think it was Heber J. Grant who really started enforcing it. Anyway, J. Golden Kimball had always liked coffee and was having a hard time giving it up, but he'd been told it needed to be done. Well, he was sent to Logan with . . . it could have been Elder McConkie's father . . . or Elder Ballard's . . . anyway, they were at a restaurant, and both ordered their meals, and both ordered hot chocolate with their food. Well, after the waitress leaves, J. Golden excuses himself to go to the bathroom and slips back into the kitchen and tells them to switch his hot chocolate for coffee. He comes back and sits down, and a few minutes later the waitress comes with their food and asks, "Now which one of you wanted the coffee?"

And J. Golden pipes up, "Hell, Elder, if you wanted coffee, why didn't you say so? I'll have some with you!"[5]

Piety

Brother Kimball was traveling around the country, visiting various groups of Saints and speaking at their conferences. During one particular conference the Saints decided to try to impress their visitor by showing him how good they were about keeping the Word of Wisdom. They met together and drew up a checklist of all the things they were going to refrain from drinking and eating. Then they put the list on the speaker's pulpit, where Brother Kimball could not possibly miss seeing it. After reading the list, true to form Brother Kimball stunned the pious Saints with, "Good hell, soup will go next!"[6]

Do Something

At a meeting of the Seventies Quorum of the Timpanogos Stake, Brother Kimball was addressing in his capacity as a general authority. Brother Kimball is reported to have said the following: "Do something! Get busy and do something! Go out and get drunk and then repent of it. But do something!"[7]

Have a Cup

J. Golden Kimball was on church business and was waiting in a train station. He had some extra time, so he went in to have a cup of coffee. Two other General Authorities on some other business happened to come in as J. Golden was sitting there drinking his coffee, and he had to think of something fast, so he just asked them if they would like to join him for a cup of Postum. He went over and ordered them coffee so that it would look just like his. The general authorities, never having tasted Postum or coffee, drank it and never knew the difference.[8]

Stake President Selection Process

J. Golden Kimball and a regional representative were driving down the road on their way to a meeting where they planned on reorganizing the stake when they saw a man off in the distance out in his field. J. Golden says, "Stop, turn around and go back, that's your man." The regional representative says, "I don't think so, he was smoking." J. Golden Kimball replies, "Brother I know that man is the one God wants as the new stake president." So they turned around and went back and J. Golden went out into the field to talk to him. He introduced himself as J. Golden Kimball a general authority and said, "I am now calling you to be the new stake president." The farmer says, "I can't do that with these damn things" (the cigarettes) and J. Golden replies, "No, you're gonna do it without them damn things."[9]

The Old Man and the Pipe

President Grant and Elder Kimball were riding along in a carriage to speak at a ward conference. They spied an old farmer with a smoking pipe clenched between his teeth walloping the tar out of his poor son behind the barn.

President Grant called out "What are you whipping that boy for?"

"I caught the rascal smoking back here and I'm learning him a lesson!" replied the old fellow.

President Grant was just about to launch into to a tirade about the gross hypocrisy of the situation before him when J. Golden Kimball piped in, "Why that is wonderful. Just what I like to see—progress between the generations!"[10]

The Coffee Shop

When Heber J. Grant called for the church to live the Word of Wisdom more faithfully, J. Golden's wife would no longer allow him to fix his coffee at home. J. Golden would sneak to downtown Salt Lake to a couple of different restaurants and have a cup of coffee. One time while he was sitting in a back booth near the restrooms, a lady spied him and confronted him, saying, "Is that you Elder Kimball drinking coffee?" J. Golden replied, "Ma'am, you are the third person today who has mistaken me for that old SOB!"[11]

FIVE

Cussing

In an interview on James N. Kimball's video *Remembering Uncle Golden*, the *Salt Lake Tribune* humor columnist Robert Kirby observes that J. Golden Kimball brought about good not because he cussed but because he could relate to people.[1] The cussing was an incidental marker of his cowboy background. Elsewhere, Kirby suggests that "the transition from campfire to council was nigh impossible. Not because Golden lacked faith, but rather because he discovered that far too many of the things that worked on the ranch also worked from the pulpit."[2]

Cussing is the most famous feature of Uncle Golden stories. Almost all in his cycle contain a cuss word or two, usually saved to the end to give extra punch to a punch line. Indeed, because of the Mormon attitude about swearing it doesn't take much to achieve an effect with an LDS audience.

One of the paradoxes of J. Golden Kimball lore is that for the stories to remain part of Mormon culture they must at the same time remain slightly scandalous and therefore intriguing. Were Mormon society to relax language taboos, the stories would cease to have the impact on Mormons that they do now. Without the Mormon aversion to cussing, many J. Golden Kimball stories would become meaningless.

This chapter focuses on stories that do not just contain swearing but

are in someway about swearing. Here, Kimball, those above, and those below him in church organization chastise, laugh at, wrestle with, and make
sense of Uncle Golden's peculiar proclivity. If swearing is seen as a kind of
folkspeech or a kind of traditional folkloric practice in and of itself, these
stories are examples of metafolklore—folklore about folklore.[3] Metafolklore
provides an indirect but useful way to glean significance and meaning from
folklore by paying attention to what those who tell it say about it. These
stories provide a kind of folk-literary criticism about the artistry of swearing
and its appropriate contexts.

Vocabulary Words

He [Uncle Golden] was asked if his swearing during sermons was intentional, if he used those two little words that caused him so much trouble
on purpose. "Well, I never intend to cuss. When I get up to speak I'm
not thinking about those words but they just come out.[4] They're left over
from my cowboy days. They used to be my native language. And I can
assure you that they come from a far larger vocabulary."[5]

Worse Sins: 1

J. Golden was talking with one of the Quorum members one time, and
the "brother" said to him, "Brother Kimball, I don't see how you can
swear so much. Why I'd rather commit adultery than swear so much."
    J. Golden answered, "Wouldn't we all brother? Wouldn't we all?"[6]

Worse Sins: 2 (different punch line)

J. Golden was talking with one of the Quorum members one time, and
the "brother" said to him, "Brother Kimball, I don't see how you can
swear so much. Why I'd rather commit adultery than swear so much."
    J. Golden responded, "I didn't know we had a choice!"[7]

Conference Talk

In an effort to control Brother Kimball's swearing over the pulpit, Heber
J. Grant wrote out a conference talk for him to read. J. Golden stumbled
over a few lines, squinting at the page and really trying to comply with

the president's request. Finally, he put the paper down, and turned to President Grant, who was sitting on the stand behind him, saying, "Hell, Heber, I can't read this thing!"[8]

On the Wall

There is this restaurant located on Center Street in Provo. I can't remember the name of it, but I guess it's pretty cool because the walls are completely covered with signatures and quotes about how delicious the food is there. Anyway, I guess J. Golden Kimball ate there once, and he wrote a message on the wall that says, "Best damn food I ever ate—J. Golden Kimball." And it is still there.[9]

Note Passing

My mother first heard this story from Brother Watts in my home ward. He said that as good a man as J. Golden Kimball was, he did make constant use of swear words.

During one conference, the conference was to be broadcast and J. Golden was to speak. The authorities were kind of worried about the language he might use, so they passed him a note as he took the stand, warning him to be careful as he was on the air. He picked up the note and said, "What the hell is this damn note?"[10]

A Word of Advice

During the Great Depression Elder Kimball was walking down the street after conference, accompanied by a banker. The banker told J. Golden, "I don't think you as a General Authority should be swearing like you do." Elder Kimball replied, "This is a hell of a time for a banker to give advice."[11]

Trouble with Swearing: 1

There once was a boy from St. George who was known for his wild past. He reformed, and one day his Mormon bishop asked him to go on a mission for the LDS Church. The bishop made it clear that the boy would have to forsake all wicked practices.

The young man said that he couldn't break himself of one thing—swearing. He said he had already tried everything and nothing worked.

So the bishop sent the prospective missionary to Salt Lake City to talk to a General Authority about his problem.

In Salt Lake, the boy explained his problem, and the interviewing general authority said. "I'm going to send you to the elder in charge of swearing."

The boy was then sent to J. Golden Kimball, one of the first seven presidents of the Seventy, who, after hearing of the problem, said, "You can stop swearing. Hell, I stopped years ago."[12]

Trouble with Swearing: 2

He [J. Golden Kimball] grew up in kind of a rough lifestyle and wasn't very rich. Once they were in a logging camp. The swearing was getting out of hand, so the advisors told them they couldn't swear anymore. And J. Golden Kimball was one of the kids supposed to be a leader or supervisor. There was this one guy who just couldn't break the habit, so they sent J. Golden Kimball to talk to him. And J. Golden was talking to him, we'll say his name was John, and he said, "John you've just got to quit. You've just got to do it." And John was like, "I just can't." And J. Golden was just like, "Damn it John, if I can do it so can you!"[13]

Oxen Problem

One day he said, "When we were hauling those temple logs, we had some oxen, and those oxen were a little lazy. They wouldn't pull. I had a team of oxen that just stood there and looked at me. Well, it was just after the manifesto on swearing, and I got mad, and I cussed those oxen up one side and down the other, and boy did they get in there and begin to pull![14] But they were church oxen and they understood the language!"[15]

Vocabulary

J. Golden blamed the mule-skinner's work environment for his cussing habit. "Mules just won't move if you speak to them in ordinary English. They understand only the most powerfully colorful language. I assure you my cussing now is only the pitiful remnant of a far larger vocabulary."[16]

Cow Trouble

One time he went out to feed the calf on Sunday morning. He was all dressed in his satins and Sunday best. The darned calf wouldn't drink. In order to get the calf to drink he had to stick his fingers in the milk and put them into the calf's mouth, then stick the calf's nose in the milk. He did that and the calf snorted or sneezed and sprayed milk and mucus all over Brother Kimball. He said, "If I weren't a Mormon, if I wasn't trying not to swear, and if I wasn't a priesthood holder, I'd push your —-damned head in the bottom of the bucket!"[17]

What We Remember

Mr. Tanner told a story about President Grant reprimanding J. Golden Kimball for the language he used in addressing the Saints. The day following the reprimand, a group of church dignitaries were sitting in the presiding bishop's office, all giving Golden the dickens for talking that way. "Why doesn't he cut out that stuff?" "Why doesn't he be more refined?"

One of the apostles spoke up and said, "What did Brother Ballard say in the meeting yesterday?" Someone replied, "Well, I don't remember just what he said, but I never heard such a fine talk in my life." Then he said, "What did Golden say?" And they all remembered.[18]

Bridges

J. Golden Kimball and some other brethren were at a meeting to determine how the church budget should be allocated. The meeting dragged on and on about trivial matters and J. Golden was getting very annoyed. When it was proposed that the church provide funds to help build a bridge over the Jordan River, Elder Kimball exclaimed, "We don't need to waste our money on this project. Hell, I could pee half way across the Jordan River." Except "pee" is not exactly the word he used.

Elder Stephen L. Richards replied, "Elder Kimball! You are out of order!"

"I know I am. And if I weren't, I could pee all the way across!"[19]

Punctuality

Some brethren were waiting for J. G. Kimball to come to church so that they could get on with their meeting. They kept asking one another if he was coming. One man who knew him quite well said that he would be coming soon and that they would be able to hear him down the road. Pretty soon they could hear yelling coming from down the road. They were able to see that it was a man herding some mules along the dusty path. As the procession approached, they recognized it to be J. G. Kimball cursing his mules for not going any faster. His loud swearing had given his entrance away.[20]

Radio Broadcast

J. Golden Kimball, an illustrious member of the church, at one time presented a weekly radio program on Sunday mornings over station KSL in Salt Lake City. One morning he became unusually worked up and swore over the radio, using "damn" and "hell" particularly. President George Albert Smith immediately called Brother Kimball into his office and chastised him for such unbecoming behavior. A newspaper reporter later learned of the encounter between the two general authorities and approached Brother Kimball about the matter, asking him how he felt about being reprimanded. The witty apostle thought but a moment before he answered, "Well, I love all the brethren, but I love some better than others!"[21]

A Shame

I got the following J. Golden joke from Amelia Smith McConkie, the widow of Bruce R. McConkie.[22] It was the one about the lady who asked J. Golden if he ever heard President [Heber J.] Grant swear. J. Golden pondered it a while in a most serious way and finally said, "Yes. There was one occasion." A shocked audience began to listen carefully. "It was on one occasion when we were traveling to St. George during a drought. Everywhere we looked rivers and canals were dry, crops were destroyed, and cattle and other animals lay dead on the side of the road." After having seen all this J. Golden said to President Grant, "This is a damn shame!" And President Grant said, "It sure is!"[23]

Freedom of Speech

On one occasion Elder J. Golden Kimball was invited to be the speaker in one of the assembly programs at Brigham Young University. One of the teachers, in order to reassure him that his remarks would be highly esteemed and that he would be restricted in no way, said to him as he went up the stairs approaching the stand, "Brother Kimball, here is a place where you can say just exactly what you want." And Elder Kimball said, "Well, if this is—this is a place that I can say just what I want, it's only—the only place on God's earth that I can."[24]

Traveling Companion

Rudger Clawson was a very dignified apostle who often traveled and talked at church conferences with J. Golden Kimball. People thought this pairing was the prophet's sense of humor at work since the two had such different styles. Elder Clawson preferred a mild manner and was so reserved that he could hardly stand to preach at the same meeting with J. Golden Kimball.

One time Elder Kimball and Clawson visited a stake that was not living the gospel. They were not paying their tithing, and attendance at church meetings was very low. When J. Golden spoke to these people he got really worked up and preached a fiery, hell-fire and damnation sermon with lots of choice cuss words and some very stern and angry lecturing.

Elder Clawson got really embarrassed and slunk down in his chair, and at the end of the meeting he bolted out the door. Realizing what was going on, J. Golden chased after him and found Elder Clawson at their hotel room, packing his bags. "I just can't do it Golden. I just can't tour with you and hear you berate people like that and use such awful language. I just can't stand it anymore; I'm going back to Salt Lake City."

Elder Kimball felt awful and tried to console his companion. "I'm so sorry. You know I love those people and you know I love you." He paused and then said, "Brother Clawson, you know if I didn't throw in a few hells and damns once in a while, they wouldn't listen to me anymore than they listen to you."[25]

Inspiration

In southern Utah, when the Quarterly Conference of the Church was to begin its broadcasting by KSL radio, Brother Kimball was to speak last, at 3:45, and the broadcasting was to cease at 4. This was to give Brother Kimball enough time for a good talk but to lessen the chance of him making one of the faux pas for which he was known. Also, to lessen the chance of a slip, President Grant had asked him to give a written talk. The Conference proceeded as scheduled until the time for Brother Kimball's talk. As he got up to give his talk, he looked at the large microphone on the stand, then at President Grant.

Then turning to the audience, he said, "I don't see how the hell I'm supposed to get inspired with this damn microphone in front of me and President Grant behind me."[26]

The Last General Conference

[J. Golden's swearing] became a problem, and the story says that President David O. McKay, the prophet at the time, went to him before a General Conference and told him that he shouldn't swear in the upcoming conference and that if he did, he would not live to see the next conference. He did swear during the following conference, and he died before the next General Conference, just as President McKay had said.[27]

J. Golden's Car Crash

J. Golden was driving his car when he drove off an embankment. He was discovered immediately because it was a busy road. Just before he passed away, when he was pulled from the car, he exclaimed, "What a hell of a way to die!"[28]

SIX

Ministering

Preaching, counseling, and traveling to help run the church took much of Elder Kimball's time and effort. He was involved in the most intimate of events in the Mormon life-cycle such as marriages, excommunications, divorces, and funerals. Many stories reflect the strains this put upon him and highlight his attempts to carry out his responsibilities with cheer and wit. His quips often seem self-consciously well crafted, and he tactically employed them to achieve a desired result ("Double Standard" and "The United Order.")

Uncle Golden Kimball, however, also often put his foot in his mouth, blurted out sharp remarks, fumbled attempts at kindly ministering in times of personal crisis, and came across as funny, even appropriate, in spite of himself ("Funeral Eulogy" and "Why Death.") In this manner he is again like the trickster figures of many cultures' folklore, but the stories contain a strong element of purposeful self-depreciation quite unlike the vanity of most tricksters.

These two images of J. Golden Kimball's skill with words—the virtuoso and the bumbler—constitute a paradox in the legend cycle. The seeming contradiction forms a fuller picture of a multifaceted human whose personality is not sterile, consistent, or monolithic.

Latter-day Saints, many of whom have served in positions of responsibility in a totally lay-organized and administered church and all of whom have interacted with lay leadership, can relate to instances where the human elements of church operation sometimes chafe against each other. Humor helps Mormons override these bumps and attain better places in interactions as fellow Saints.

Almost all of the stories in this chapter convey no information about whether the member being ministered to appreciated Elder Kimball's ministering. In fact, most punch lines seem to strive for the maximum divergence of at least two possible interpretations of his actions. The words can be highly offensive as well as just right in soothing a suffering person in need of comfort and counsel (e.g., "Why Death?"). In fact, the genius of the stories lies in the fact that the hearer is invited to imagine how they might respond were Kimball to say something similar to them.

Far from being offended, one real-world recipient of J. Golden Kimball's solicitude remarked, "The day before [my surgery], a mutual friend brought Brother J. Golden Kimball to administer to me. First, he talked and visited a considerable time and then blessed me. There was nothing frivolous about his talk, and yet he soon had me smiling. Later, the smiles were interspersed with laughter. I began to see things in proper perspective and to realize that all was well. . . . . I felt I was in the presence of a sane, well-balanced man of exceptionally strong faith. In truth, never did I feel the power of faith more than that day."[1]

The Missing Congregation

J. Golden once arrived at the Tabernacle in St. George one Sunday and found that the hall was nearly empty. Instead of giving his talk to a nearly empty building, he went in search of the congregation.

He found them at a local ball field, about to watch a baseball game.

J. Golden calmly walked out to the pitcher's mound, and the crowd, realizing who it was, fell silent.

So, Golden preached his sermon right there from the pitcher's mound.

When he finished, he yelled "play ball" and climbed back into the stands to enjoy watching the game.[2]

Double Standard

Somebody said, "Brother Golden, people always laugh at you. Do you intend to be funny?" "No, I don't. I don't expect to say those things, but they just come out. Take Brother Ballard, for instance. Now he can say the same thing I do and people like it. He can get up in the Tabernacle and he can say, 'Brothers and sisters, I have not prepared a sermon for you today. The Lord will put the words into my mouth, and only the Lord has an idea as to the message that I will bring.' And then he'll go ahead and preach a fine sermon. I can get up and say the same thing: 'Brothers and Sisters, God only knows what I'm going to tell you!'"[3]

Trip to Salina

Years ago, the brethren sent J. Golden to Salina, Utah, to visit the Saints. When he got there he found the bishop very upset and at wit's end.

"What's the matter bishop?" said J. Golden.

"Elder Kimball, we have a woman in the ward who is just so promiscuous it is terrible. She's destroying the community," said the bishop.

"Come now bishop, it can't be as bad as you say!"

"It is Elder Kimball. I hate to say it, but she's slept with half the men in town."

Thinking quickly and trying his best to console the distraught bishop, J. Golden said, "Now bishop, that's not so bad. Salina isn't a very big town."[4]

Special Delivery

There was this one old lady that when J. Golden was getting up there in years she came up to him and goes, "You're getting old and your time's about up J." She had an envelope and she said, "I was wondering if you could deliver this envelope for me?" J. Golden says, "Sure, I could do that. Who's it for?" She says, "Well, it's for my father and I was wondering if when you passed on you'd take this to him." And J. Golden Kimball said, "Ma'am when I pass on I ain't going to have time to go looking all over hell for your father!"[5]

Why Death?

A woman with two brothers came to see J. Golden Kimball. One of
the brothers, who was a good and loving man with a young family, had
just died. The other brother, who was a scoundrel at best, was still very
healthy.

The sister asked J. Golden why this could happen. Why couldn't the
Lord take the other brother, the scoundrel, and leave the good brother
here?

J. Golden thought for a moment and said, "Well, I reckon the Lord
didn't want that jack-ass of a brother any more than you do!"[6]

Condolences

After a friend died, Golden called on his widow to express his condo-
lences. The widow was grief stricken and said she was sad that she would
never see her husband again.

Golden then replied, "I'm awfully sorry to disappoint you, sister, but I
know you will!"[7]

Sealings

I heard that when J. Golden Kimball would perform [marriage] sealings
in the temple, as the couple would kneel at the altar he'd say, "Okay, take
each other by the hand. . . . I said *take* hands not *shake* hands. You'll have
time to get acquainted later!"[8]

Marriage Problems

For approximately twenty years after the church announced the termi-
nation of the practice of polygamy, there were still many problems with
plural marriages, and especially in southern Utah. Around 1915 there
occurred in southern Utah many more of these marriages of which the
church was not aware. By this time the church looked upon polygamy as
adultery, and when word was received in Salt Lake City of the problem
which existed in southern Utah, the General Authorities, of course, were
very upset and concerned. They knew that the problem must be solved

immediately and that the Saints in that area must be brought to the realization that adultery is a grievous sin.[9]

J. Golden Kimball was selected to travel to southern Utah to try and solve this problem for the church. A special meeting was called for all the husbands and wives in that area to hear a General Authority from Salt Lake City talk about a serious problem in their area. Of course, most of the people attending knew what to expect as far as the subject matter for the evening, but little did they expect the treatment which was given that subject by J. Golden Kimball.

J. Golden really captivated his audience and brought everyone to an equal understanding level when he began his speech with the following sentence: "If my wife looked like your wife, I'd commit adultery too."[10]

Treating Women Right

While attending a Relief Society conference in the tabernacle Brother Golden noticed that most of the sisters were snoozing or inattentive.[11] When it came his time to address the female congregation Brother Golden began his talk with "I don't know one man in a hundred that knows how to treat a woman right." This comment aroused the sisters, and when Brother Kimball was satisfied with this attention he then said, "And I don't know of a woman in a thousand that knows when she's being treated right."[12]

The Perfect Couple

Brother Golden had quite a lot to say about marriage. One day he said, "I've often wondered what would happen if the perfect man married the perfect woman. I'll bet he'd shoot her within a week if she didn't poison him first."[13]

Funeral Eulogy

One time as J. Golden was preaching the sermon of a deceased man, the man for whom he thought he was preaching walked in and sat down on the back row. Elder Kimball stopped, turned, and said, "Bishop, just who the hell's funeral is this?"[14]

Adultery Case: 1

A [Scandinavian immigrant] brother had been called before the high council on a charge of adultery. It seems that he had been paying too much attention to a certain sister while her husband was away on a mission.[15] This was a very serious offense, the penalty for which would be excommunication. Although Brother Golden was in attendance as a representative of the general authorities of the church, the local bishop was conducting the hearing.

"Now, brother," he began, "pretty serious evidence has been presented that you have been unduly attentive to this sister since her husband has been away."

"Yeah, biscop, dot is true dot I haf been. De brudder iss on his mission unt I tink dot it is right fur us to take care of dose dat stays at home. I yist do my Christian dooty und dot is all right, I do notting wrong."[16]

"But you have been seen around the sister's home all hours of the day and night, and on one occasion you were seen to leave the house at five or six in the morning. You must have been there all night. Now what about that?"

"Vell, now, biscop, dat's all right, too. I do all de things vot a good brudder should do. Unt I do de chores and sometimes it takes a long time to do de chores und maybe it do take me all night sometimes. But dat is all right. I have do notting wrong. I yist do my dooty and dere's notting wrong in dat."

"Well, you know," continued the bishop, "it has been testified that someone was passing by the sister's house and they looked in the window and saw you in bed with her. Now how do you explain that?"

"Vell, biscop, it's like dis. I do not deny dat maybe I have been seen in bed with her. But I vant to say right here and now dat I have do notting wrong! I am not guilty of de thing of which you accuse me of!"

Whereupon J. Golden Kimball unwound his long legs, stretched, and said, "Brethren, I move that the brother be excommunicated. It's obvious that he does not have the seed of Israel in him."[17]

Adultery Case: 2

The brethren find out this old boy's been seen around a particular sister's house, even staying overnight. They investigate the matter, call a church court, and the fellow admits to having had intimate relations with the woman for over a year. Some brethren feel that since no child was born they might ought to go lenient on him.

J. Golden says, "I vote that we excommunicate him because if he had the true seed of Israel in him it would have been made manifest by now."[18]

An Enthusiastic Eulogy

Brother Kimball was invited to speak at a certain funeral up in Idaho. At the service, J. Golden ranted and raved and praised this poor deceased gentleman for some time then finally sat down. After the meeting, the bishop of the involved ward suddenly noticed that Brother Kimball had disappeared. The bishop went investigating and finally found him outside, knocking his head against a fence post. In concern, the bishop asked what the problem was. With a downcast look on his face Brother Kimball replied, "Oh, Brother, I just preached that man right into the celestial kingdom but I just know he's going straight to hell."[19]

Small-town Dispute

Several years ago in a small valley community that lies just outside of Ogden, Utah, there arose a dispute between the local stake presidency and high council and the elders quorums.[20] It seemed as if the stake president was met with opposition in every plan that he tried to implement. . . . [There] was open rebellion between the elders quorums and the presidency. A formal request to have a General Authority was sent. . . . J. Golden Kimball was the General Authority that was sent.

President Kimball met with the elders quorums and then with the stake presidency. He told the elders quorums that he would like to hold a meeting in two days to review a plan of action. . . . Later he met with them, and after an opening prayer he proceeded to take down the names of every member present. After he did this, he stated that he now had the names of all those present and that they had better damn well repent or that they would be promptly excommunicated from the church. After stating this, he walked out of the room and returned to Salt Lake City.[21]

The Russian Name

J. Golden Kimball was once giving a blessing to a Russian with a name that was very difficult to pronounce. He tried several times to get it right when he finally gave up and said, "Oh Father, you know who this is anyway" and proceeded with the blessing.[22]

Sustaining a Bishop

J. Golden Kimball was extending a calling for bishop. He presented the first individual, who was rejected by the congregation [a very rare occurrence]; he then presented them with a second, and the members rejected each candidate with a unanimous vote. He then looked to the audience and asked them for a candidate that they would accept. A gentleman from the back of the room raised his hand and suggested a name for bishop. Kimball asked the congregation where the man was, and they replied that he was plowing his fields. Brother Kimball said okay, departed to the farm, and interviewed the individual that they suggested for bishop. Satisfied with the man, he returned to church with him still dressed in farm clothing. J. Golden asked the congregation if this was the man that they desired. They said yes, and Brother Kimball set him apart right then and there on the stand.[23]

The United Order

Mr. Cannon said that one time J. Golden Kimball was discussing the United Order in a sermon. He said, "Brothers and sisters, I believe in the United Order! I will throw all my debts in with you any time!"[24]

Promise Keepers

J. Golden Kimball was sent out to call a missionary from an outlying stake in the valley. He told the stake president to find a list of eligible men, then he and the stake president sat down and eliminated all but one. This one was a poor farmer saving up to buy a wagon. J. Golden says to call him in anyway. When they told him what they wanted, the man says, "I want to buy my wagon, I don't want to go on a mission." J. Golden tells him, "If you go you'll be able to buy a better one when you get back." So the man accepted the call and went but had to sell his horses and use his savings in order to go. The man goes and comes back, and goes to work to buy back his horses. Then he goes to see J. Golden Kimball and tells him, "It's been a year and I still can't buy my horses, let alone the wagon." J. Golden takes him out to his stable and picks out his best horses and wagon and gives them to the man. The guy doesn't want to accept them and has to be persuaded to take them. He finally takes them and leaves. Elder Kimball goes inside, and his wife is waiting for him to scold him for being so dumb as to give away their best horses. She really lays into him, and J. Golden tells her, "Be quiet woman, if the Lord won't keep his promises, by hell I will."[25]

Patriarchal Blessing

One day he said, "You young fellows. I want to advise you to go down to the patriarch and have your patriarchal blessing, and find out what's in store for you if you live the gospel the way you should.[26] When I was a boy I did—I went down to the patriarch and had my patriarchal blessing. And the patriarch put his hands on my head, and he said, 'Brother Golden, verily I say unto you, you will live the gospel, you will become a pillar of the church, you will preach the gospel to every nation, kindred, people. And the church will be proud of you. And verily I say unto you, that you are truly your father's son.' Now that's always been a great comfort to me!"[27]

A Miracle

After a church meeting a sister approached Uncle Golden saying, "Brother Kimball you know cattle and soil. Can you come take a look at my farm? I can't get anything to grow." J. Golden went to the farm, looked around and kicked the poor soil around a little, and said, "Well, what can I do for you sister?"

"Couldn't you say a prayer and ask for a miracle so my crops will grow?"

"Sister, you don't need a miracle, you need manure."[28]

The Cigar

There once was a man whose office buddy gave him a big fat Cuban cigar because his wife had just given birth. The guy who got the cigar was a Mormon and, of course, was not going to smoke it, but he didn't want to be rude so he put the cigar in his suitcoat pocket and forgot about it. That Sunday he was to be set apart as a bishop. J. Golden Kimball happened to be the General Authority present to perform the ordinance. As J. Golden stood behind the man with his hands on his head he noticed the cigar in his coat pocket and thought it rather strange, but he had already started to pray.

"Brother so-and-so, with the holy priesthood power vested in me I ordain you and set you apart as a bishop in the Church of Jesus Christ of Latter-day Saints, *cigar and all.*"

At this point, the new bishop had to stand up and explain how he came to have a cigar in his pocket to everyone there.[29]

Helping St. Peter

J. Golden was helping St. Peter out up at the recommend desk one day, and along came this fellow who wanted to get in to the kingdom, but the man couldn't find his recommend, and St. Peter was having trouble finding the man's name in the Lamb's Book of Life, and everybody was starting to get just a little bit flustered.[30] So J. Golden thought of one idea. Says he, "Perhaps we can find you in the attendance records. You did attend your meetings didn't you?"[31]

"Well, I had to work on Sundays," said the man, "And I couldn't attend very often."

That sparked a few ideas, and St. Peter says, "Maybe we can find you in the tithing records. You paid tithes and offerings didn't you? . . . Ah! Here it is! I found it!" St. Peter pulls up the man's record which shows that the man paid 10 cents for a fast offering once.[32] He looks it over carefully for a few minutes and begins to be troubled. After a moment he turns to J. Golden for a bit of counsel and says, "This man paid 10 cents of fast offering once, and he expects me to let him in. What do you think I should do?"

J. Golden responds, "Well I say we give the fellow his dime back and tell him to go to hell!"[33]

Flowers

J. Golden once stepped up to the pulpit to give an Easter sermon, only to find a beautiful large arrangement of lilies on the pulpit.

He looked at the lilies, then out at the congregation, and then back at the lilies. Finally, he picked up the arrangement and carefully set it down on the floor beside the pulpit, out of sight of the congregation.

He then stood behind the pulpit and addressed the congregation, "The contrast was too great."[34]

Growth Problems

Once while on his travels, J. Golden Kimball was invited to sit in on a city council meeting in which the problem of Logan, Utah's stagnant growth was being discussed.

The mayor said, "Elder Kimball, can you help us? For fifteen years our town has not grown at all, and we can't figure out why."

"Well," said J. Golden, "maybe the problem is that every time one young woman gets pregnant, one young man leaves town."[35]

J. Golden Kimball at General Conference

The story that I've always heard about J. Golden Kimball is that they always scheduled him to speak last in General Conference, hoping that they'd run out of time and he wouldn't be able speak because they were afraid of what he might say.[36]

The Red Podium Light

I think one time I heard he used to cover the red light on the podium and would say, "I'll talk however long I damn well please."[37]

I'll Call For You

Once J. Golden was leaving a regional conference after speaking, and as he was leaving he overheard a group of brethren teasing an older sister who had never been married. Their taunting turned cruel, and the sister began to cry. They were saying things like "you've never been married," "you've never been wanted," and "who's going to call for you at the morning of the first resurrection?" He walked over to the sister, who was in tears, and he put his arm around her shoulders. He said, "Sister, you don't have to worry about that. When the time comes, if no one calls for you, I will." Needless to say, the tormentors left.[38]

SEVEN

Chastising

Hellfire preaching and stern rebuke is often misunderstood by those unaccustomed to it. Modern high school English students have long wondered why New Englanders of the mid-1700s put up with such gruesome sermons as "Sinners in the Hands of an Angry God." The sermon's metaphor depicts a wrathful Deity knocking back an arrow ready to let fly at a gossamer cord that holds a tiny spider, which represents doomed man wriggling over the inferno. In fact, people packed church buildings to hear Jonathan Edwards's stinging jeremiads.[1] In a day when many avoid the psychic discomfort of moral introspection at almost all costs, the benefits of subjecting one's soul to brutal scrutiny and the verbal artistry of a sharp religious chastisement might be lost on today's audiences. For those who perpetuate, or have re-created, many aspects of the Puritan's stern concern for the seriousness of getting right before God, however, diatribes such as those for which Brigham Young and later J. Golden Kimball were famous might be much appreciated.

Mormon preaching styles have mellowed much since then, maybe even to the opposite extreme. There is, however, still cultural nostalgia for the days when brimstone was a little more free-falling, and some of Kimball's stories display verbal mercilessness and harsh admonition. Many Mormons take great glee in the spoken fire that rains down to refine and delight them in the safely distanced form of J. Golden Kimball stories.

Uncle Golden unleashed his tongue on Gentiles as well as on Saints; in "Ranching and Tithing" he even rebukes the devil. Sometimes the J. Golden Kimball of folklore unleashes chastisement more in response to personal slights than as a corrective to general backsliding. A fellow folklorist in the BYU English department told of a student, a descendant of J. Golden Kimball, who complained about the tone of stories about him because they do not show him to be a kind, caring man. That is a fair criticism, and it underscores again the limits of using oral narrative cycles as windows to the past. Mormons today, however, may be quicker than others to confuse sharpness with unkindness. A well-known passage in the Doctrine and Covenants spells out the preferred Latter-day Saint method of chastisement for priesthood leaders: "beproving betimes with sharpness, when moved upon by the Holy ghost; and then showing forth afterwards an increase of love toward him whom thou hast reproved lest he esteem thee to be his enemy" (121: 42). Knowing chastisement to be necessary still does not make the first half of the admonition an easier pill to swallow than the second. But the first half is no less part of kindness than the second, and perhaps no one illustrates that more than the J. Golden Kimball of folklore.

Revolvers

One day up in southern Idaho J. Golden Kimball was preaching a sermon, and the bishop had told him that some of the boys were getting a little wild, and asked him whether he would say a few words that might calm the boys down. So Brother Golden was preaching his sermon, and about half way through he remembered what the bishop had asked, so he stopped right in the middle of what he was saying, and said, "By the way, the bishop tells me that some of you young bucks are getting a little too wild up here. He says you're carrying six-shooters around in your hip pockets. I want you to be careful. The damn things might go off and blow your brains out."[2]

Obnoxious Traveling Companions

J. Golden Kimball was riding on a stagecoach somewhere in Missouri. A group of men were riding along with him, and they began to complain about the Mormons. One man said he hated the Mormons with a passion, thus he was going to Texas to get away from them. Another man said he was going to Kentucky to get away from the Mormons. And finally, a third man said he was going to Boston to get away from all the "blank" Mormons. J. Golden Kimball then said, "You can all just go to hell because there won't be any Mormons there."[3]

City Streets: 1

One day Uncle Golden was standing on South Temple and Main. He waited for a chance to cross and then started across the street. A car whizzed by in front of him and struck his pant leg. J. Golden looked at the retreating car, shook his fist at it, and said, "You—you—damn you! Have you no respect for the priesthood?"[4]

City Streets: 2

One day old J. Golden Kimball was walking down the street, and he started to cross the street, you know, and this buggy (or whatever they had back then) went whizzing by him and almost knocked him on his face. He let out a stream of colorful words and said, "Don't you Gentiles know the difference between a heathen and the Lord's own anointed?!!!"[5]

City Streets: 3

Mr. Cannon said that on one occasion he was talking with J. Golden Kimball on the corner of South Temple and Main in Salt Lake City—by the Hotel Utah. As Kimball left Mr. Cannon to cross the street towards ZCMI he stepped into the path of an automobile which knocked him down but did not harm him. Kimball got up and returned to the Hotel Utah corner, and as he brushed himself he said, "Some people's eye sight is so poor that they can't tell the Lord's anointed from the Gentiles!"[6]

Missionary Prayers

Brother Golden was out in the field (while he was serving his mission in the southern states), praying and praying. He finished, then looked up and saw two men eyeing him and his companion, the men were armed. Brother Golden said, speaking to his companion, "Hell, didn't I tell ya those longwinded prayers'd get us in trouble?"[7]

Ranching and Tithing

Brother Kimball was out on his ranch, separating out the best of his calves to pay his tithing. He would isolate the desired animals from the rest of the herd and then turn around to open the gate to let them out of the field. But when he would turn around the calves would be back in the herd. This same occurrence would happen several other times exactly as it happened the first time. Finally, Brother Kimball lost his temper and shouted, "Satan, if you do this one more time, I'll give the whole damn herd to the Lord."

Brother Kimball proceeded as before, separating the best calves for the bishop's storehouse. But when he turned around after opening the gate, the calves were still separate and Golden could pay his tithing.[8]

Choir Practice

J. Golden Kimball was called down to St. George, Utah, to a dispute among the Saints who were trying to build a chapel in southern Utah. He got together two choirs for the meeting. He asked one choir to sit in the back of the church and had the other choir sit at the front. At his signal, they both stood up and sang a small portion of a song, each choir singing a different song.

"How did it sound, brothers and sisters; it sounded like hell didn't it? That's the way you sound over this damn building; you can't agree."[9]

Horns

J. Golden Kimball once yelled at a menacing mob gathering at an LDS baptismal service in the Southern States mission, "We've got horns! Come here and we'll gore the hell out of you!"[10]

A Special List

J. Golden once spoke in a sacrament meeting with a sheaf of papers in his hand. He got worked up about his subject, which was exhorting the members to obey the commandments. After a while, he said, "You may be wondering, brothers and sisters, what this sheaf of papers is that I keep waving around. Well, I'll tell you. It's the Lord's #@!* list, and all of your names are on it!"[11]

The Splinter

J. Golden Kimball was asked to go as a general authority to take care of a problem in a particular ward. Before the ward's sacrament meeting, he met with some members who explained that the Relief Society president had such a domineering personality that she basically dictated everything that happened in church and told everyone what to do.[12] But everyone was so afraid of this self-righteous busybody that they did not know what to do to stop her, including the bishop. Elder Kimball said he'd think and pray about the matter and make an announcement when he spoke at the meeting.

During his talk he gave an analogy: "Sometimes, if you are not careful you can sit down on bad wood and get a really painful splinter in your @*! and there is nothing you can do about it except have someone pull it out for you because you can't.[13] This is exactly what has happened here. Sister so-and-so has become a big splinter in this ward's @*! and I have come to take her out for you. All of those in favor of releasing sister so-and-so as Relief Society president please make manifest by raising your right hand."

And that's how they released her. And the lady was so shocked by Elder Kimball's choice of words that she did not object.[14]

EIGHT

Repenting

J. Golden Kimball in trouble with his superiors and local members is a rec-
ognizable theme of his story cycle, but it is not as common as some others.
What usually put him in the dog house was his sharp, loose tongue. These
stories recount his attempts, both self-initiated and brethren-imposed, at repentance for transgressions. He is not always successful in this, as "Thoughts
on Southern Utah" and "Congregational Salvation" show, but his attempts
entertain and resonate with anyone who has tried to make better something
they have done wrong.

A Principle of Repentance

It seems that some people were not comfortable with his use of colorful
language. Someone asked with an accusing tone, "Don't you think that in
the next life you will be held responsible for use of such language?" His
response, "Hell, no! I repent too damn fast."[1]

Telephone Trouble

J. Golden was said to have complained about the invention of the telephone because before, when he would speak in a town and say a few
things he shouldn't have over the pulpit, it would take a few days to get
back to the brethren. By then he could find a way out of the trouble he
caused. But with the telephone, the bad news would reach Salt Lake
before he could even get there by train.[2]

Thoughts on Southern Utah

J. Golden Kimball was sent to southern Utah to supervise a stake conference in the midst of a dry and hot southern Utah summer. As the time for
the keynote address approached, so did the noon hour and the ensuing
heat. J. Golden got up to speak and (wiping the sweat from his face) said
in his high-pitched voice, "This weather is unbearable. If I were the devil
and owned hell and southern Utah, I'd live in hell and rent out southern
Utah!"

The stake members were (naturally) highly insulted and reported the
event to President Heber J. Grant, demanding an apology from Brother
Kimball. Under strict orders from President Grant to return to southern
Utah and apologize to the Saints, J. Golden did return.

The weather, however, had not changed, and so in his most apologetic
manner, J. Golden stood before the congregation and told them, "I am
indeed sorry for any offense I may have caused any of you fine people. I
certainly meant to do no harm to anyone's feelings. But it is so damn hot
down here that if I were the devil and owned hell and southern Utah, I
would live in hell and rent out southern Utah!!"[3]

Congregational Salvation

Brother Kimball was attending a conference in southern Utah. As he
spoke to the congregation about his recent tour of the town, he exclaimed, "and in conclusion, if you don't mend your ways only 10 damn
percent of you are going to make the celestial kingdom!" Of course this
quite upset the people and they promptly wrote to church headquarters
in Salt Lake. The General Authorities sent Brother Kimball back down
there the next conference with instructions to apologize to the people.

When he came into town, he again looked around and then in conference stated, "I have been sent here to apologize for a statement I made a few months ago. After looking things over again and with careful thought and much prayer, I will have to apologize for my rash remark. If you don't mend your ways only 5 damn percent of you will make it to the celestial kingdom!"[4]

Goodness

Uncle Golden used to say, "I have heard so much about goodness that sometimes I get unhappy, even at conference, and I feel like a little girl I heard of who did wrong. Her mother importuned her and labored with her so much that she said, 'Mother, don't try to make me good; just shoot me.'"[5]

NINE

Remembering

Most J. Golden Kimball stories are told in third person, and the teller is not a character in the narrative. In the accounts that follow, storytellers reminisce about interactions they or their close acquaintances had with Kimball. In some instances the storyteller is merely reporting a witnessed event; in others, they take more direct part in the action.

These personal-experience or once-removed narratives reflect the complexity and flow of intertwined human lives. They do not have the same stereotyped patterns and truncated structure as the jokes and legends in previous chapters. Some capture J. Golden Kimball's attempts at humor specific to a certain event. Others are surprisingly anomalous, and storytellers probably remember them for being out of the ordinary. Still others capture Uncle Golden's gentleness and compassion, attributes sometimes obscured by the fire and brimstone stereotype of much of the folklore concerning him. In "Young Missionaries" his trickster nature is employed for pedagogical purposes.

As time passes the historical connection of any living person to Elder Kimball dimishes, and fewer and fewer stories circulate in which the narrator is also part of the narrative. It should be little surprise then that most of these stories were collected between the 1940s and 1960s; there are none from the 1980s and 1990s. They present one exception to the general rule that J. Golden Kimball stories are not dying out, but thrive and continue to develop. Jokes and legends, however, have no such necessary connection to any one person's personal remembrance and thus cannot be killed by time so easily. These anecdotes occupy a middle ground between oral history and folklore. Many jokes and legends in the J. Golden Kimball cycle undoubtedly trace the history of their telling to such personal-experience stories.

Forgiveness and Repentance

He [J. Golden Kimball] spoke at my cousin's funeral. My cousin was disfellowshipped on account of taking a polygamist wife after the manifesto. . . . So Golden got up and talked a few minutes, and he said, "I am not treasuring polygamy, but if it wasn't true Joseph Smith was a fake and my father and my mother, and you wouldn't pin a red badge on her for it. God is kind and loving. He is human. He is forgiving. And if I get up on the other side and find that that is not so I'll climb back over the fence again." [When the informant sent Kimball a stenographic copy of the funeral service he responded], "The theme I try to put over is love, forgiveness and repentance. If you take that out, what is left?"[1]

Silver Dollars

You know that St. George was originally settled as a place to raise grapes for the sacrament wine.[2] St. George settlers drank and smoked etc. on the side before the Word of Wisdom was stressed as a commandment. Now all the rowdy behavior stopped when general authorities came to visit. Elder Kimball and another elder had come to ask for temple building funds and had stayed a couple of days. The people were missing their tobacco and stuff and getting impatient for the elders to go home. The other man, an apostle, spoke long and fluently on the blessings of having a temple in the area and made every appeal for the building fund. J. Golden knew what the Saints were going through and sensed their impatience. When it was his turn to speak, he stood up and said, "If you donate now and donate generously, we'll be out of town in half an hour." The Saints responded by covering the stage with silver dollars.[3]

The Active Woman

A woman living in Salt Lake City was known by her friends to be involved in just about every church and civil activity that one could get involved in. Her entire time and energy went to these affairs, to the neglect of her husband and family. Lately this had caused a great deal of friction in her household. One day she was walking down a Salt Lake City avenue. She was preoccupied with memorizing a speech she was to deliver at one of her meetings. Because of her preoccupation she accidentally ran into a man whom she immediately recognized to be J. Golden Kimball. They both apologized, but both knew it was her fault. Brother Kimball just smiled and said to her as he walked away, "Lady, you just can't do so many things at once. You've got to look where you're going before you can get there." Brother Kimball never knew what a profound effect those words had upon the life of that woman. That woman was me.[4]

Young Missionaries

My father was called on a mission for the church, and although he hadn't been active he said he believed the church to be true because his mother told him it was.[5] He went to the mission home in Salt Lake City and was given instructions there. He was placed in charge of seventeen other missionaries to see that they all arrived safely at their destination. They were told that their train would be met in Chattanooga, Tennessee, by some experienced missionaries. When they arrived there, they could see no one save a priest standing on the platform of the station. The missionaries were all frightened and wondered what they should do. My father was not. He stepped over to the priest and asked how he could find the LDS Mission Headquarters. The priest replied, "Oh, so you're more of those damned Mormons come out to pester us, eh?" He then started in on a long bit of name-calling derision of Mormons. My father had a violent temper, and he was trying hard to control it. At that point the priest started quoting scripture to them. This was more than my father could bear. He could not even read a scripture let alone quote one. He did the only thing he knew—doubled up his fist and let fly. The priest dropped in his tracks.

All of the missionaries rushed to him, helped him to his feet, brushed him off, and returned his books and hat. He said, "I am J. Golden Kimball, your new mission president. I wanted to find out what kind of missionaries I was getting."

My father was confined to his room for three days. All of his companions said he would surely be sent home. He said he promised the Lord then and there that if he ever got to stay he would learn to read and quote scripture as well as J. Golden Kimball. Brother Kimball came to him at the end of three days and said, "Young man, I believe you are a defender of the truth, but you had better learn to keep that temper in check." He did learn to read and quote scripture and completed an honorable mission.[6]

J. Golden's Funeral

When J. Golden Kimball died, Rufus went to see the First Presidency about getting the tabernacle for the funeral. David O. McKay said, "Why, you couldn't fill the tabernacle for a Seventy. We can't even fill the Assembly Hall for an apostle!" Rufus said, "We can fill it for Golden." And he said, "Well, you can have it." I was one of the honorary pall-bearers, and I saw David O. come in the tabernacle and get nearly to the stand and then he stopped and looked around and looked around. They said he had as big a funeral as there was for President Young.[7]

Too Popular

Zeke said that he was in Salt Lake one time not very long before the death of J. Golden Kimball. He was coming out of the post office and ran into Levi Edgar Young tottering along.[8] He took hold of his arm, and they walked up the street together. On the Sears and Roebuck corner they met J. Golden Kimball, who was in quite ill-health. Young said, "Let's each take a hold of Brother Golden's arms and help him up to his office." So they did, and as they walked along they met various people who all seemed to have messages either for Young or Zeke. Finally, J. Golden said, "Well, you're too damn popular for me! If it hadn't been for your popularity I'd have been in my office twenty minutes ago."[9]

How to Raise Kids

I remember very distinctly an instance of the J. Golden Kimball-esque type story. I happened at the time to be president of a Mutual Improvement Association in one of the Salt Lake wards.[10] As Sunday night speaker we had invited Elder J. Golden Kimball to speak. A good deal of his discourse was, as very frequently, related to his personal experiences and to his family, and he reiterated a good many of his family troubles. And at the close of his discourse he uttered a sentence that was so tremendously impressive that no one in the audience for two or three minutes could recover composure because of its sudden ludicrousness. He had been talking about the rearing of children and the difficulty of discipline and so on, and this closing remark was as follows: "If you want to know how to raise children, go ask an old maid, and God save the queen!"[11]

Gold-'n'-Blue

On one occasion when I was a teacher in the Latter-day Saints University high school in Salt Lake City, Elder J. Golden Kimball was invited to be the speaker. My father had known him as a boy and had been told that because of physical and mental distress he had developed a rather melancholy and blue disposition. His speech immediately followed the singing by the student body of the student song, "The Gold and Blue," which mentioned the colors of the school. So when Elder Kimball got up to speak he said, "You've just been singing 'The Gold-'n'-Blue.' That's me."[12]

The Worth of a Child

Mr. Morris said that he remembered seeing J. Golden Kimball and hearing him preach. He said he remembered one particular meeting when Kimball was talking about the worth of an individual. Kimball said that he had a son—the finest son in the world—really a marvel—and that he wouldn't take a million dollars for him. And, he added, he wouldn't give ten cents for another like him.[13]

Heavenly Goals

On the 1938 conference tape Elder Kimball is introduced. He gets up and bears his testimony for several minutes, mentioning the celestial kingdom as the goal for all Latter-day Saints. In conclusion Elder Kimball says, "As my father used to say, 'If any of you make it I'll be surprised!' in the name of Jesus, Amen."[14]

TEN

Resembling

The number of jokes and humorous stories that circulate around and comment on the Mormon experience is far larger than the number told specifically about J. Golden Kimball.[1] Many often attributed to someone else would fit well into the Kimball story cycle. What follows are examples of stories of a similar spirit to J. Golden's yet not specifically about him. In many cases however, variants do circulate and are attached to Uncle Golden.

"Walking on Water," attributed here to Gordon B. Hinckley and in chapter 1 to J. Golden Kimball, is a good example of a story attributed to Kimball as well as someone else. In this case it most often circulates about a contemporaneous church president. In recent years the joke has become particularly associated with the current church president, Gordon B. Hinckley, who makes liberal use of humor when speaking in public. Many Mormons have taken this as an invitation to leaven their own lives with more humor, which has perhaps contributed to the emergence of a cycle of jokes about President Hinckley. Several are presented here and reflect his zest for life and his humorous spirit.

Much Mormon humor features well-known figures in social and religious life. Flourishing cycles of stories and jokes circulate around not only specific church presidents but also anonymous beleaguered bishops,[2] set-upon missionaries,[3] and unenviable BYU coeds.[4] Stories from these cycles and elsewhere are only included in this chapter if they provide examples of, and context for, themes that emerge in the J. Golden Kimball cycle.

Walking on Water

There's the pope, President Hinckley, and a rabbi all sitting in a boat off the shore. And the pope gets out and walks across the water. And they don't have any oars or anything. And then President Hinckley saw what he did and said, "Oh that's a good idea." And so he walks out across the water too. And the rabbi is sitting here watching this and decides to do the same thing. So he gets out, and he falls right into the water. And the pope turns to President Hinckley on the shore and says, "Well, do you think we should tell him where the rocks are?" And President Hinckley looks at him and says, "What rocks?"[5]

The Chauffeur

One day President Hinckley was going to a really important meeting, and they sent a limo to come pick him up. President Hinckley was sitting in the back and was talking to the driver about all the neat things in the limo. He leaned forward and told the driver, "You know, I've always wanted to try driving a limo." So the driver asked him if he wanted to try it out. They pulled over and President Hinckley got behind the driver's seat while the driver got in the back. President Hinckley started speeding and was pulled over by a policeman. When the policeman saw who was driving, he looked confused and excused himself to go talk on his radio. He called his boss and said, "I just pulled over someone really big." "Who Lavell Edwards?" his boss asked. "No, way bigger than that!" said the policeman. "Merrill Bateman?" the boss asked. "No, even bigger than that," said the policeman. "Governor Leavitt?"[6] "Nope, bigger." "Then who in the heck is it?" asked the boss. "I sure don't know," said the policeman. "But it's got to be someone really big because President Hinckley is driving!"[7]

Captured

Once there was a plane flight across the Atlantic Ocean, and it happened that a stake president, a high counselor, and a bishop all wound up on the same flight. It also happened that the plane had some hijackers onboard, and they hijacked the plane. Well, they lined the stake president, the high counselor, and the bishop up against the wall and said that they were going to shoot them all but that they would grant them each a last wish. First they asked the stake president what his last wish was. The stake president said, "Well, I wish I could organize one more welfare project." So the hijackers said they would see what they could do. Next, the hijackers asked the high counselor, "What is your final wish?" The high counselor said, "Well, I wish I could give just one last talk." So the hijackers said OK. Then they asked the bishop, "Well, what is your final wish?" The bishop said, "Please, please, shoot me before the high counselor starts talking!"[8]

Golfing on Sunday

There was a bishop who just loved to golf but lately he'd been so busy that he hadn't had any chance to go. So he decided that just once he'd take off on Sunday morning to go play. So he chose a place way out of town where no one he knew would catch him. Sunday came and off he went.

Well, the Lord was watching all of this, and he called one of his angels to him and said for him to go down there and give this bishop a hole in one, maybe even two or three of 'em. So the angel goes down and he gives the bishop a hole in one and then a couple more. He could see how happy and excited the bishop was. He just couldn't believe it. So the angel went back up to heaven and asked the Lord, "Now tell me, why did you want me to give him these holes in one? I'd think you'd rather punish him." The Lord just smiled and said, "Who's he going to tell about it?"[9]

An Airplane Conversation

A Catholic priest and President Hinckley are sitting next to each other on a plane flying to California. On the way there, one of the stewardesses comes up the aisle selling alcoholic drinks. She first asks President

Hinckley if he would like a drink and he politely refuses the beverage. The Catholic priest on the contrary buys two alcoholic drinks and downs them in a couple of minutes. After he finishes his drinks, he turns toward President Hinckley and wipes his mouth and says, "Gee President Hinckley you sure don't know what you're missin'!" Later on, the same stewardess comes up the aisle selling cigars and cigarettes. She again asks President Hinckley if he would like to buy a cigar or cigarette and again he politely refuses the offer. The Catholic priest sitting next to President Hinckley buys a cigar and smokes it for almost the rest of the trip. Just before they land, the Catholic priest leans over to President Hinckley and says, "Gee President Hinckley, you sure don't know what you're missin'!" After the plane lands, they both walk out to the terminal together, and President Hinckley sees his wife waiting for him. When he reaches her, he gives her a big hug and a kiss and then turns to the Catholic priest and says, "Gee, you sure don't know what you're missin'!"[10]

Heber and the Pope

A long time ago when the Mormons were in Rome the pope said that they all had to leave.[11] So, obviously, all the Mormons were mad 'cause they didn't want to leave and so the pope decided to make a deal with them. He decided that they would have a religious debate and if the Mormons won they could stay and if they lost they would have to leave. So the Mormons picked a young missionary from Idaho named Heber to debate with the pope. But because Heber couldn't speak Italian very well he decided to make it more interesting by saying that neither side could talk, and the pope decided that was fine. So the day of the great debate Heber and the pope sat facing each other, and they just stared at each other for a couple minutes. And then the pope raised up three fingers, and Heber looked at him and raised up one finger. So then the pope waved his fingers in a circle around him and Heber pointed to the ground. So then the pope pulled out a glass of wine and some bread and Heber pulled out an apple, and that's when the pope stood up and said, "I give up. You Mormons are too good for me, you can stay."

So later the people, like Roman people I guess, asked the pope what had happened, and the pope said, "First I held up three fingers for the trinity, and he responded by holding up one finger to show that we have the same God and it's one common God. And then I waved my fingers around me to show him that God is all around us, and he pointed to the ground to show that God is also right here. Then I pulled out a glass of wine and some bread to show that God absolves us from our sins, and he pulled out an apple to remind me of original sin. He had an answer for everything, what could I do?"

And then back at the, like, the Mormon community all the missionaries gathered around to ask Heber what had happened. And Heber said, "First he held up three fingers to say that the Mormons had three days to get out of here. And I said not one of us is going anywhere. And then he said this whole place is going to be cleared of the Mormons, and I told him we were staying right here." "And then what happened?" somebody asked. And Heber said, "I don't know—he took out his lunch and I took out mine."[12]

Religious Wives

One day three men and their wives died. One couple was Catholic. One couple was Jewish. One couple was Mormon. So they all went up to heaven's gates to see if they could get in or not.

First the Jewish guy went up, and God asked him if he had done good works in his life. He said that he thought he had. They looked over his life, and God said, "Well I guess you're right. What's your wife's name?" The guy said, "Penny." Then the Lord said, "You can't go into heaven because you think about money more than you think about me."

So the Catholic goes up there. The same thing happened to him. At the end the Lord said, "OK, what's your wife's name?" The guy goes, "Brandy." So the Lord said, "You drink too much to get into heaven." So he went away.

Then this Mormon guy turns to his wife and says, "Well, Fanny, I think we better get out of here."[13]

The Danish Lady Gossip

Down in San Pete County, where all the Danes lived at the turn of the century, three dear old Latter-day Saints from the old country were gathered in the backyard to hang out their wash. When they were finished hanging out their wash, they drifted together, and Sister Olsen said, "I'm so sorry for that sister in our ward who was so sad yesterday in sacrament meeting. She was so sad to hear all of the babies being blessed because she has not a baby of her own. I'm afraid the problem she has is that she's 'inconceivable.'" They all nodded their heads, and sister Johnson said, "That's so sad that she has no babies and she's been married a long time now, but I think your English may be a little wrong. She's not 'inconceivable.' I think what you say in English is she's 'impregnable.'" Then Sister Johansson interrupted and said, "I've been crying a lot about this cause I've been through this before myself and I think the Lord will bless her and she'll be alright. In fact, I heard Brother Jenson and the bishop talking in the hall and Brother Jenson said she's 'unbearable.'"[14]

Mottoes

Question: What's a cross between Spencer W. Kimball and J. Golden Kimball?
 Answer: "Do it damn it!"[15]

Doctrinal Opinions

Elder Harold B. Lee was questioned about his writing "BS" in the margins of one of Brother Cleon Skousen's "Thousand Years" books, to which he replied, "'BS' stands for passages in which *Brother Skousen* voices his own opinion, not doctrine."[16]

Republicans

Oscar [McConkie]'s father said in one of these meetings in southern Utah, one of the brethren in the morning session said, "I'm going to put a ledger in the foyer, and we'd like some of you to sign up to be Republicans." (Because, oddly, at that time the Democratic Party was the one that Mormons favored.)

 When they came back for the afternoon session, no one had signed the book. So the General Authority, whoever it was, said, "Brothers and sisters, you have misunderstood." He said, "God needs Republicans."

 And Oscar said his father would wink and say, "And you know those damned Republicans think they've had God on their side ever since."[17]

Home Teaching

A visiting general authority commented that we had a remarkable record in our stake of 100 percent home teaching for ten out of twelve months for the past three years!

The stake president responded, "And if it weren't for Halloween and New Year's Eve we'd have made 100 percent every month!"[18]

Smart Aleck

Once when two missionaries were tracting, they came across a smart aleck who said, "Hey it says here in the Bible that true believers will drink poison and not die. Tell you what, I have got some poison here, if you drink it and don't die I'll get baptized in your church."

The missionaries thought for a second and then one said, "I've got a better idea. Why don't *you* drink the poison, then we'll raise you from the dead and baptize you if you are interested."[19]

Horned Missionaries

A pair of missionaries was out tracting in a particularly difficult neighborhood. Finally, one lady opened her door but refused to let the elders in.

"I just have one question," she explained.

"What's that?" replied one of the elders.

"Is it true, what my pastor told me, that all Mormons have horns?"

"Yes," replied the sly elder. "In fact, I had mine clipped a few weeks ago before I came here from Salt Lake. If you touch up here on my head, you can still feel the stubs!"

"Really?" asked the woman, incredulous.

"Sure. Go ahead. Put your hand right here."

After a minute of fingering his head the woman said, "I don't feel anything."

And the elder said, "Keep feeling, you are sure to feel something soon."

She felt around some more, "No, I don't feel anything."

The missionary smiled, "Really? Not even a little bit silly?"[20]

An Important Phone Call

About three months ago President Hinckley, the Mormon prophet, was traveling in Italy when he passed by the Vatican. He remembered that he needed to talk to God. He stopped, went in, and asked the pope if he could use the phone to call God. Of course the pope was delighted to let him use it. So President Hinckley called and talked to God for about an hour. When he got done the pope asked, "So how is God doing?" President Hinckley replied, "He is doing wonderful and says to tell you hi. How much do I owe you?" "That will be $1,000!" "$1,000?" To which the pope replied, "It was a long-distance phone call to God." So President Hinckley thanked him again, paid him his money, and went on his way.

The next month the pope was in Salt Lake City and decided to stop by and pay a visit to President Hinckley. While he was there he asked to use the phone to call God. With pleasure President Hinckley let him use the phone. After a two-hour conversation with God the pope finally hung up and asked, "How much do I owe you?" President Hinckley responded, "Don't worry about it! It was a local call."[21]

A Bad-news Call

Well, you see, the pope was one day sitting in the Vatican with his cardinals around him, and he said, "Brethren, I have some good news and I have some bad news. The good news is that Christ has come to earth again."

And the cardinals go, "Wonderful, wonderful!"

"Now for the bad news. . . . He called from Salt Lake City."[22]

ELEVEN

Repeating

Elder Kimball must have been much less troublesome to church leadership than the folklore suggests. Few were as fond of telling J. Golden stories as his peers, and when Kimball died, Claude Richards compiled eulogies from other General Authorities.[1] Invariably, the eulogies acclaimed J. Golden Kimball's wit, honesty, and special connection with the Mormon people.

The following stories are all gathered from public writings and sermons of LDS Church leaders. They show how Kimball's comrades and successors in the church's presiding bodies participate in, and use for homiletic purposes, the oral tradition about J. Golden Kimball. In their similarity to those told by "regular" Mormons, the stories also show how General Authorities are part of the folkloric processes that permeate all of Mormondom. In fact, the institutional memory of the presiding bodies of Latter-day Saint ecclesiastical leadership seems to have preserved stories that appear in no folklore archive. Unlike earlier views of folklore that suggested it belonged specifically to non-elite groups, all sorts of Mormons cherish J. Golden Kimball stories.

In keeping with the standards of comportment of their office, however, the J. Golden Kimball stories from Latter-day Saint General Authorities tend to lack the hells and damns common among other Mormons. Those of fellow and subsequent General Authorities are more likely to press the humor into homiletic service rather than merely allow mirth to be an end in itself. There are, however, some exceptions. The daughter of a member of the First Presidency, James E. Faust, recounts a story in the spirit of J. Golden Kimball in her father's biography:

> Lisa tells of going with her parents and her high school boyfriend (now her husband) to visit Hugh B. Brown, who by this time was becoming quite elderly. As they visited, President Faust commented on how beautiful an Oriental rug was, to which President Brown replied, "It is, isn't it? I think I'll take that with me to heaven." Then he chuckled and said, "That's presumptuous, to think I'm going to heaven. I'll probably show up at the pearly gates with that rug under my arm, and St. Peter will look at me and look at the rug and tell me where to go."
>
> President Faust shared in a good laugh and then said, "President Brown, if you're not getting in, there's no hope for the rest of us."[2]

In a similar vein, former church president Spencer W. Kimball was known to tell the ironic story that "[Uncle Golden] once said he figured that no other Kimball stood a chance of high Church office, since the Brethren would not risk the chance of another one like him."[3] This story, like those that follow, suggests that the theme of General Authority consternation with J. Golden Kimball, so common in stories about him, has perhaps been over-emphasized while their delight in Kimball has been underappreciated.

Magazine Drive (from Joseph B. Wirthlin, Quorum of the Twelve Apostles)

Years ago Elder J. Golden Kimball was traveling with one of the presiding brethren in southern Utah. In those days meetings often didn't have a time limit; they went on as long as the speaker wanted to speak. . . .

One fast Sunday they had been preaching nearly all day. Everyone was hungry, especially Elder Kimball, who felt that he was "pretty near dead."

Finally, at about four o'clock in the afternoon, the presiding apostle turned and said, "Now, Brother Kimball get up and tell them about the *Era*."

The *Era* magazine had just been launched and the Brethren wanted to encourage subscriptions. Elder Kimball approached the pulpit and then, after a short pause, said, "All you men that will take the *Era* if we will let you go home, raise your right hand." There was not a single man who did not raise his hand that day and subscribe to the *Era*.

You see, the power of gratitude is immense.[4]

Trouble with Kids (from Boyd K. Packer, Quorum of the Twelve Apostles)

The story is told that someone stopped Elder J. Golden Kimball on the street on one occasion. There had been a little difficulty in Elder Kimball's family that had become publicly known, and whoever it was who stopped him, no doubt with a mind to injure, said, "Brother Kimball, I understand you're having some problems with one of your children." His answer was, "Yes, and the Lord is having some problems with some of his, too."[5]

Bills (from Spencer W. Kimball, President of the Church)

I want to mention a story I have told about Uncle Golden. You have heard about my Uncle J. Golden Kimball, who was a rather interesting person. I don't think it is true, but it was told of him that his creditors kept coming and bothering him all the time and they wanted payments on their accounts. And he began to get a little tired of it, and he said, "Now listen here fellows. You know the way I handle my accounts. I take all of the bills at the end of the month and I put them in the waste basket. Then I stir them around and if I see one that looks good and I can, I'll pay it. But," he said, "if you don't quit bothering me I won't even put yours in the waste basket."[6]

Say Amen (from Spencer W. Kimball, President of the Church)

Golden Kimball . . . got up to speak one time as a General Authority, and when he sat down nobody said anything. Nobody said "Amen." So he got right up again and he said, "Well, I'll start again. You didn't want me to close so I'll just go on and speak again." So he spoke for a little while, and then he said "Amen." There were about a dozen or two people that remembered. He stood up again and tried it again.

Now, that would be kind of a pity, wouldn't it? Will you always say "Amen"? Never fail.[7]

A Tithing Heart (from Charles W. Nibley, Presiding Bishop of the Church)

I think it is Brother Golden Kimball who tells the story of his father's owning a beautiful horse. Tithing was paid with horse, cattle, sheep, and everything obtainable in those days. The horse Brother Kimball had was a very fine one, and he said to the boys: "I believe I will turn that horse in for tithing; pay it to bishop Hunter." The next morning one of the boys paraded the beautiful animal around and wanted to keep it, but President Kimball said: "See here, you take that horse right down and pay it in for tithing, before my heart puckers up."[8]

Too Much Singing (from Heber J. Grant, President of the Church)

Upon my recent trip to Arizona, I asked Elders Rudger Clawson and J. Golden Kimball if they had any objections to my singing one hundred hymns that day. They took it as a joke and assured me that they would be delighted. We were on the way from Holbrook to St. Johns, a distance of about sixty miles. After I had sung about forty tunes, they assured me that if I sang the remaining sixty they would be sure to have nervous prostration.[9]

The Lord's Joke (from Hugh B. Brown, Counselor in the First Presidency)

Golden Kimball came down to our conference in Granite Stake. I introduced him as the Will Rogers of the Church. I said he likes a joke. When he got up he said, "I think the Lord himself likes a joke. If he didn't, he wouldn't have made some of you folks."

I think even Golden Kimball wouldn't dare say that to this group.[10]

Dreams (from Anthony W. Ivins, First Counselor in the First Presidency)

Brother J. Golden Kimball told us yesterday that he was a great believer in dreams . . . the ones that come true.[11]

Mt. Nebo (from Thomas E. McKay, Assistant to the Quorum of the Twelve Apostles)

Brother J. Golden Kimball, my dear friend, was attending a conference in one of the stakes in southern Utah, so the story is told. He was presenting the names of the General Authorities and presented the Presidency of the Church. They voted upon them separately—then the Council of the Twelve, the First Council of the Seventy—there were fewer hands coming up each time, and then he slipped this in: "It has been proposed that we move Mount Nebo in the southern part of the valley to the northern. All in favor, manifest it." And they voted it. "Any opposed by the same sign." And nobody voted against it. So he presented the names of the Presiding Bishopric and then asked the president of the stake to continue with the presentation of the stake authorities.[12]

Church Office Building Workers (from Harold B. Lee, Then a Member of the Quorum of the Twelve Apostles)

As I think of the dedication of these brothers and sisters, I have thought often of something that is reported to have been said by the late President J. Golden Kimball. He was asked on one occasion how many people worked in the Church Office Building, and his answer was, "Oh, about a third of them." At least, we can say to you that these folks represent the "third" of which Brother Kimball was speaking—a thoroughly dedicated "working third."[13]

Paying Tithing (from Franklin D. Richards, Assistant to the Quorum of the Twelve)

An interesting experience is told of Brother J. Golden Kimball in speaking to a meeting of Saints on the subject of tithing. He said, "All of you who would be willing to die for the gospel please put up your hands." Nearly every hand in the congregation was raised.

Then he said, "All of you who have been paying an honest tithing please raise your hands." It seems that only a few hands were raised.

Brother Kimball turned to the bishop and said, "See, they would rather die than pay their tithing."[14]

Knowing Brother Golden

On one occasion, one of the General Authorities was asked, "Do you know J. Golden Kimball?"

The GA replied, "Be hanged if I know whether I do or not! I've been with him and heard him speak off and on for forty years, and I'm still in doubt!"[15]

Notes

PREFACE

1. For an introduction to Mormon folklore see Wilson, "Folklore," 1477–78; Wilson, "Mormon Folklore: Cut from the Marrow," 521–40; and Wilson, "Folklore a Mirror for What?" 13–21.

2. For a general introduction to folklore studies see Oring, *Folk Groups and Folklore Genres;* Toelken, *The Dynamics of Folklore;* Brunvand, *The Study of American Folklore;* and Georges and Jones, *Folkloristics.*

3. William A. Wilson Folklore Archive item numbers 8.7.2.1.2–8.7.2.1.7.

4. On contemporary fieldwork techniques and theories of representation see Lawless, *Holy Women, Wholly Women;* Rosaldo, *Culture and Truth;* and Jackson, *Fieldwork.*

5. Joseph Smith's account of his First Vision experience can be found on "The Official Website of the Church of Jesus Christ of Latter-day Saints" at http://www.lds.org/en/1_Joseph_Smith_Testimony/0–S_Testimony_Contents.html.

6. The church claimed 11,394,518 members at the end of 2002 (http://www.mormon.org/learn/0,8672,968–1,00.html [accessed March 1, 2007]). A conference at the College of St. Hild and St. Bede at the University of Durham in England on April 19–23, 1999, was devoted to the question of whether Mormonism constituted a world religion. Amid much discussion about the viability of the concept of "world religion" itself by scholars such as Bryan Wilson, Ninian Smart, Douglas Davies, Malise Ruthven, and John Hinnells, a consensus emerged that Mormonism makes as good a case (if not better) for being a world religion as any other faith.

7. Although the term *Gentile* has largely disappeared from the Latter-day Saint vocabulary except as a tongue-in-cheek archaic relic, in J. Golden Kimball's day it was common for Latter-day Saints to use the term as Jews do, to refer to anyone outside their faith. Eliason, "Nameways in Latter-day Saint History, Custom, and Folklore."

8. May, "Mormons," 720–31.

9. In composing this historical sketch I have drawn on Alexander, *Utah: The Right Place;* Givens, *The Viper on the Hearth;* and Allen and Leonard, *The Story of the Latter-day Saints.*

10. Allen and Leonard, *The Story of the Latter-day Saints,* 127–28.

11. Alexander, *Utah: The Right Place,* 108.

12. Eliason, "Curious Gentiles and Representational Authority," 158–60.

13. A "cycle" is a folklore term referring to all of the anecdotes, jokes, and legends told about a particular person.

14. For bibliographic information concerning Mormon contributions to folklor-

istics as well as the study of Mormons by folklorists see Terry, "Exploring Belief and Custom," 1–4; and Wilson, "A Bibliography of Studies," 389–94.

15. Fife and Fife, *Saints of Sage and Saddle*, 304–15.

16. Dorson, *American Folklore*, 120–21; Dorson, *Buying the Wind*, 498, 512, 518.

17. Wilson, "The Paradox of Mormon Folklore," 127–47.

18. Randolf, *Hot Springs and Hell*, xxv.

19. General Authorities are LDS leaders who belong to presiding councils of the LDS Church, which have general jurisdiction over the whole of the church rather than specific local areas. They are analogous to cardinals in Roman Catholicism. The bodies that compose the General Authorities are, in descending order of authority, the First Presidency, Quorum of the Twelve Apostles, Seven Presidents of the First Council of the Seventy, and the First and (more recently formed) Second Council of the Seventy. Mormons sometimes refer to General Authorities as "the brethren."

INTRODUCTION

1. Richards, *J. Golden Kimball*, 123.

2. In presenting this biographical sketch I am indebted to Kimball, "J. Golden Kimball: Private Life of a Public Figure," 55–84, and to Powell, "J. Golden Kimball," 302.

3. Eliason, "Nameways in Latter-day Saint History."

4. Many of the polygamous marriages that were performed were done primarily for the woman to have a husband in the hereafter. Those in plural marriages did not necessarily act as married couples, either socially or intimately. Twelve of Heber C. Kimball's wives formed the "core" of this plural family. Kimball, *Heber C. Kimball*, 229.

5. Collected by Rebecca Kent in 1998, William A. Wilson Folklore Archives, Brigham Young University (hereafter WAWFA): FA1, project 1642.

6. Arrington, Fox, and May, *Building the City of God*, 91–110.

7. Kimball, *Conference Reports*, Oct. 1931, 57.

8. Eliason, "Mormons," 612–16.

9. Roberts, *Autobiography*, 139.

10. Kimball, *Conference Reports*, Oct. 1925, 158. An oral folk historical version of these events is perpetuated in "Missionary Prayers" (chapter 7).

11. Kimball, *Conference Reports*, Oct. 1917, 133.

12. Roberts, *Autobiography*, 138.

13. Ibid., 160.

14. Cheney, *The Golden Legacy*, 100.

15. On the economic hard times of 1890s' America see Steeples and Whitten, *Democracy in Desperation*.

16. Kimball, *Conference Reports*, Oct. 1921, 85.

17. Kimball, *Conference Reports*, Oct. 1918, 31.

18. Kimball, "Private Life of a Public Figure," 68.

19. Kimball is the most mentioned person in Roberts, *Autobiography*, 261.

20. Bitton, "Brigham Henry Roberts."

21. Roberts, *Autobiography*, 138, 142–45, 152–54, 160–63.

22. Ibid., 145.

23. Ibid., xv; Van Wagoner and Walker, *A Book of Mormons*, 246; Madsen, *Defender of the Faith*, 379.

24. Kimball, *Conference Reports*, Oct. 1933, 42–44.

25. J. Golden Kimball Diary, Nov. 30, Dec. 5, 1902; Roberts, *Autobiography*, 237–53. In the Doctrine and Covenants—a book of Latter-day Saint scripture made up of revelations to Joseph Smith and others—it states concerning the relationship of the Seventy to the Twelve, "And they form a quorum, equal in authority to that of the Twelve special witnesses or Apostles just named" (107:26). On quorum reorganizations see Hartley, "The Seventies in the 1880s," 79–83.

26. Kimball, *Conference Reports*, April 1930, 61.

27. This argument has been made many places and is the basis for the disciplinary emergence of oral history and ethno-history over the past several decades. A good place to start is Vansina, *Oral Tradition as History*.

28. Kimball, *Conference Reports*, Oct. 1906, 117.

29. Kimball, *Conference Reports*, April 1921, 178. J. Golden Kimball interpreted being relegated to speak last as a dubious honor. The final speaker at a meeting holds a position of honor usually reserved for the highest-ranking authority. If, however, other speakers exceed their time limitations, the final speaker is often obligated to curtail his or her remarks to allow the meeting to end on time. This is also part of the oral tradition. See "J. Golden Kimball at General Conference" (chapter 6).

30. Kimball, *Conference Reports*, Oct. 1905, 81.

31. Kimball, *Conference Reports*, Oct. 1912, 27.

32. Gundry, Parry, and Lyon, *Best-Loved Humor of the LDS People*, 2, 3, 5, 7, 12, 15, 16, 20, 31, 35, 56, 68, 71, 79, 87, 91, 94, 100, 113–15, 119, 121, 142, 145, 149, 150, 152, 161–62, 168, 188, 193, 195, 200, 205, 207, 210, 212–13, 216, 217, 224, 228, 245–46, 253–54, 259, 260–61, 262, 263, 269, 273, 276, 277. The index of this book contains more references to J. Golden Kimball than any other person or topic, which suggests his stature at the center of any understanding of Mormon humor.

33. For a biographical treatment see Richards, *J. Golden Kimball*, and Cheney, *The Golden Legacy*. Unfortunately, Cheney, in presenting his book as history, is less than careful in sorting documented utterances and occurrences from folklore. A biography that promises to be more scholarly, "Remembering Uncle Golden," is forthcoming from J. Golden Kimball's nephew, James N. Kimball.

34. I am happy to thank my colleague Paul Baltes, a humor scholar and stand-up comedian, for helping explain the role of a straight-man in stand-up comedy.

35. Brunvand, *The Study of American Folklore*, 197.

36. Mormon folklorist David Neal pursued his graduate training at Memorial University, Newfoundland, Canada. He noticed that many stories told about a popular politician there, Joseph Smallwood, were the same he'd heard about J. Golden Kimball in Utah. Philip Hiscock, a folklorist at MUNF, sees many similarities between the J. Golden Kimball legend cycle and that of Joseph Smallwood and backs up this observation (chapter 2, note 21). Austin and Alta Fife (*Saints of Sage and*

Saddle, [307]) identify the story "dog attack" in chapter 2 of this book as a borrowing from the legend cycle of Abraham Lincoln. For further examples of stories from elsewhere that resemble stories told about J. Golden Kimball, see chapter 5, note 19, and chapter 6, note 4. Because many Utah Mormon families have roots in New England, it may be that contemporary New Englanders and Utahans have traced their stories to the same origin.

37. Civil servant, male, Up Hatherley, England, 2002; Gardner, *J. Golden Kimball Stories*.

38. Eyring, "Religion in a Changing World," 157, 155–70.

39. See track 6, "On Being Wrongly Accused," on the compact disk *J. Golden*, starring Bruce Ackerman, contributing research compiled by James N. Kimball, video by Kevin Mitchell. The video was written and directed by James Arrington and stars Dalin Christianson.

40. On the distinctions and problems of generic classification see Finnegan, *Oral Traditions*, 135–57; see also Bauman, *Story, Performance, and Event*, 55.

41. Although not uncontested by a handful of folklorists who persist on defining "folk religion" as apart from "official" mainstream religion and, by implication, "backward" or "primitive" (e.g., Titon, *Powerhouse for God*, 144–49), the insight that all religious groups have "folk" and "official" aspects has become central to the approach toward religion by folklorists who specialize in religious folklore and is among Danielson's main points ("Religious Folklore," 45–70).

42. Folklorist of religion Leonard Primiano considers as "derogatory" the characterization of folklorists' interest in religion as interest in the "unofficial" aspect of religiosity. He suggests instead "vernacular religion." Primiano, "Vernacular Religion and the Search for Method," 37–56.

43. J. Golden Kimball stories told by his peers and subsequent General Authorities are discussed in chapter 11. Keith H. Basso, a linguistic anthropologist, deals with the issue of generic rarity in *Portraits of the Whiteman*. His analysis of Apache joking imitations of white people shows that a folklore genre might be relatively uncommon within a group of people but still important or informative about central issues to that culture. Even the most obscure cultural practices can illuminate volumes about the workings of a society.

44. To contact this list, e-mail owner-mormon-humor@lists.panix.com.

45. In Kimball's day not all young men were expected to serve—only those who were called. On the Mormon missionary experience as a rite of passage see sociologists Shepherd and Shepherd, *Mormon Passage*. The church takes no action against a young man who does not go, but those who do are much more likely to find that faithful young women will consider them marriageable material than those who do not.

46. Folklorist Hector Lee's recording *Folk Humor of the Mormon Country* is the first recording of Kimball's stories for a popular audience. See also Arrington's *J. Golden*, as well as *Remembering Uncle Golden*, produced and edited by Elizabeth Searles (videocassette) and *On the Road with J. Golden Kimball* (videocassette).

47. Davies, *Jokes and Their Relation to Society*, 165–66.

48. Dundes, "A Study of Ethnic Slurs," 186–203.

49. Davies, *Jokes and Their Relation to Society*, 168.

50. For an account of this metamorphosis see Limerick, *The Legacy of Conquest*, 134–75; see also White, *"It's Your Misfortune and None of My Own,"* 236–97.

51. Smith, *Teachings of the Prophet Joseph Smith*, 129.

52. Smith, *History of the Church*, 5: 423.

53. Stegner, *Mormon Country*, 191–92.

54. Burton, *The City of the Saints*, 290.

55. Bagley, "No 'Flip' or 'Frick,'" B2.

56. Flexner, *Listening to America*, 462. Flexner does not provide references for this claim, so it must be taken as speculation at best. Special thanks is due Steve Florman and Don Norton for information about Mormon swearing.

57. Lillie, "The Utah Dialect Survey," 41–42.

58. Smith, *Conference Reports*, Oct. 1901, 2.

59. Richards, *Conference Reports*, Oct. 1938, 117.

60. Brown, *The Abundant Life*, 65; McKay, *Conference Reports*, Oct. 1948, 118–19, 120.

61. Rich, *Conference Reports*, Oct. 1905, 71.

62. Doctrine and Covenants, 89: 2.

63. Burnham, *Bad Habits*, 1–15.

64. Program administrator, male, Orem, Utah, 2000.

65. Kimball, *The Miracle of Forgiveness*, 32.

66. Baker, "Humor," 2: 664.

67. Bunker and Bitton, *The Mormon Graphic Image*, 1–6.

68. "Brigham Brigham Young," folksong collected by Austin and Alta Fife from Lewis W. Jones, Monroe, Utah, Aug. 1, 1946, Fife Mormon Collection, 1: 539, FMR 8-8-1, and 1006–A, FTC 21: 173–277, Fife Folklore Archive, Utah State University, Logan.

69. Jansen, "The Esoteric-Exoteric Factor in Folklore," 205–11. Welsch applied this concept to joking traditions ("Enter Laughing," 64–65).

70. For more on the opinion that "surviving forms or relics of the past could help to reconstruct the course of man's development" (163) see Stocking, *Victorian Anthropology*, 156–64.

71. Wilson, "A Sense of Place of a Sense of Self," 3–11.

72. Wilson, "The Study of Mormon Folklore," 95–110.

73. Male, Logan, Utah, 1946, told by George J. Jensen, Fife Mormon Collection, 1: 254.

74. Internet user, 1998, collected by Rebecca Kent in 1998 (WAWFA: FA1, project 1642). For other examples of stories that are remarkably similar yet span several decades compare the story told by Charlie Smith (Fife Mormon Collection [1: 429]) with the story collected by Rebecca Kent in 1998 (WAWFA: FA1, project 1642) and the story told by George Jensen (Fife Mormon Collection [1: 590]) with the story collected by Rebecca Kent in 1998 (WAWFA: FA1, project 1642).

75. Vansina, *Oral Tradition as History*.

76. Darnton, *The Great Cat Massacre*, 9–72.

77. For an example of a story in which a detail has changed to keep the story understandable to contemporary Mormon audiences see the discussion about changing Mormon political party preferences in the notes to "Convention Prayer" (chapter 2).

78. As cited in Brunvand, *The Study of American Folklore*, 190.

79. Ibid.; Dorson, "Davy Crockett and the Heroic Age," 95–102.

80. Paredes, *With His Pistol in His Hand*, 15–16, 23–32.

81. Tatar, "Born Yesterday," 96.

82. Even for the Greeks, heroes were more a local than a national matter. Some we regard as universal to ancient Greece may have more to do with the historical accidents of record preservation and the preferences of chroniclers such as Ovid. The classicist John Talbot points out that Panhellenic heroes such as Heracles were exceptional. "The ordinary case," H. J. Rose contends, involved heroes worshipped locally "by their own descendants or former subjects" ("Hero-Cult," 506). For an account of how the poet Pindar may have preserved accounts of local heroes for what, through the accidents of history, has proven a worldwide audience see Carne-Ross, *Pindar*, 79–85.

83. Richard Dorson calls this active prowess of American folk heroes the "ethos of limitless individual capacity" (*Handbook of American Folklore*, 59).

84. Wilson, "The Paradox of Mormon Folklore," 54.

85. Hickman's career is discussed in Hilton, *"Wild Bill" Hickman and the Mormon Frontier*.

86. Larson, "Orrin Porter Rockwell," 179–90.

87. Hamblin and Little, *Jacob Hamblin*; Wixom, *Hamblin*. Jacob Hamblin has also been popularized by an outdoor musical spectacular *Utah!* which has been performed seasonally at the Tuachan Amphitheatre near St. George, Utah.

88. Alter, *Jim Bridger*; Vestal, *Jim Bridger, Mountain Man*; Smith, *Joe Hill*.

89. Brown, *The Tall Tale in American Folklore and Literature*; Eliason, "Jim Bridger," 103.

90. Eliason, "Joe Hill," 369.

91. Shah, *The World of Nasrudin*; Shah, *The Exploits of the Incomparable Mulla Nasrudin*; Ramazani *Six Hundred Mulla Nasreddin Tales*; www.afghan-network.net/funny/1html; www.afghan-web.com/culture/jokes.html. Many Afghan stories from the Hodja cycle are very similar to those collected by Shah and others.

92. Consider an online review of Ramazani's *Six Hundred Mulla Nasreddin Tales* by one indignant Turk: "Nasreddin Hoca is not an Iranian character!!!! He lived in Aksehir, which is a small city in Anatolia (Turkey). I am very surprised to see that an Iranian writer try to show Nasreddin Hoca as an Iranian character. Let's not forget that two or three years ago it was celebrated as the Nasreddin Hoca year in Turkey!" www.amazon.com/exec/obidos/tg/detail/-/0936347090/qid=1066163356/sr+1-2/ref=sr_1_2/102-4214255-5444100?vv=glance&s+books#product-details.

93. There have been several anthologies in English containing Nasreddin Hodja (Hoca) tales. Most are popular literary retellings rather than transcriptions of oral

tales: Downing, *Tales of the Hodja;* Juda, *The Wise Old Man;* and Güldiz, *Nasreddin Hodja* (a comic book). For a more scholarly treatment of Hodja tales see Marzolph and Baldauf, "Hodscha, Nesreddin." Nazreddin Hodja has become a focal point in a broader, rather contentious debate about the relationship of Turkish folklore scholarship to contemporary nationalism and conservative sensibilities about lewd and erotic folklore. Conrad, "The Political Face of Folklore—A Call for Debate," 409–13; Basgöz, "More about Politics and Folklore in Turkey," 413–15; Dégh, "Politics Alive in Turkish Folklore," 527–29.

94. Muallimoglu, *The Wit and Wisdom of Nasraddin Hodja,* 78, 79, 7–8.

95. Ibid., xi–xiv.

96. For an overview of the history of American folkloristics, including the emergence of performance-centered approaches, see Zumwalt, *American Folklore Scholarship,* and Bronner, *American Folklore Studies.* The performance-centered approach is still the leading methodology of the discipline. The issues of authenticity and identity, however, are emerging as central discussions about the nature of the discipline, and the historiography of folkloristics reflects that (e.g., Bendix, *In Search of Authenticity*).

97. An articulation of this view of the nature of folk societies can be found in Redfield, "The Natural History of the Folk Society," 224–28, and Redfield, *The Little Community.*

98. Richard Bauman has been the leading theoretician of this sea change in folklore scholarship. He develops his theoretic contributions in "Folklore" and "Performance" in *Folklore, Cultural Performances, and Popular Entertainments,* ed. Bauman, 29–40, 41–49.

99. Abrahams, *The Man-of-Words in the West Indies.*

100. Briggs, *Competence in Performance.*

101. Ben-Amos, "Folktale," 111–12.

102. Long, "Ballad Singers, Ballad Makers, and Ballad Etiology," 225–36.

103. Although I appreciate Long's insight, it would have been even stronger had she emphasized that singers and storytellers do not always fall into one category and one category only. Depending on context, a storyteller may shift from one mode to another. Someone who may act the confabulator while camping with hunting buddies may well try to be a strict perservator if called to testify in a court of law.

104. Even though J. Golden Kimball was a success in his efforts there were moments when his speaking was not immediately understandable as doctrine or humor (e.g., "How to Raise Kids" [chapter 9]).

105. Freud, *Jokes and Their Relation to the Unconscious,* 9. For more information on the psychology of humor see Oring, *Jokes and Their Relations;* Briggs, *Competence in Performance,* 171–232; Abrahams and Dundes, "On Elephantasy and Elephanticide," 225–41; Wolfenstein, *Children's Humor;* Piddington, *The Psychology of Laughter;* Bergson, *Laughter;* and Zwerling, "The Favorite Joke," 104–14.

106. Faust, "The Need for Balance in Our Lives," 4.

107. Davies, *Jokes and Their Relation to Society,* 172–73.

108. College graduate, male, Provo, Utah, 1978, collected by Marguerite Sadler

in 1978 (WAWFA: FA1, project 621). A stake is an administrative unit in the Church of Jesus Christ of Latter-day Saints analogous to a Catholic diocese in that a stake does not have a congregation but is made up of several congregations overseen by a stake president. The stake's membership will gather in large meeting houses ("tabernacles" in J. Golden Kimball's day or a "stake center" today) for regular conferences and special occasions. General Authorities are likely to speak on both sorts of occasions.

109. See, for example, "Troublesome Tourists" (chapter 2), "Boring Speeches" (chapter 3), and "What We Remember" and "Traveling Companion" (chapter 5).

110. "I am thinking of one of the things in Sunday School that influenced me as a child," said George Albert Smith, who was born in 1870. "I was not a very good singer, but I enjoyed music, and I remember some of the hymns that influenced my life. . . . I remember George Goddard and William Willis, two dear old brethren who used to come to the Sunday School in the Seventeenth Ward when I was there and lead us in singing 'I Am a Mormon Boy,' and other hymns." Smith, "Tribute to Richard Ballantyne," 503, also available at http://www.byu.edu/fc/ee/z_music .htm.

111. Briggs, *Competence in Performance*, 171.

112. Stehl, interviewed by Fabrizio, "Utah and the World Press," Feb. 7, 2002. This conception in France has less to do with Mormons than France's postrevolutionary history of antisectarianism and current hostility to new religious movements in general. Hysteria about and hostility toward "cults" has reached unfortunate levels in France. French law has become so restrictive of religious freedom that the U.S. State Department has grown concerned, and the Communist Chinese government in Beijing has given its approval as it, too, seeks to develop new anti-religious legislation. Palmer, "No Sects, Please—We're French"; Bosco, "China's French Connection."

113. Although generally regarded by insiders as the result of efforts to follow Christ's example of kindness, some Mormon cultural critics have suggested that the ethic of niceness may impede a healthy sharing of differences of opinion and strongly stated preferences. Bell, "When Nice Ain't So Nice," 40–46.

114. Bay and Eliason, *Culturegram 2000*.

115. On the pervasive negative popular perceptions of Mormons in the past see Givens, *The Viper on the Hearth*, and Bunker and Bitton, *The Mormon Graphic Image, 1834–1914*.

116. Cray, "The Rabbi Trickster," 340.

117. Kent S. Larsen II to author, e-mail, Oct. 16, 1997.

118. Dorson, *American Negro;* Dundes, "African Tales among the North American Indians," 207–19.

119. Cray, "The Rabbi Trickster," 331–45, 338–39 (story).

120. Danielson, "The Dialect Trickster," 39–59, 43–44 (story).

121. "Trickster" in *Funk and Wagnall's Standard Dictionary of Folklore, Mythology, and Legend*, ed. Leach and Fried, 1123–25.

122. Toelken, "The 'Pretty Languages' of Yellowman," 145–70; "All de Bes' Story," in Joyner, *Down by the Riverside*, 172–95.

123. Leach and Fried, eds., *Funk and Wagnall's Standard Dictionary of Folklore, Mythology, and Legend*, 1124.

124. Attorney, male, Los Angeles, Calif., 2000.

125. Lundquist, *The Trickster: A Transformation Archetype.*

126. Oring, *Jokes and Their Relations.*

127. A Mormon trickster of a more standard variety can be found in the "renegade missionary" stories told by Mormon missionaries. In these stories legendary elders spectacularly violate church rules and the even stricter rules of missionary life. They are invariably brought under control and chastised. Wilson, "Trickster Tales and the Location of Cultural Boundaries," 55–66.

128. Aarne and Thompson, *The Types of the Folktale*, 486–507.

129. In trickster tales from cultures under subjugation, where sets of norms are imposed, the trickster is less likely to get caught and thereby vicariously break unpopular rules. Where a people are more autonomous and in control of defining and deciding the values and rules by which they live, a trickster is more likely to get caught and punished. This reflects the relative esteem in which free and subjugated people hold the rules by which they live. When the J. Golden Kimball of folklore violates the values of the church to which he freely gives his assent, he is likely caught, but when he is showing up snobs and Gentiles, he gets away with doing so.

130. Dorson, "The Rise of Native Folk Humor," 39–73.

131. Larry A. Landen to author, e-mail, Oct. 30, 1997.

132. Lankford, "Trickster," 716–17.

133. Vicarious action for others who cannot act is, after all, a central doctrinal concept of Latter-day Saint religiosity that undergirds such practices as baptism for the dead and other vicarious temple ordinances. In addition to Sunday services that to many might seem conventionally Protestant, Latter-day Saints also engage in a dimension of worship that makes them distinctive among Christian faiths: vicarious ordinances. Mormons perform sacred ceremonies in temples that the church has built worldwide but are open only to faithful Latter-day Saints. After Mormons receive their own temple rites, all subsequent visits to the temple are on behalf of people who did not have a chance, while living, to make the choice to accept what Latter-day Saints hold to be the universally applicable message of their religion and to accept the necessary ordinances for salvation. The baptisms and other ordinances to which Mormons submit on behalf of those who have died are gifts of service, and they do not know whether such gifts will be accepted (or even appreciated) by those for whom they are intended. Latter-day Saint doctrine stresses that those for whom vicarious ordinances are performed are under no obligation to accept them and may well go unused. Mormons engage in such activities in the belief that missionary work continues in the afterlife and that people who accept the message and wish to be baptized cannot do so, being disembodied spirits. That is why Latter-day Saints still embodied on earth are baptized on the behalf of others who have died. Only those with bodies can do this service for those who may wish to but cannot. (A standard reference on the theological significance of Mormon temple work can be found in Packer, *The Holy Temple*). These concepts at the core of Latter-day Saint theological

distinctiveness may add a fuller dimension to the J. Golden Kimball of folklore's role as a trickster hero doing vicarious duty for those who cannot. There may be a deeper underlying resonance between the vicarious function of J. Golden Kimball jokes and Latter-day Saints' vicarious religious practices. Several Latter-day Saints have been skeptical about this idea, however, and I cannot present this interpretation as having passed the ethnographer's "does-it-fly-with-the-natives" test.

134. Abrahams, "Some Varieties of Heroes in America," 341–42, as quoted in Wilson, "The Paradox of Mormon Folklore," 54.

135. Wilson, "Mormon Folklore," in *Mormon Americana*, 437–54.

136. *The Encyclopedia of Mormonism* defines being active as "observing a full religious lifestyle of attendance, devotion, service, and learning" (14). Moreover, approximately "44 percent [of LDS church members] experience a period of inactivity at some time and then resume religious involvement" (1527). In addition, approximately "eight out of ten current members will become disengaged for a period of at least one year," "about one of every five members retains his or her religious belief but does not attend meetings," and "only 14 percent remain disengaged nonbelievers" (1527). The encyclopedia is also careful to note that "in areas outside the United States where the Church is less well established and where most growth is from recent conversion, retention of members may not be as high" (1527). For more information see Luclow, *Encyclopedia of Mormonism*, vol 4.

137. *The 2003 Church Almanac* gives membership figures as 1,655,606 for Utah, 5,310,598 for the United States, and 11.6 million for the world for year end 2002 (pp. 248, 172, 441).

138. I thank David Allred, my research assistant for this project, who scanned the stories and crunched the numbers for these percentages.

139. These lists can be contacted at owner-mormon-humor@Mailing-List.net and aml-list@cc.weber.edu.

140. The Varsity Theater has discontinued this practice, not because Mormons objected but because movie studios and film makers objected to what they saw as violations of the artistic integrity of their products.

141. This follows a suggestion made in conversation by Mormon essayist Edgar A. Snow Jr., who has also struggled with the issue of representing swear words in writing.

142. In the early 1960s the *Journal of American Folklore* devoted a special issue to this matter ("Symposium on Obscenity," 189–282).

143. Green, "Folk Is a Four-Letter Word," 525.

144. Brunvand, *The Study of American Folklore*, 197.

145. Wilson, "Mormon Folklore—Faith or Folly?" 47–54.

146. Kimball, *Conference Reports*, Oct. 1919, 205.

147. I owe this insight to historian Richard L. Bushman.

148. When asked if he would give up poetry for a cure for cancer, Wilson, who has experienced cancer in his family, replied, "For one poem maybe not; but for poetry, yes." Wilson also notes, "[Neil] Postman also argued that the stories told by ordinary people about the events of their lives are not more profound than novels,

plays, and epic poems. I think not. I believe these stories are important precisely because they have the power of literature, because, as I shall try to argue, they actually are, or can be, novels or epics. This explains why I have not been able to get my mother's stories out of my head these many years. Like other works of literature I cherish, they have stayed with me because of their artistic power" (135). For both quotations see Wilson, "Personal Narratives: The Family Novel," 127–49.

CHAPTER 1: TRICKING

1. The Mutual Improvement Association was the name of the official church youth organization. The money would have been used to provide social and religious programs and activities for teenagers.

2. Male, Chico, Calif., 1950, told by Hector Lee, Fife Mormon Collection, 1: 943, Fife Folklore Archives, Utah State University, Logan. Kimball lets dawn on his audience that fifty cents is nothing if one can give one's life for the gospel. People are much more motivated to charitable action when they recognize its importance on their own rather than being harangued about it. Apparently, that is true even if clever trickery prompts the realization. J. Golden uses a different motivational technique in "Magazine Drive" (chapter 11).

3. Plumbing contractor, male, Mesa, Ariz., 1998; David E. Smith, conversation with author, Mesa, Ariz., Dec. 29, 1998.

4. Student, female, Atlanta, Ga., 1969, collected by Susan Spear in 1969 (William A. Wilson Folklore Archives, Brigham Young University [hereafter WAWFA]: FA5, 4.11.2.17.1).

5. This version of the story is noteworthy because it is a story about a story. It is told as a personal experience about having heard J. Golden Kimball speak. A sacrament meeting is the main Sunday meeting in the Latter-day Saint devotional calendar. What other Christians call the communion or the Sacrament of the Lord's Supper, Mormons call "the Sacrament." The bishop or a counselor begins the service by conducting church business, and then bread and water are blessed and passed in remembrance of Jesus' atoning sacrifice. Next, members of the congregation give prepared talks on gospel topics. The meeting always begins and ends with a prayer and a hymn. Mormons use water instead of wine because of a revelation given to Joseph Smith in response to an attempt to poison Latter-day Saint sacrament wine. The revelation states "it mattereth not what ye shall eat or what ye shall drink when ye partake of the sacrament, if it so be that ye do it with an eye single to my glory—remembering unto the Father my body which was laid down for you, and my blood which was shed for the remission of your sins" (Doctrine and Covenants 27: 2).

6. Unlike among Catholics, where the term *bishopric* refers to a bishop's jurisdiction, among Mormons it refers to the governing body over a ward (geographic congregation), which is made up of the bishop and two counselors. These three men in dark suits and white shirts are a ubiquitous presence at the front of Mormon meeting houses all over the world. The one in the middle is the bishop. The three take turns conducting the meeting but assign ward members to speak. Mormons

give "talks," not sermons. During a talk, the busy men—who have full-time jobs and families as well as their church callings—sometimes nod off.

7. Attorney, male, Atlanta, Georgia, 2000; anonymous e-mail collection provided by (presumably) an attorney, Sept. 12, 2001. In soteriology, Mormons are virtual universalists. Only people who have a full knowledge of God's plan and then consciously reject it and side with Satan will be everlastingly damned in "outer darkness," where there is "weeping and wailing and gnashing of teeth" (Doctrine and Covenants 101: 91). Everyone else will eventually receive some gradated measure of salvation. Mormons often casually use the term *hell* in theological contexts in much the same way as other Christians, but when speaking of the specific view articulated in Latter-day revelations "outer darkness" is more common.

8. In the past, the names of all of the General Authorities of the church were read—quite a long list—during the sustaining of church leaders over the pulpit at stake conference time. Now, the process has been shortened by reading only the names of the First Presidency and Quorum of the Twelve. The First and Second Quorums of the Seventy and their presidents are referred to collectively as a group.

9. Japanese student, male, Provo, Utah, 1977, collected by Akiko Blais in 1977 (WAWFA: FA5, 4.11.2.14.3). To fully understand this story, the Latter-day Saint principle of "common consent" and how it is implemented needs to be understood. The Doctrine and Covenants mandates, "And all things shall be done by common consent in the church" (26: 2). Although Mormonism is administered by a hierarchal theocracy with clearly delineated lines of authority, potential abuses of power and encroachments on individual freedom are checked by the principle of common consent. Church authorities at each level of church service are called by other authorities above them; they are never nominated or elected for office. Before anyone can assume a position or office—done by an ordinance called "setting apart" by the "laying on of hands" on the person's head—their name must be presented to their ward for a sustaining vote, or to their stake or the whole church, depending on the purview of the office to which they are called.

Members are invited to "make manifest" their sustaining vote from the pews by raising their right hands. Those opposed are invited to "make manifest by the same sign." Members generally trust their leaders to be informed by revelation, and leaders rarely try to foist someone unacceptable on those to be served. The principle of common consent allows members to reject people proposed for setting apart or sustaining in an office, which has happened occasionally in church history. In fact, however, it is extraordinarily rare for there even to be a dissenting vote. Most members have probably never seen it happen, despite having participated in hundreds of sustainings. Historian Dale Morgan provides an interpretation of this process from an outsider's perspective: "Opponents usually failed to take into account the specific trust of the Mormons in their leaders, and the sense of responsibility held by the leaders to ward their people—a conception of inter-responsibility and mutual faith, which was certainly a more vital ethical relationship than is ordinarily observed between governors and governed" (*The State of Deseret*, 12–13). In other words, the Mormon hierarchy was less a form of autocratic despotism than a legitimate expression of the people's popular will. By the time people have reached the level of General Authority it is especially unlikely that someone objectionable to the church will be among their number.

Because the process of sustaining runs so smoothly, many Mormons sometimes regard it as a perfunctory process and fail to pay attention when general officers are presented at stake conference time. Hands often shoot up without much thought. In this story Kimball reminds Latter-day Saints of the seriousness of this practice and the responsibility they bear to exercise common consent and sustain their leaders even though the outcome is almost certain.

10. Seminary teacher, male, Provo, Utah, 1961, collected by Elain Christensen in 1961 (WAWFA: FA5, 4.11.2.14.1). This Mt. Nebo version is significantly wordier than most versions of the story, but Mt. Nebo shows up more often in tellings of this story than Mt. Timpanogos. Curiously, Mt. Nebo, although bigger, is more remote and less familiar. It is possible that the prevalence of the more obscure Mt. Nebo in the legend cycle is evidence of the story being based on an actual occurrence. Societies change the features of a story as they pass it on, and changes tend to occur in the direction of making details more familiar to more people. Nebo's prevalence over Timpanogos may indicate that the event took place in view of Mt. Nebo in Juab or southern Utah County. Angie Margetts has found one story about Mt. Timpanogos, collected by Charles Aaron in 1977 (WAWFA: FA5, 4.11.2.14.3), and six about Mt. Nebo: the first was collected by Elain Christensen in 1961 (WAWFA: FA5, 4.11.2.14.1); the second by Valerie Webster in 1964 (WAWFA: FA5, 4.11.2.14.2); the third by Dawn Brashear in 1964 (WAWFA: FA5, 4.11.2.14.4); the fourth by Sara Otis in 1989 (WAWFA: FA5, 4.11.2.14.5); the fifth told by Mrs. Thomas E. McKay (Fife Mormon Collection, 1: 436); and the sixth collected by Ben Cardon (e-mail to author, Dec. 15, 1998). For a version of the story with a variant ending in which J. Golden Kimball does not expose his trickery see "Mt. Nebo" (chapter 11).

11. In accordance with Malachi 3: 10–11, the Church of Jesus Christ of Latter-day Saints' finances rest on the principle of each member paying a full tithe. This is now understood to mean 10 percent of one's gross increase each given year. Sometimes members will pay a portion of that amount, but Mormons call a full 10 percent a "full tithe."

12. Student, female, Provo, Utah, 1974, collected by Beckie Van Dyke in 1974 (WAWFA: FA5, 4.11.2.6.2). This story is retold in a slightly different version in "Paying Tithing" (chapter 11). For another story on the difficulty of paying tithing see "A Tithing Heart" (chapter 11); for a depiction of J. Golden Kimball's struggle with tithing see "A Full 10 Percent" (chapter 2); on Kimball's determination to pay tithing see "Ranching and Tithing" (chapter 7).

13. Joseph Smith returned the Golden Plates to the Angel Moroni without having been allowed to translate two-thirds of the record. Mormons await the day when the "sealed portion" will be translated. McConkie, "Understanding the Book of Revelation," 85–89.

14. Student, female, Provo, Utah, 1976, collected by Anna Tueller in 1976

(WAWFA: FA5, 4.11.2.21.1). Even though Joseph Smith proclaimed that the Book of Mormon is "the most correct of any book" (Smith, *Teachings of the Prophet Joseph Smith*, 194), Kimball's era marked a low point in Latter-day Saints' appreciation of it. Some Mormon intellectuals tended to question its historical reality, and most of the general membership may well have regarded it as genuine in its historical setting in ancient America but by and large did not read it. In the late twentieth century, however, President Ezra Taft Benson helped bring about a Book of Mormon revival by encouraging every Mormon to read it daily. Today, most devout Mormons have read carefully in the book; many have read it through many times and made it a centerpiece of their devotional lives. Reynolds, "The Coming Forth," 6–15.

15. Marrying outside the faith or in a civil ceremony invites no church sanction on members, but Latter-day Saint theology holds that the highest level of salvation is open only to those who enter into the New and Everlasting Covenant of celestial marriage whereby a man and a woman can be sealed together for time and all eternity (Doctrine and Covenants 132: 6). Sealing needs to be done by one who has the proper priesthood authority (132: 7–8). That authority can only be exercised in temples specially dedicated for the purpose of performing holy ordinances. Church leaders of all levels are eager to encourage young people to marry in the temple; a high percentage of temple marriage in a church unit is regarded as a promising sign of success.

16. The Church of Jesus Christ of Latter-day Saints is famous for the effective welfare program it administers for members who fall on hard times. Before they turn to governmental support, the church encourages them to rely on its extensive system of aid, which involves a network of warehouses, farms, and canning factories where people may volunteer service and receive food. Administering the system is one of the main responsibilities of church leaders.

17. Student, male, Austin, Tex., 1997. The use of statistics to measure spiritual success is a double-edged sword. If church leaders do not gather statistics it can be difficult to recognize areas needing improvement and to meet spiritual needs. When statistics are used, however, the temptation exists to see them as fruits of righteousness. Anyone who has served in a church leadership position, or in a business setting where statistics guide policy, will recognize the point of this story. Those who have witnessed the sword of statistics cutting the wrong way will appreciate Kimball's unique way of dealing with the issue. A similar story, "You Take Off Ten Pounds. . . ," can be found in Richard M. Dorson's "Maine Master-Narrator" (202): "Two fishermen met at the Parker House in Boston and started to talk about their luck. One said he had caught a twenty pound salmon in Mooselockmeguntic. The other said that the year before he had been out night fishing and the lantern fell out of the boat. A couple of months later he was trolling and felt a heavy tug at the line, and pulled up the lantern—still lit. 'Come now, you don't expect me to believe that,' said the fisherman. 'All right,' answered the other, 'You take off ten pounds and I'll put out the light!'"

18. Student, male, Provo, Utah, 2000, collected by Davina Weinert in 2000 (WAWFA: FA5, 4.11.2.7.51.1). This story is a good example of a J. Golden Kimball

folktale understood to be fictional rather than a legend believed to be true. It follows the common joking pattern of three individuals; the first two perform similar actions, and the last does the same in a surprising and novel way. As Axel Olrik explains, "Nothing distinguishes the great bulk of folk narrative from modern literature and from reality as much as does the number three. Such a ruthlessly rigid structuring of life stands apart from all else" ("Epic Laws of Folk Narrative," 133). This J. Golden Kimball joke is especially noteworthy in that it has a double punch line. Such jokes almost always have the teller's folk group represented as the best—in this case the one with authentic miraculous power.

The William A. Wilson Folklore Archive provided thirty-seven versions of this story. Eighteen tell a story similar to the one in chapter 9. The first figure crosses the water using stepping stones or "rocks." Seventeen out of eighteen times the figure is depicted as a pope. In one instance, however, where a Catholic priest sinks into the water, a rabbi successfully crosses the water using the stepping stones. The second figure, usually a Mormon, walks on water. That person is, of course, oblivious to the stepping stones. In nine of the seventeen versions collected the figure is described as President Kimball (J. Golden Kimball's nephew); in three he is a "Mormon bishop"; three portray him as a "Mormon prophet"; and two depict President Hinckley. The third man in the scenario cannot walk on water and does not see the stepping stones. As a result, he sinks and sometimes drowns. In five of the eighteen versions the third figure is described as a rabbi, and in five others he is the Ayatollah Khomeini. Two versions depict Billy Graham, and two others depict a Pole. In addition, Jim Baker, a monk, and a Catholic priest are each represented in one version.

There are a few exceptions to the three-figure pattern. In one instance the third figure, the Ayatollah Khomeini, does not actually attempt to walk on the water but rather swims. In another instance the third figure, a rabbi, asks the other two men "to tell him their secret of how they were able to walk on the water." Only one of the thirty-seven versions describes two figures, a pope and Billy Graham, using rocks to cross the water while the third, President Kimball, walks across unaided.

The punch line in the first eighteen stories comes when the first figure exclaims to the second, "Maybe we should have told him about the stepping stones" and the second figure replies with the question, "What stones?" The other eighteen stories carry a different punch line. Again, the stories describe three ecclesiastical figures. Invariably, however, two use the rocks to cross the water and one sinks. The punch line comes when the first two turn to each other and say, "Do you think we should tell him where the rocks are?" There are two notable exceptions, however. In one story the first two figures look at the third and remark, "You just have to know where the rocks are." In the other story, one of the figures who successfully crosses the water exclaims, "Hey stupid, step on the rocks."

In fourteen of the eighteen variants it is the Mormon who sinks (twelve Mormon bishops, one branch president, and one stake president). In the other four versions, one rabbi, one Baptist minister, and two Catholic priests sink. The types of figures who walk successfully on water include a Catholic priest, a Protestant "reverend," a

Mormon bishop, a rabbi, a Mormon missionary, a Protestant minister, an Episcopal priest, and a Protestant deacon.

CHAPTER 2: QUIPPING

1. Thompson, *Motif-Index of Folk Literature*, 117–33.

2. Plumbing contractor, male, Mesa, Ariz., 1997; David E. Smith, conversation with author, Mesa, Ariz., Dec. 29, 1997. For blessings of healing and sacred ordinances such as confirmation of the gift of the Holy Ghost and ordination to the priesthood, Latter-day Saints employ the laying on of hands with solemnity and dignity. That is not what J. Golden Kimball means here.

3. Gila Valley is dry and hot and would have been a difficult place to settle as a pioneer. As Gregory McNamee notes, "Owing to accidents of wind flow and geology, these mountains receive at best twenty-three inches of precipitation a year, a quantity that, say, New Orleans might receive in a few days of summer. At the Gila's end, six hundred miles to the west along the solar flats of the Arizona desert near Yuma, the rainfall may not exceed three inches a year; the region is one of the most arid in North America" (*Gila*, 3–4).

4. Plumbing contractor, male, Mesa, Ariz., 1997; David E. Smith, conversation with author, Mesa, Ariz., Dec. 29, 1997.

5. Implied in this story is awareness of the effects of higher criticism on Christian thought. During J. Golden Kimball's tenure as a General Authority, theories questioning the veracity of biblical miracles began to be discussed in Latter-day Saint circles. Christians of a more literal bent, like Latter-day Saints, if their beliefs are influenced by deliteralizing trends at all, usually question first miracles that seem meant as fiction or do not have as profound a theological significance as the central miracle of Christianity, the Resurrection. For an overview of higher criticism see Reventlow and Farmer, *Biblical Studies and the Shifting of Paradigms, 1850–1914;* for a historical account of the development of higher criticism see Berry, *Higher Criticism and the Old;* for a critique of higher criticism see Boer, *The Bible and Higher Criticism;* for an explanation of the Mormon interaction with higher criticism see Reynolds, "The Coming Forth of the Book of Mormon," 6–47; see also Swensen, "Mormons at the University of Chicago Divinity School," 37–47, and Kenney, "Mormons, Genesis and Higher Criticism," 8–12.

6. Larry A. Landen to author, e-mail, Oct. 30, 1997.

7. Kent S. Larsen II to author, e-mail, Oct. 21, 1998.

8. Rancher, male, Coalville, Utah, 1977, collected by William G. Petuskey in 1977 (William A. Wilson Folklore Archives, Brigham Young University [hereafter WAWFA]: FA5, 4.11.2.9.3).

9. Student, male, Salt Lake City, Utah, 1982, collected by Lisa Wilhite in 1982 (WAWFA: FA5, 4.11.2.35.2).

10. Civil servant, male, Up Hatherley, England, 1998; John Gardner to author, e-mail, Dec. 8, 1998.

11. Male, Logan, Utah, 1946, told by George J. Jensen, Fife Mormon Collection, 1: 252, Fife Folklore Archives, Utah State University, Logan. The form and

content of the two versions of this story, separated by more than fifty years and the Atlantic Ocean, are nearly identical—further evidence of the remarkable stability and longevity in much of the J. Golden Kimball Legend cycle.

12. College graduate, male, Provo, Utah, 1978, collected by Marguerite Sadler in 1978 (WAWFA: FA1, project 621).

13. Just across the street east of the temple, the grand Hotel Utah has long been a Salt Lake City landmark. For many years the president of the church has lived in a penthouse suite, and the foyer was a place where one might encounter church dignitaries. Renamed the Joseph Smith Building, it has been remodeled as offices and a tourist center.

14. College graduate, male, Provo, Utah, 1978, collected by Marguerite Sadler in 1978 (WAWFA: FA1, project 621).

15. Librarian, female, Logan, Utah, 1964, collected by Jo Dee Madsen in 1964 (WAWFA: FA5, 4.11.2.10.1). The two versions of "Round and Round" are essentially the same joke and examples of Kimball's frustrations with modern living. The only major difference in detail is the type of offending device that lays J. Golden low. These two versions can also be seen as oikotypes, or regional variants. The church's woolen mills, long shut down, were in Utah County near Provo. Arrington, "The Provo Woolen Mills," 97–116.

16. Stake conferences are notoriously long, and the weather in St. George notoriously hot. Utah Mormons would assume these factors in appreciating this story.

17. Health-care executive, male, Kingston, N.Y., 1997; Alan Burgess to author, e-mail, Nov. 5, 1997.

18. Attorney, male, Lahabra, Calif., 2000; anonymous e-mail collection provided by (presumably) an attorney, Sept. 12, 2001. This story apparently circulates among southern Protestants as well:

> A young minister was courting two women, one tall, shapely, beautiful, but not too much inclined to be a preacher's wife. The other was somewhat homely but a wonderful organist, choir leader, and soloist. He sought counsel of an older pastor. Listening to descriptions of the two women, he offered his advice.
>
> "Marry the one with the musical talent. She'll be a fine partner for you in your ministry."
>
> So the young preacher married this woman. On their wedding night, he got into bed. After a while she came out of the bathroom in a see-through gown and with her hair in curlers. He stared at her and said, "Sing, Myrtle, sing." (Jones, *The Preacher Joke Book*, 30–31)

Because Loyal Jones provides no date for the collection of this story it is impossible to tell who told it first, Mormons or southern Protestants. Mormon versions go as far back as 1950 (told by Hector Lee, Fife Mormon Collection, 1: 943). Assuming J. Golden Kimball actually told the story, and assuming it had one rather than multiple origins, it is possible that Kimball adapted it from one he heard while a missionary in the South. The Mormon version of the story is notable for omitting details that would link it to Protestantism—the terms *minister, ministry, preacher,* and *pastor* as well as the idea of preaching as a profession one can chose to enter. The Mormon version also features details that make the woman's unattractiveness more vivid.

19. Kent Larsen to author, e-mail, Jan. 12, 1999.

20. Civil servant, male, Up Hatherley, England, 1998; John Gardner to author, e-mail, Dec. 8, 1998. This story, or stories like it, have been told about different famous individuals across the world. I thank David Neal for pointing out similarities between stories told about J. Golden Kimball and stories recounted by Newfoundland's colorful politician Joseph Smallwood. Philip Hiscock recalls, for example, that Smallwood told a story similar to "Troublesome Tourists" on *The Barrelman*, Hiscock's daily radio program on VONF in St. Johns, Newfoundland (Philip Hiscock to author, e-mail, Aug. 20, 2002). Smallwood explained that "the foundation for a new building was being dug in the morning as he passed, and in the afternoon the tenants were being turned out for nonpayment of rent." Smallwood "attributed the story to one of his regular listeners, Mr. Author B. Walker." The story, Hiscock says, "was meant to point out the bragg[ing] nature of some New York construction workers." In addition, "as a boy in St Johns" Hiscock heard a story even more similar to the story about J. Golden Kimball. That story, like the J. Golden story included here, is "a joke on the braggadocio of American tourists." The story's punch line is especially similar: "the building wasn't there this morning when I passed." Folklorists often use the term *Munchausen effect* to describe characters like Smallwood. The term refers to individuals who, upon "hearing and telling jokes and anecdotes, change them to be about themselves, or to whom many stories seem to gravitate." Of course, the term works much better for Smallwood than Kimball. The types of stories included here were always told about him, not by him. Attribution of stories that did not occur to J. Golden Kimball came from Mormon people rather than Kimball.

21. Student, male, Richfield, Idaho, 1998, collected by Rebecca Kent in 1998 (WAWFA: FA1, project 1642). The humor here relies on the semantic ambiguity of the word *bastard*. On one level, Kimball is clearly using it in its technical but somewhat archaic meaning, a male child born out of wedlock. But Mormons' familiarity with J. Golden Kimball's reputation as someone who swore would bring to mind the word's informal meaning as a swearword referring to "an offensive or disagreeable person—used as a generalized term of abuse." The idea of applying this connotation to anyone in the family of one of the most revered men in Mormon history is scandalous, but the multiple meanings of the word—and J. Golden's apparent guilelessness—allow him latitude. Also implicit is a response to anti-Mormons' assertion that plural marriages were illegitimate and children born to them were illegitimate as well. Mormons vehemently resisted that characterization, holding that plural marriages were not only legitimate but also sanctioned by God, both in their time and in the time of biblical patriarchs.

22. Writer, male, Provo, 1999. This story is similar in its implications to "Family Ties."

23. Actor, male, Salt Lake City, 1996, paraphrased from *Remembering Uncle Golden*, produced and edited by Elizabeth Searles. This story is a variation on a widespread Latter-day Saint aphorism: "The Church must be true, otherwise the missionaries

would have ruined it a long time ago." The quip is a recognition that the church does not rely on self-selected professionals of seasoned maturity and focused enthusiasm to represent it throughout the world. Rather, the Latter-day gospel is borne by nineteen-year-olds of varying levels of maturity, intellect, and motivation and very little training. The aphorism suggests to Mormons that the religion's rapid growth must be due to its recognizably true message, given that there is little to recommend its messengers in terms of persuasive appeal.

24. Some cases of divisions of wards into political parties may have happened, although documentation is hard to come by. The church was very concerned in the 1880s and 1890s that Mormons be seen as nonpartisan.

25. Church history professor, female, Provo, Utah, 1997. The humor in this situation comes in part from Kimball's assertion that somehow an all-knowing God would not know he was present unless he prayed. There is also rich historical context concerning why Kimball would not want God to know he was present at the convention. The development of political parties independent of church affiliation was held out by Congress as a prerequisite for statehood. Before statehood, Utah had two main political parties, both of which were local and had no national following. The People's Party was made up overwhelmingly of Mormons, and the Liberal Party was overwhelmingly Gentile. Then Utah began to integrate national party politics. Mormons identified the Republican Party as the more anti-Mormon of the two national parties, and many were deeply averse to affiliating with it because it held slavery and polygamy to be "twin relics of barbarism" since 1856. Eager for statehood, however, and realizing that would never be granted until Congress perceived the operation of at least two legitimate parties in Utah, church leaders urged members to become Republicans. According to tradition, many were so reluctant that they had to be assigned.

This situation is thick with irony. Although the Gentile perception of Mormon theocracy was of people who walked in unthinking uniform lockstep according to the edicts of church leaders, the clearest case of church leadership trying to influence Mormon political action is characterized by a reluctant, independent-minded flock being persuaded to act less uniformly—less like Mormons and more like mainstream Americans. To accomplish that, church leaders issued political edicts, exactly the sort of thing that Congress, jealous of its power, did not want done. May, *Utah: A People's History;* see also Alexander, *Grace and Grandeur.*

The second irony is that in the last few decades of the twentieth century Mormon voting habits, in the American West at least, became overwhelmingly Republican (Mayfield, "Electoral Patterns," 169–77). In part that was due the Republican Party changing from being the party of federal intervention to the party of less government and federal restraint. Another factor had to do with the Democrats' embrace of social policy issues with which religiously conservative Mormons disagree. These historical developments have caused changes in the way this joke is told. Most Mormons who tell the story are unfamiliar with the history of changes in Mormon patterns of party affiliation, and most versions project contemporary party affiliation patterns onto the past, with J. Golden Kimball being assigned as a Democrat. It appears that the informant for this story intended to tell the older version of this joke with Uncle Golden as as Republican but slipped into the current version.

26. Male, Logan, Utah, 1946, told by George J. Jensen, Fife Mormon Collection, 1: 254. According to Austin and Alta Fife, this story is a variant of one told about Abraham Lincoln. Fife and Fife, *Saints of Sage and Saddle*, 307. A similar story can be found in Zall's *Abe Lincoln Laughing* in a passage (1119) quoting H. W. Beckwith's "Personal Recollections of Lincoln":

> "What made you kill my dog?" said the farmer.
> "What made him try to bite me?"
> "But why did you not go at him with the other end of the pitchfork?"
> "Why did he not come after me with his other end?"

27. Male, Ogden, Utah, 1946, told by Nathan A. Tanner, Fife Mormon Collection, 1: 396. Mormon culture entertains conflicting views on wealth. The Book of Mormon marks it potentially a sign of both sin and righteousness. For example, 2 Nephi 26: 20, reads: "And the Gentiles are lifted up in the pride of their eyes, and have stumbled because of the greatness of their stumbling block, that they have built up many churches; nevertheless, they put down the power and miracles of God, and preach up unto themselves their own wisdom and their own learning, that they may get gain and grind upon the face of the poor." Conversely, according to 2 Nephi 1: 9: "Wherefore, I, Lehi, have obtained a promise that inasmuch as those whom the Lord God shall bring out of the land of Jerusalem shall keep his commandments, they shall prosper upon the face of this land, and they shall be kept from all other nations, that they may possess this land unto themselves. And if it so be that they shall keep his commandments they shall be blessed upon the face of this land, and there shall be none to molest them, nor to take away the land of their inheritance, and they shall dwell safely forever." Despite constant warnings from general authorities about the dangers of get-rich-quick schemes, Salt Lake City has gained a reputation for being home to a disproportionate amount of financial fraud. Some have suggested that Mormons' tendency to trust authority and equate wealth with righteousness makes them susceptible to perpetrate as well as fall victim to the bad financial propositions that stir religious rhetoric into the mix of what seems to be sound financial planning. Gottlieb and Wiley, *America's Saints*, 118–22; see also Ostling, *Mormon America*. The story depicts the existence of such tendency among Mormons and also the presence of wry savviness about its dangers.

28. Male, Logan, Utah, 1946, told by George Jensen, Fife Mormon Collection, 1: 590. The self-reflexive nature of this story provides a good example of what Alan Dundes calls meta-folklore, or folklore about folklore ("Metafolklore and Oral Literary Criticism," 505–16). The story reflects on the significance of a cycle of which it is itself a part and mentions West, a contemporary of Kimball, who scandalized America's moral sensibilities with barely concealed sexuality and double entendres (Watts, *Mae West*).

29. Male, Washington, Utah, 1947, told by Andrew Sproul, Fife Mormon Collection, 1: 633.

30. Male, Chico, Calif., 1950, told by Hector Lee, Fife Mormon Collection, 1: 943. Latter-day Saints take literally that the act of baptism causes the remission of sins when done by proper authority and confirmed by the Holy Spirit. The Fourth Article of Faith of the Church of Jesus Christ of Latter-day Saints states, "We believe that the first principles and ordinances of the Gospel are: first, Faith in the Lord Jesus Christ; second, Repentance; third, *Baptism by immersion for the remission of sins* [emphasis added]; fourth, Laying on of hands for the gift of the Holy Ghost." The remission of sins can be lost, however, by subsequent sinful behavior. A true change of heart that leads away from sin must be experienced to retain a remission of sins. The story suggests a scenario in which the baptized has not experienced this change. To some Latter-day Saints, the theology behind the story might seem doctrinally correct from a technical perspective, but the situation is absurd. In this interpretation the humor comes from the incongruity of a General Authority proposing a doctrinally untenable position.

31. Actor, male, Salt Lake City Utah, 1996, *Remembering Uncle Golden*. Again the story seems to be a variant of one also told by Protestants. Loyal Jones records the following from Senator Sam J. Ervin Jr.:

> There was a Presbyterian and a Methodist down in North Carolina who got to arguing about the Presbyterian doctrine of predestination, and like all religious arguments the longer it lasted the more wrathful the participants became. Finally the Methodist said, "Well, I will admit there may be something to the doctrine of predestination. I think Presbyterians are predestined to go to hell."
>
> Then the Presbyterian said to the Methodist, "Well, I would rather be a Presbyterian and know I am going to hell than to be a Methodist and not know where in the hell I am going." (*The Preacher Joke Book*, 37)

In this case, the story seems to have originated with Protestants instead of Mormons because the punch line in the Protestant version has richer texture in relation to predestination. In the Mormon version, the predestination element is absent, and the nearly identical punch line does not integrate as well with the story's build-up.

32. Kent S. Larsen II to author, e-mail, Aug. 10, 1998. This rare quip in which Kimball is on the receiving end rather than the giving end relies on the hearer being familiar with his extraordinarily tall and thin frame.

33. Plumbing contractor, male, Mesa, Ariz., 1999; David E. Smith, conversation with author, Mesa, Ariz., April 20, 1999. This malapropism is similar to the "flowers at the funeral" story attributed to Pastor Bergin in the Introduction. People who speak at funerals often make use of metaphor, but apparently J. Golden did not fully consider the end of this one when he began it.

34. Photographer, male, Mapleton, Utah, 2000.

35. Student, female, Provo, Utah, 2000.

36. Attorney, male, Cedar City, Utah, 2001; anonymous e-mail collection provided by (presumably) an attorney, Sept. 12, 2001. This story contains a fairly common motif that Mormons occasionally experience: the difficulty of paying a full tithe. For more on tithing see chapter 1, note 11.

CHAPTER 3: TEASING

1. Welsch, "Enter Laughing," 64–65.

2. Internet user, female, Orem, Utah, 1998, collected by Rebecca Kent in 1998 (William A. Wilson Folklore Archives, Brigham Young University [hereafter WAWFA]: FA1, project 1642).

3. College graduate, male, Provo, Utah, 1978, collected by Marguerite Sadler in 1978 (WAWFA: FA1, project 621). Like most Christians, Mormons believe in praying about important life decisions. Later-day Saints also believe that each individual can receive personal revelation from God in making such decisions. The issue of whether receiving such a revelation is a possibility before, or a prerequisite to, matrimony has long been important for Latter-day Saints. Schoemaker, "Made in Heaven," 38–53.

4. Student, male, Logan, Utah, 1980, collected by Mathew Sharpe in 1980 (WAWFA: FA5, 4.11.2.46.1).

5. Student, female, Provo, Utah, 1971, collected by Kumen H. Jones in 1971 (WAWFA: FA5, 4.11.2.5.2).

6. Health-care executive, male, Kingston, N.Y., 1997; Alan Burgess to author, e-mail, Nov. 5, 1997.

7. University student, female, Provo, Utah, 1998.

8. College professor, male, Provo, Utah, 1998.

9. College professor, male, Provo, Utah, 1999.

10. Student, female, Brigham City, Utah, 1977, collected by Leda Hall in 1977 (WAWFA: FA5, 4.11.2.36.1). This seemingly simple joke provides for rich interpretation. Its humor relies on multiple levels of absurdity and incongruity. To see it as evidence of Mormons' hostile attitudes or threatening intentions toward southerners would be a mistake. As Christie Davies points out, jokes rarely, if ever, convey veiled hostility toward other groups of people (*Jokes and Their Relation to Society*, 8–9). Those who are genuinely and unabashedly hostile make use of readily available direct and offensive epithets as well as actual violence. Those sensitized to political correctness or worried about the social censure that can come from having hostile attitudes toward particular groups would refrain from telling such jokes. This story, however, cannot be understood except as a Mormon response to the overt southern hostility and violence toward Mormons described in the Introduction. The violence common in the past is long gone, but southern-style Evangelical Protestantism is still the main source of anti-Mormon pamphleteering worldwide, and Mormon missionaries in the South continue to have encounters with hostile preachers who consider them minions of Satan.

This story bears comparison to "Baptism" (chapter 2). Both rely on audience familiarity with the Latter-day Saint doctrine that baptism is essential to salvation, yet both show the principle applied in an outlandish, even horrifying, way. The stories imply a violation of the fundamental Mormon tenet that individual freedom of choice or moral agency must be exercised in choosing whether to accept the gospel. This story contains the added nuance of a reference to baptism for the dead, a doctrine explained in more detail in the Introduction. This joke, however, ignores the fact that someone resistant to Mormonism in life will not be more responsive in the afterlife, especially if Mormons were instrumental in their death. Again, a Mormon audience would recognize the absurdity, a central aspect of the humor. Kimball's zeal for victory, untempered by the patience and kindness that make for what a Mormon audience would recognize as an authentic Christian victory, provides another level of absurdity.

11. Student, male, Long Beach, Calif., 1980, collected by Alan Ray in 1980 (WAWFA: FA5, 4.11.2.41).

12. Missionary, male, Nauvoo, Ill., 1980, collected by Darrel Allen in 1980 (WAWFA: F5, 4.11.2.47.1).

13. Male, Chico, Calif., 1950, told by Hector Lee, Fife Mormon Collection, Fife Folklore Archive, Utah State University, Logan, 1: 943.

14. Student, female, Provo, Utah, 2000, collected by Ben Horton in 2000 (WAWFA: F5, 4.11.2.52.1).

15. Male, Logan, Utah, 1946, told by George Jensen, Fife Mormon Collection, 1: 590. The phrase *laying on of hands* refers to the method by which priesthood holders such as Smoot give blessings, ordain others to the priesthood, and set people apart for callings. This story juxtaposes the sacred and the sexual with the double implication of "laying on of hands." Reed Smoot is a rare figure in the J. Golden Kimball legend cycle. This is the only joke in which he appears, but he is in every version of it. In 1930 Utahans elected Smoot as their senator, and before taking his oath of office on March 5 of that year he was accused of, among other things, being a polygamist. Although the accusation was false, the investigation that followed attacked the entire Mormon church. Hearings ensued that eventually brought church president Joseph F. Smith before a senatorial committee to answer intrusive and demeaning questions about his private life and religious beliefs (Merrill, *Reed Smoot*, 11–99). It is easy to see, in light of these events, why Reed Smoot might have been hesitant to marry again.

16. Consulting firm CEO, Farmington, Utah, 1999; Steven Shippley to author, e-mail, Sept. 13, 1999.

17. Kent S. Larsen II to author, e-mail, Aug. 10, 1998.

18. Computer support representative, female, Provo, Utah, 1998; Sharon Boyle to author, e-mail, Nov. 30, 1998. Apparently, at some point some of the J. Golden Kimball stories circulating on the Internet were transcribed from earlier Kimball books and then passed on without attribution. Cheney collected the story from the Marion Ward, and the story is found almost word for word in *The Golden Legacy* (115–16).

19. Male, Logan, Utah, 1946, told by George J. Jensen, Fife Mormon Collection, 1: 253. Although seniority and longevity are indeed the manner in which one becomes president of the Seven Presidents of the Seventy, to mention this so bluntly would be considered gauche.

20. Plumbing contractor, male, Mesa, Ariz., 1998; David E. Smith, conversation with author, Mesa, Ariz., Dec. 29, 1998.

21. Student, male, Provo, Utah, 2000.

22. Female, Salt Lake City, Utah, 1946, told by Mrs. Thomas E. McKay, Fife Mormon Collection, 1: 437.

23. Male, Provo, Utah, 1946, told by B. F. Cummings, Fife Mormon Collection, 1: 456.

24. Religion professor, male, Provo, Utah, 1978, collected by Miriam Pierce in 1978 (WAWFA: FA5, 4.11.2.13.1).

25. Medical researcher, male, Arlington, Mass., 1998; Richard B. Anderson to author, e-mail, Dec. 10, 1998. This joke presents an alternate view of many stories, such as "Boring Speeches" and "Quorum Succession" (chapter 3) and "Traveling Companion" (chapter 5), in which Kimball is portrayed as more popular than his more senior colleagues. In general, the more senior a General Authority, the more interest there is among Mormons in what he has to say.

26. Student, male, Salt Lake City, Utah, 2000.

27. Attorney, male, Cedar City, Utah, 2001; anonymous e-mail collection provided by (presumably) an attorney, Sept. 12, 2001.

CHAPTER 4: PARTAKING

1. Davies, *Jokes and Their Relation to Society*, 101.

2. Andy Piantanida to author, e-mail, May 11, 2000.

3. Plumbing contractor, male, Mesa, Ariz., 1998. David E. Smith, conversation with author, Mesa, Ariz., 29 Dec. 1998.

4. Male, Chico, Calif., 1950, told by Hector Lee, Fife Mormon Collection, Fife Folklore Archives, Utah State University, Logan, 1: 943.

5. Retired farmer, male, Spanish Fork, Utah, 2000.

6. Religion teacher, male, Provo, Utah, 1964, collected by Janice Gilliland in 1964 (William A. Wilson Folklore Archives, Brigham Young University [hereafter WAWFA]: FA5, 4.11.2.24.1).

7. Student, female, Pleasant Grove, Utah, 1972, collected by Laura Wadley in 1972 (WAWFA: FA5, 4.11.2.37.1).

8. Student, male, Tooele, Utah, 1982, collected by Holly Smith in 1982 (WAWFA: FA5, 4.11.2.38.1).

9. Student, male, Idaho Falls, Idaho, 1984, collected by Cliff Munson in 1984 (WAWFA: FA5, 4.11.2.44.1).

10. Educator, male, Springville, Utah, 2000.

11. Program administrator, male, Orem, Utah, 2000.

CHAPTER 5: CUSSING

1. *Remembering Uncle Golden*, produced and edited by Elizabeth Searles.

2. Kirby, "LDS Authority's Words Were Not Always Golden."

3. Dundes, "Metafolklore and Oral Literary Criticism," 505–16.

4. Such comments about failed efforts to stop swearing and the involuntary nature of its continuance are fairly common in the legend cycle. These features and the punch line of "Trouble with Swearing" later in this chapter bring to mind the phenomenon of involuntary swearing often associated with Tourette's Syndrome

(Kushner, *A Cursing Brain*). Along with involuntary jerking or "ticcing," a common feature of the syndrome is involuntary ejaculations of the most offensive kinds of language in exactly the most inappropriate settings (coprolalia). Swearing during a sermon would be the kind of thing a sufferer from Tourette's might do. It is, however, unlikely that Kimball had Tourette's. First, the diagnosis was known at the time, and no contemporary of his ever suggested that it could apply to him. Second, Kimball showed none of the other common symptoms of the syndrome. And, third, despite the impression created by his story cycle, he rarely swore in the most inappropriate contexts such as at a church meeting, and when he did it seemed calculated for maximum effect rather than random. His uses and abuses of the English language, although seemingly uninhibited, direct, and down-to-earth, do not seem to be involuntary outbursts.

5. Male, Chico, Calif., 1950, told by Hector Lee, Fife Mormon Collection, Fife Folklore Archive, Utah State University, Logan, 1: 943.

6. Health-care executive, male, Kingston, N.Y., 1997.

7. Ibid.; Alan Burgess to author, e-mail, Nov. 5, 1997.

8. Film production employee, male, Orem, Utah, 1978, collected by Marguerite Sadler in 1978 (William A. Wilson Folklore Archives, Brigham Young University [hereafter WAWFA]: FA1, project 621). The humor of this story relies on the incongruity of Kimball cussing just as he is being told not to and the public expression of exasperated familiarity with the church president, which, if it occurred, should have been kept part of their private interaction. Those who remember one of President Grant's favorite motivational stories will appreciate the story even more. Grant made improving the legibility of his handwriting a personal goal and repeatedly described how he met that goal when discussing the possibility and importance of self-improvement. This story references what would have been a well-known tale about Grant at the time. Even though most Mormons now would not catch the allusion, the story remains popular. Madsen, *The Lord Needed a Prophet*, 109; for more on this particular story see Wilson, "The Paradox of Mormon Folklore," 54–55.

9. Student, female, Provo, Utah, 2000.

10. Student, female, Logan, Utah, 1960, collected by Sherry Harger in 1960 (WAWFA: FA5, 4.11.2.1.12).

11. Film production employee, male, Orem, Utah, 1978, collected by Marguerite Sadler in 1978 (WAWFA: FA1, project 621).

12. Kent S. Larsen II to author, e-mail, Sept. 24, 1997.

13. Student, male, Richfield, Idaho, 1998, collected by Rebecca Kent in 1998 (WAWFA: FA1, project 1642).

14. What the "manifesto on swearing" might mean is unclear, but the story does make clear that its teller believed Kimball lived during a period when the church stepped up efforts to curtail swearing among its members.

15. The punch line could be interpreted in several ways. One is that the overlap in terminology used in theological discourse and swearing at livestock ("damn," "damnation," "hell," "hellfire," etc.) allowed oxen owned by the church, and presumably exposed to theological language, to understand Uncle Golden. A more likely

explanation is that the oxen, like many church members, were reared in a time when the church did not proscribe cussing as vigorously and perhaps remembered a day when it was common for church members to cuss. Other interpretations may be lost to time. The story is not commonly told anymore, perhaps due to the opacity of the punch line to today's Mormon audiences.

16. Educator, Springville, Utah, 2003.

17. Film production employee, male, Orem, Utah, 1978, collected by Marguerite Sadler in 1978 (WAWFA: FA1, project 621).

18. Male, Ogden, Utah, 1946, told by Nathan A. Tanner, Fife Mormon Collection, 1: 397.

19. Professor, male, Provo, Utah, 1998. This story, part of *Fritz Wetherbee's Speak N'Hampsha Like a Native*, is not unique to the J. Golden cycle. Perhaps reflecting the shared ancestry of many New Englanders and Utah Mormons, this story has a New England as well as a Utah version.

> Every March in the towns of New Hampshire, the citizens get together for a town meeting. This is where the town decides what it will do with its tax money. Every citizen in the town may attend and may be heard on any subject. A few years ago in Sawyer, New Hampshire, there was on the town warrant an article to raise the sum of five hundred dollars to repair the bridge over the North Fork River.
>
> The moderator that year was Dexter Peckum, and he was running a pretty good meeting up until this article came up. Seems the bridge had been there for over a hundred years and it only served a few families—saved them a few minutes getting to the general store over in West Mylan. Most of the citizens didn't like the idea of spending town money to increase the prosperity of the next door town whose high school baseball team had beaten them soundly the year before.
>
> Mooney Bittle was the most incensed. He got carrying on about how the town had only two hundred people and "that would mean more than two and a half dollars a piece just for a damned bridge," he said. "Now we won't have that kind of talk in my public meeting," said moderator Peckum. And he banged the gavel. "Besides," says Monney, "the damned river is only a few feet wide there. Bygeez, I could pee half way across it," he says. "You're out of order," said the moderator Peckum. "Damn right I am," says Mooney. "If I was in order, I could pee all the way across it."

20. LDS missionary, male, Northwestern States Mission, 1959, collected by Valerie Webster in 1959 (WAWFA: FA5, 4.11.2.23.1).

21. Student, female, Boise, Idaho, 1964, collected by Nelda Wayment in 1964 (WAWFA: FA5, 4.11.2.30.1).

22. Bruce R. McConkie was a well-known, doctrinally minded apostle in the late twentieth century.

23. Computer programmer, male, St. Paul, Minn., 1999; David Adams to author, e-mail, Jan. 14, 1999.

24. Male, Provo, Utah, 1946, told by B. F. Cummings, Fife Mormon Collection, 1: 526.

25. Professor, male, Springville, Utah, 1998.

26. Student, male, Logan, Utah, 19— (specific year not listed), collected by Thomas K. Brown in 19— (WAWFA: FA5, 4.11.2.7.3). To Latter-day Saints, the prophet of the church is by definition inspired and inspiring. The humor of this story comes from Kimball's inadvertant suggestion that this is not the case. The presence of surveillance, recording, and broadcasting makes him nervous, not President Grant himself.

27. Attorney, male, Los Angeles, Calif., 2000; anonymous e-mail collection to author from (presumably) an attorney, Sept. 12, 2001.

28. Chemist, male, Salt Lake City, Utah, 2000.

CHAPTER 6: MINISTERING

1. Richards, *J. Golden Kimball*, 102.

2. Kent Larsen II to author, e-mail, Jan. 3, 1999. Mormons are Sabbatarians whose leaders have always encouraged church members to refrain from sports on Sunday.

3. Male, Chico, Calif., 1950, told by Hector Lee, Fife Mormon Collection, 1: 943, Fife Folklore Archive, Utah State University, Logan.

4. Plumbing contractor, male, Mesa, Ariz., 1997; David E. Smith, conversation with author, Mesa, Ariz., Dec. 29, 1997. The humor comes from J. Golden's attempts to console the bishop by minimizing his problem in absolute terms. Of course in relative terms the bishop still has a big problem. This story is not unique to the J. Golden cycle. Perhaps reflecting the shared ancestry of many New Englanders and Utah Mormons, it has a New England as well as a Utah version: "Seems some years ago, Webster Powers met Foster Kidder in a store over in Lemster. 'Webster,' says Foster, 'I understand you're going to marry Fern Prichard.' 'Ya, that's true,' says Webster. 'But Webster,' says Foster, 'Fern Prichard has been to bed with every man in this town.' 'Well, I know that,' says Webster, 'but this is a very small town'" (*Fritz Wetherbee's Speak N'Hampsha Like a Native*).

5. There are at least three dimensions of humor in this story. One comes from the ambiguity between the nonliteral meaning of "looking all over hell" as a figure of speech and its possible literal interpretation in this context. Another is that the hearer might expect Kimball to reject the woman's petition on the theological grounds that you can't take material things to the spiritual world but be surprised by his answer that assumes a down-to-earth afterlife where one can exchange letters. Possibly, his rebuff is the result of taking offense at her assumption that he is near death. Whatever his motivation, another appropriate incongruity comes from using well-known General Authority busy-ness as an excuse for not helping a lay member. To Mormon listeners, the woman's request violates a well-known taboo against bothering General Authorities with personal matters. Yet Kimball's response also violates another well-known taboo against abrupt directness in general and General Authority ungraciousness and impatience in particular.

6. Kent S. Larsen II to author, e-mail, Oct. 16, 1997.

7. Kent S. Larsen II to author, e-mail, July 29, 1998. This story can certainly be appreciated by anyone who believes in an afterlife. For Latter-day Saints, the story may take on added significance considering two of Joseph Smith's most repeated teachings: "That same sociality which exists among us here will exist among us there, only it will be coupled with eternal glory" (Doctrine and Covenants 130: 2) and, "Whatever principle of intelligence we attain unto in this life, it will rise with us in the resurrection" (130: 18). Latter-day Saints have understood these teachings to mean that people who did not get along before death will not have their relationship miraculously transformed in the afterlife.

8. Plumbing contractor, male, Mesa, Ariz., 1998; David E. Smith, conversation with author, Mesa, Ariz., Dec. 29, 1998.

9. This sketch of the church's attitudes toward the continuance of plural marriage fits very well with historical evidence. The Church of Jesus Christ of Latter-day Saints by this time had completely reversed its practice of plural marriage and excommunicated members who continued to perform or enter into polygamist marriages. The policy continues to the present. For a history of plural marriage after its discontinuance by the church and an account of church efforts to stop it see Bradley, *Kidnapped from That Land.*

10. Student, male, Logan, Utah, 1964, collected by Russell Bice in 1964. William A. Wilson Folklore Archives, Brigham Young University (hereafter WAWFA): FA5, 4.11.2.33.1

11. The Relief Society is "the women's organization of the Church, which complements the priesthood." The Prophet Joseph Smith organized the Relief Society in 1842. The primary objectives of the Relief Society, the largest women's organization in the world, are compassionate service and strengthening the women and families of the Church." "An Official Internet Site of the Church of Jesus Christ of Latter-day Saints" at http://www.mormon.org/glossary/0,10233,1445–1–R,00.html

12. College graduate, male, Provo, Utah, 1978, collected by Marguerite Sadler in 1978. WAWFA: FA1, project 621.

13. Male, Chico, Calif., 1950, told by Hector Lee, Fife Mormon Collection, 1: 943.

14. Student, male, Logan, Utah, 1980, collected by Darrel Allen in 1980 (WAWFA: FA5, 4.11.2.15.2).

15. From the beginning of Mormon history into the early twentieth century, men were sometimes called on missions far from their homes for several years, leaving one or more wives to fend for themselves and their children. It was a great sacrifice for everyone in the family. Since the latter part of the twentieth century, however, only single people and married couples have been called as missionaries. In Mormon theology, any infidelity outside marriage is seen as a sin second only to murder (Alma 39: 3–5), but to cuckold a man on a mission would be found especially galling.

16. This version of the story is worth special mention because it is not only a J. Golden Kimball story but also an example of another traditional Utah Mormon joking cycle. After Great Britain, Scandinavia was the most fertile mission field for

nineteenth-century missionaries. Thousands of Saints gathered in Utah from Norway, Sweden, and particularly Denmark. Sanpete County in central Utah and the Brigham City area in the north became hubs for settlement. As immigrants tried to acculturate to the dominant language and culture, "Brudder Ole Olsen" and "Biscop Peter Petersen" became stereotypes for the supposed bumpkins and their quaint brutalization of the English language. Jenson, *Sanpete Tales.*

17. Male, Chico, Calif., 1950, told by Hector Lee, Fife Mormon Collection, 1: 943. The meaning of this story's punch line is not clear. There are several possible interpretations, all of which rely on an understanding of Latter-day Saint conceptions of Israel. It is common for Latter-day Saints to refer to the church and its members as "modern Israel" and to consider Mormons a "covenant people." In the past, that conception was underscored by the belief that most Mormons were literal descendants gathered from among the scattered tribes of Israel and that missionary work gleaned those who had true lineage from among the Gentile tares. The idea of Mormons being of literal Israelite lineage is not as prevalent in official discourse and lay discussion as it once was. (On Mormon conceptions of lineage and Israel see Millet and McConkie, *Our Destiny;* for a review of Millet and McConkie's work see Epperson, "Some Problems with Supersessionism in Mormon Thought," 125–36; see also Mauss, *All Abraham's Children.*)

The idea of excommunicating someone for failing to take advantage of the opportunity provided by lying in bed with a woman is ludicrous, but the situation in the story makes joking sense in that make-believe context. The word *seed*, which reveals another dimension of the story, suggests an overlap between worldly and righteous ideals of manhood—being fertile and producing children. A man who produces no results when lying with a woman is lesser by either standard. Ideally, Latter-day Saint men exercise fertility, if they have it, within the bounds of marriage, but it is no sin to be infertile through no fault of one's own. That makes Kimball's desire to excommunicate the man understandable but illogical from a doctrinal point of view. Another version of this story, "Adultery Case: 2," in which the defendant admits to the adultery, more clearly supports this interpretation with the punch line "I vote that we excommunicate him because if he had the true seed of Israel in him it would have been made manifest by now."

18. Plumbing contractor, male, Mesa, Ariz., 1998; David E. Smith, conversation with author, Mesa, Ariz., Dec. 29, 1998.

19. Student, female, Smithfield, Utah, 1982, collected by Jeanne Hill in 1982 (WAWFA: FA 5, 4.11.2.39.1). Where other Christians are more likely to refer to say *heaven*, Mormons often use the term *celestial kingdom*. This refers to the highest level of salvation ("degree of glory") one can attain in the afterlife. The term comes from a vision Joseph Smith had of what are essentially three levels of heaven or degrees of glory: the telestial kingdom, the terrestrial kingdom, and the celestial kingdom (Doctrine and Covenants 76).

20. This storyteller is describing a conflict over roles and authority among various levels of church governance. The stake president has two counselors as well as a twelve-man high council to conduct the ecclesiastical affairs of the stake. In the

contemporary church, each ward will have an elders quorum composed of ordained men who meet for instruction on Sundays. Basically, all devout Mormon men are ordained elders and later high priests. Elders quorums are led by a president and two counselors.

21. Business manager, male, Ogden, Utah, 1980, collected by Steven B. Jacobs in 1980 (WAWFA: FA 5, 4.11.2.45.1). The circumstances described here are very unusual. Such mutinies would be inconceivable to most Mormons. Equally uncommon are draconian threats by those in higher levels of authority. To threaten the most extreme punishment of excommunication like this over the pulpit is unheard of and would astonish witnesses. The unusual problem described here challenges Mormonism's culture of "niceness" and nonconfrontation. Kimball's direct, swift, and effective (but completely out of pattern) resolution of the problem is perhaps the kind of thing people uncomfortable with unresolved conflict would like to see more of. The story is also noteworthy for its unlikeliness and audacity.

22. Pet store clerk, male, Provo, Utah, 2000. It is customary for the person giving the blessing to address the person being blessed and use their full name before proceeding. Part of Mormon lived religion is the practice of giving and receiving blessings by the laying on of hands by an ordained priesthood holder. A blessing may be given for an illness or injury or at the onset of a new church assignment. Blessings, although intimate and spiritual, are somewhat formal and dignified. Such a familiar conversation with the Deity would be unusual.

23. Student, male, Provo, Utah, 2000. As in "Small-town Dispute," this story describes a theoretically possible but highly unusual situation. Unlike "Small-town Dispute," Kimball resolves this dilemma with patience, persistence, and input from the congregation. Asking the congregation to accept a new bishop usually goes off without a hitch, and asking a man who is breaking the Sabbath by plowing on Sunday is highly unusual. The story, however, highlights the belief that God does not always see as mortals do.

24. Male, Los Angeles, Calif., 1947, told by W. Tenney Cannon, Fife Mormon Collection, 1: 636. The United Order was a nineteenth-century Mormon effort at cooperative economics. A story told by Brigham Young in 1855 likewise questions the intentions of some United Order participants: "Some were disposed to do right with their surplus property, and once in a while you would find a man who had a cow which he considered surplus, but generally she was of the class that would kick a person's hat off, or eyes out, or the wolves had eaten off her teats. You would once in a while find a man who had a horse that he considered surplus, but at the same time he had the ringbone, was broken-winded, spavined in both legs, and had the pole evil at one end of the neck and a fistula at the other, and both knees sprung" (taken from a Brigham Young sermon, June 3, 1855, in *Journal of Discourses* 2: 306–7).

25. Film production employee, male, Orem, Utah, 1978, collected by Marguerite Sadler in 1978 (WAWFA: FA1, project 621). There is a story in LDS history similar to this bit of J. Golden Kimball folklore in that people go out of their way to make sure that God's words are fulfilled. Section 118 of the Doctrine and Covenants records a revelation to Joseph Smith on July 8, 1838, in which God directs a group of

missionaries to set off for "over the great waters" from the temple site in Far West, Missouri, on April 26, 1839. In the intervening time, however, the Saints had been run out of Missouri and established themselves in Nauvoo, Illinois. To fulfill the revelation they had to travel hundreds of miles in the wrong direction, away from England, and sneak into Missouri. Although they were threatened by the hostile Missouri state government's Extermination Order against Mormons, the prophecy was fulfilled to the letter. Cook, *The Revelations of the Prophet Joseph Smith*, 231–32. The cynical interpretation of such stories is that they demonstrate that revelation and prophecy are only real insofar that they are self-fulfilling through human action. A faithful interpretation of the accounts is that of course they are fulfilled by human actions; God always uses believers to carry out his righteous purposes on earth. The punch line of "Promise Keepers" suggests that Kimball did not see the forest for the trees. A Mormon would consider Kimball wrong and believe that God was keeping the promise through Kimball's generosity.

26. After the pattern of the biblical patriarchs, especially Jacob's blessing of his sons before his death (Genesis 49), Mormons believe that prophetic patriarchal blessings from biological fathers and appointed church patriarchs are a privilege of their religion. Although a father's blessing may be given at any time, each stake has a patriarch to whom LDS youths (and converts of all ages) go for an officially recorded patriarchal blessing. After the patriarch places his hands on the person's head and pronounces the blessing, the young person will receive a transcribed copy; another copy will be archived in Salt Lake City. The patriarch calls the person by name and pronounces prophetic blessings as directed by the Spirit. Often the blessing will impart advice for righteous living; remark on the personality of the blessed; and provide advice for future career, marriage, and children. All of the future blessings described in the ordinance are predicated upon the faithfulness of the person so blessed and may be lost by disobedience or find their ultimate fulfillment in the next life. Latter-day Saints are encouraged to consult and reflect on their patriarchal blessings, which are regarded as a kind of personal scripture, throughout their lives for encouragement and guidance. Patriarchal blessings also declare a lineage through which the blessed will receive blessings, either by literal descent or by adoption into the House of Israel. For more on the Mormon conception of lineage, note 17.

27. Male, Chico, Calif., 1950, told by Hector Lee, Fife Mormon Collection, 1: 943. The humor of this story can come from at least two incongruities. Declarations of lineage usually identify one of the sons of Jacob—usually Jacob's grandson and adopted son Ephraim—as the ancient line through which blessings will come. That J. Golden Kimball would interpret "you are truly your father's son" to be a declaration of lineage underestimates the power of patriarchal blessings to reveal ancient information and is an over-literal understanding of the character assessment "you are truly your father's son." What most Mormons would glean from this story is that the patriarch meant to convey that J. Golden was a "chip off the old block"—like father, like son. That someone would interpret the statement to resolve questionable parentage in the immediate preceding generation would be preposterous to those familiar with patriarchal blessings and the morals of Kimball's mother.

28. Actor, male, Salt Lake City, 1996, paraphrased from *Remembering Uncle Golden*, produced and edited by Elizabeth Searles.

29. Plumbing contractor, male, Mesa, Ariz., 1997; David E. Smith, conversation with author, Mesa, Ariz., Dec. 29, 1997. This story shows Elder Kimball figuring out a way to demonstrate his trust in the man's worthiness for the calling but at the same time inviting him to explain the cigar.

30. A volunteer sits at a recommend desk in the entrance of every LDS temple, checking the temple recommends of anyone who tries to enter. A recommend is a credit card–sized document signed and dated by the member's bishop and stake president, who vouch for the member's good standing and worthiness. Without an up-to-date recommend, one cannot enter the temple. Latter-day Saints see the ceremonies that go on in the temple as symbolic of one's entrance into heaven, but the idea of an actual recommend desk at the Pearly Gates would be regarded as humorous over-literalism. St. Peter's presence as gatekeeper at the entrance to heaven comes from the common cycle of St. Peter jokes that American Mormons would know well.

31. Meeting attendance and participation is commonly seen as a prime measure of a Mormon's commitment to his or her faith. Among Mormons, one more often hears the term *active Mormon* rather than *devout Mormon* used to describe someone's commitment level.

32. In addition to paying 10 percent of their income as tithing to the church, Mormons are asked to pay the equivalent cost of two meals a month to support the needy. This "fast offering" accompanies a twenty-four-hour fast that is observed on a churchwide basis on the first Sunday of every month. A 10 cent fast offering once in a lifetime would indicate an extremely tightfisted individual.

33. Computer programmer, male, St. Paul, Minnesota, 1998; David Adams to author, e-mail, Dec. 18, 1998. Part of the humor in this joke relies not just in the un-expectedness of a cussword coming out of a church leader's mouth but also the double meaning of the final phrase. "Go to hell" is, of course, a common figure of speech, but in this case it is intended quite literally. A similar punch line is used in much the same way in a different joke in "Obnoxious Traveling Companions" (chapter 7).

34. Kent Larsen II to author, e-mail, Dec. 29, 1998.

35. Plumbing contractor, male, Mesa, Ariz., 1999; David E. Smith, conversation with author, Mesa, Ariz., April 20, 1999.

36. Secretary, female, Provo, Utah, 2000.

37. Student, male, Provo, Utah, 2000. A part of the standard building plan used in constructing Latter-day Saint meeting houses in past decades was a little red light on the podium, put there to inform speakers whether they have gone on too long. The bishop's seat had a control switch with which he could flip on the light as a subtle reminder, or he could flip the switch rapidly to catch the speaker's attention. Apparently, Kimball resisted attempts to shorten his talks.

38. Student, female, Provo, Utah, 2000. This troubling story is particularly rich with references to Mormon understandings. The tormentors are not only being cruel to the woman but also abusing theology to do so. To be eligible for the highest level

of salvation and hence resurrection with the first group to come forth after Christ's coming, Latter-day Saints, both men and women, believe that they must enter into celestial, or eternal, marriage (Doctrine and Covenants 132). As George Q. Cannon has explained the temple marriage ordinance, when couples are sealed they are promised the blessings of the resurrection and eternal life, conditioned upon their faithfulness. "When the servant of God pronounces these words upon those who come to the altar and he seals the wife to the husband, just as sure as God lives, just as sure as the heavens are above our heads and the earth beneath our feet, so sure will those words be fulfilled upon the heads of those upon whom they are pronounced, if they are faithful to the covenants which they make; and they will come forth in the morning of the first resurrection clothed with glory, immortality and eternal lives." Cannon, *Gospel Truth*, 1: 109.

Implicit in "I'll Call for You" are the doctrines of plural marriage and vicarious marriage for the dead, both of which hold out the hope of the highest salvation for those having difficulty finding a spouse. The story demonstrates one way in which a promise made by President Spencer W. Kimball might be fulfilled: "We promise you that insofar as your eternity is concerned, that no soul will be deprived of rich, eternal blessings for anything which that person could not help, that eternity is a long time, and that the Lord never fails in his promises and that every righteous woman will receive eventually all to which she is entitled which she has not forfeited through any fault of her own." Kimball, *The Teachings of Spencer W. Kimball*, 294.

President Joseph Fielding Smith once explained, "You good sisters, who are single and alone, do not fear, do not feel that blessings are going to be withheld from you. You are not under any obligation or necessity of accepting some proposal that comes to you which is distasteful for fear you will come under condemnation. If in your hearts you feel that the gospel is true, and would under proper conditions receive these ordinances and sealing blessings in the temple of the Lord; and that is your faith and your hope and your desire, and that does not come to you now; the Lord will make it up, and you shall be blessed—for no blessing shall be withheld." Smith, *Doctrines of Salvation*, 2: 76. The reference to husbands calling for their wives on the morning of the First Resurrection comes from the popular conception that husbands will call forth their wives on resurrection morning. The apparent tenderness of this story contrasts with "The Singing Bride" (chapter 2) and "Marriage Problems" (chapter 6).

CHAPTER 7: CHASTISING

1. Historian Gerald R. McDermott calls Jonathan Edwards "America's greatest theologian before the Revolution" and "a prominent leader of the revival" (*One Holy and Happy Society*, 4). As Stephen R. Yarbrough and John C. Adams explain, "Throughout the spring of 1735, [Edwards's] entire town was in a religious frenzy. Over three hundred people were converted as Edwards continued to mix humiliation with consolation, God's sovereignty with human dependency" (*Delightful Conviction*, 27). For more information on the popularity of Jonathan Edwards, see Baym, ed., *The Norton Anthology of American Literature*, 174–76.

2. Male, Chico, Calif., 1950, told by Hector Lee, Fife Mormon Collection, 1: 487, Fife Folklore Archives, Utah State University, Logan.

3. Student, male, Provo, Utah, 1990, collected by Kevin Michael Ross in 1990 (William A. Wilson Folklore Archives, Brigham Young University [hereafter WAWFA]: FA5, 4.11.2.42.1).

4. Computer support representative, female, Provo, Utah, 1998; Sharon Boyle to author, e-mail, Nov. 30, 1998.

5. Student, male, Provo, Utah, 1974, collected by Kathy Benhardt in 1974 (WAWFA: FA5, 4.11.2.3.3). To emphasize the holiness of their calling, General Authorities are sometimes referred to as "the Lord's anointed." The term is not used casually and is most often reserved for instances where the sacredness of the office is to be emphasized. Using the appellation is this context is highly incongruous and classic J. Golden Kimball.

6. Male, Los Angeles, Calif., 1947, told by W. Tenny Cannon, Fife Mormon Collection, 1: 637.

7. College graduate, male, Provo, Utah, 1978, collected by Marguerite Sadler in 1978 (WAWFA: FA1, project 621). This seems to be an oral version of one in *Conference Reports*, Oct. 1925, 158. As Kimball recorded it, the story ends, "I thought he would never get through; and when he said Amen, we looked back, and there were four men standing behind us with guns on their shoulders. I said to my companion, 'That is another lesson, from this time on in the South; I shall pray with one eye open.'"

8. Museum curator, male, Provo, Utah, 1974, collected by Steven L. Olsen in 1974 (WAWFA: FA5, 4.11.2.11.1). Latter-day Saints now tithe in cash. In the past, the church was equipped to receive tithing "in kind" and accepted a larger variety of goods and services. In the agricultural economy of turn-of-the-century Utah, tithing was often paid in crops and livestock. Brigham Young once remarked that the tendency among members was sometimes to give up only livestock that was sickly or that misbehaved. "Once in a while," he said, "you would find a man who had a cow which he considered surplus, but generally she was of the class that would kick a person's hat off, or eyes out, or the wolves had eaten off her teats. You would once in a while find a man who had a horse that he considered surplus, but at the same time he had the ringbone, was broken-winded, spavined in both legs, and had the pole evil at one end of the neck and a fistula at the other, and both knees sprung." Arrington, Fox, and May, *Building the City of God*. In light of this story, Kimball's attempt to donate the best of his heard would be considered a particularly honorable sacrifice by members of his community. Apparently, he believed that Satan noticed those efforts as well because he threatens Satan by upping the stakes. Latter-day Saints believe in a literal and personal Satan who attempts to thwart human efforts to do good.

9. Student, female, Provo, Utah, 1966, collected by Joyce Oldroyd in 1966 (WAWFA: FA5, 4.11.2.28.1).

10. College student, male, Provo, Utah, 1998. An old stereotype holds that Mormons have horns. Karl E. Young ("Why Mormons Were Said to Wear Horns")

speculates that because cuckolded men in the Elizabethan era were said to sprout horns, perhaps (in the imaginations of non-Mormons) multiple wives might be unfaithful to their husbands, turn-about being fair play. Young's explanation, however, is perhaps needlessly complex and subtle. Sprouting horns has also been associated with evil designs and lustful ambition, which much of the Gentile world regarded polygamous men as having. The contemporary term *horny* (i.e., amorously aroused) is related to this idea. In the end, the belief among Mormons that Gentiles thought them to have horns may have been even more prevalent than the Gentiles' belief that Mormons actually did. The issue may indicate more about Mormon views of themselves than about an ostensible negative stereotype from outside. For another story relying on this folk belief see "Horned Missionaries" (chapter 10).

11. Cancio Filholar to author, e-mail, Dec. 4, 1998.

12. The Relief Society president is called by her bishop to lead the group in her ward area. "The Official Internet Site of the Church of Jesus Christ of Latter-day Saints" at http://www.lds.org.

13. The first telling of this story of which I am aware occurred on KUED, Utah's public television station, in 1996 on the first airing of Jim Kimball's television special. I have heard it many times since, perhaps as an example of popular media influencing the oral tradition. The story is noteworthy because it is the only one I have come across that uses this particular word. There is no evidence for its usage anywhere else in the cycle. In the 1990s, network television allowed the use of the word on-air for the first time, indicating that it has perhaps lost some of its bite. Whether the J. Golden Kimball story cycle will pick up on that remains to be seen. The word still has bite for many Mormons, and its use would have focused the congregation's attention. When a student at Utah Valley State College told me this version of the story I asked if she used such language at other times. "No way!" she said. "Only when telling J. Golden Kimball stories!" This is a good example of how Kimball functions as a release valve among Mormons.

14. College student, female, Orem, Utah, 2001.

CHAPTER 8: REPENTING

1. Physician, male, Paradise, Calif., 1997. Richard N. Gray Jr. to author, e-mail, Dec. 29, 1997.

2. Senior English major, female, Provo, Utah, 1997.

3. Student, female, Provo, Utah 1976, collected by Kathy L. Collins in 1976 (William A. Wilson Folklore Archives, Brigham Young University [hereafter WAWFA]: FA5, 4.11.2.2.1). A similar story can be found in Mody C. Boatright's "More about 'Hell in Texas'": "General Sherman is credited with saying that if he owned hell and Texas, he would rent out Texas and live in hell. 'That's right,' retorted a Texan, 'every man for his own country'" (134).

4. Student, female, Provo, Utah, 1964, collected by Dawn Brashear in 1964 (WAWFA: FA5, 4.11.2.8.1).

5. Kent S. Larsen II to author, e-mail, Aug. 3, 1998.

CHAPTER 9: REMEMBERING

1. Male, Ogden, Utah, 1946, told by Nathan A. Tanner, Fife Mormon Collection, 1: 401, Fife Folklore Archives, Utah State University, Logan.

2. On Mormon sacramental wine, see chapter 1, note 5.

3. Film production employee, male, Orem, Utah, 1978, collected by Marguerite Sadler in 1978 (William A. Wilson Folklore Archives, Brigham Young University [hereafter WAWFA]: FA1, project 621).

4. Student, female, Vernal, Utah, 1965, collected by Judy Evans in 1965 (WAWFA: FA5, 4.11.2.32.1). Being members of a lay-run church, committed Latter-day Saints often spend many hours a week organizing and participating in church activities. They are also encouraged to gain an education, be active in their communities, and spend time with their families. In addition, Mormons are much more likely to join clubs and organizations such as veterans' groups, volunteer organizations, professional societies, and farm organizations. The mean number of organizations to which adult Mormons belong is 1.03; for the non-LDS it is 0.4. The sample has a .0001 margin of error and is tabulated from the General Social Survey conducted by the National Opinion Research Center at the University of Chicago. The story seems to articulate issues more common among Mormons than among the population as a whole.

5. In Mormon parlance "active" refers to those who live their faith and are not Mormon in name only (chapter 6, note 32).

6. English teacher, female, Spanish Fork, Utah, 1974, collected by Georganna A. Huff in 1974 (WAWFA: FA5, 4.11.2.40.1). B. H. Roberts also enjoyed the ritual of testing new missionaries by playing the part of an anti-Mormon and performed it well. J. Golden may have learned the trick from Elder Roberts, or this story may have substituted J. Golden for the protagonist. Kimball, *Conference Reports*, Oct. 1933, 42–44.

7. Male, Ogden, Utah, 1946, told by Nathan A. Tanner, Fife Mormon Collection, 1: 402.

8. Levi Edgar Young (1874–1963) was a both a Mormon General Authority and a professor of western history at the University of Utah. For more information on Young, see the register of the Levi Edgar Young Collection at the William A. Wilson Folklore Archives, Brigham Young University, compiled by Dennis Rowley and Richard A. Tolman in 1994.

9. Male, Ogden, Utah, 1946, told by Zeke Johnson, Fife Mormon Collection, 1: 425.

10. At the time, this was the name of the Latter-day Saints' Young Men and Women's Organization.

11. Male, Provo, Utah, 1946, told by B. F. Cummings, Fife Mormon Collection, 1: 527.

12. Male, Provo, Utah, 1946, told by B. F. Cummings, Fife Mormon Collection, 1: 578.

13. Male, Providence, Utah, 1972, told by LaVal Morris, Fife Mormon Collection, 1: 985.

14. Film production employee, male, Orem, Utah, 1978, collected by Marguerite Sadler in 1978 (WAWFA: FA1, project 621).

CHAPTER 10: RESEMBLING

1. As of October 7, 2002, the William A. Wilson Folklore Archives at Brigham Young University had cataloged 625 individual Mormon jokes, at least 116 of which were J. Golden Kimball stories. That makes Kimball stories the most popular Mormon humorous story cycle, but they still account for only about 19 percent of all the Mormon jokes and humorous stories collected.

2. For stories about bishops, see William A. Wilson Folklore Archives, Brigham Young University (hereafter WAWFA), FA9, 3.2.3.8.11–3.2.3.8.9.1; see also Wilson, "The Seriousness of Mormon Humor," 6–13.

3. For stories about set-upon missionaries, see WAWFA, FA9, 3.2.3.3.1.1– 3.2.3.3.1.

4. Although BYU has always been a coeducational institution, the Utah college scene began in the 1970s to borrow jokes about female college students; the jokes were emerging from formerly all-male, state-sponsored universities "going coed" as a result of the demands of the women's movement. "Coed jokes" portray a stereotype of an overweight, stupid, gluttonous, and undesirable person. They also articulate anxieties about, and reflect resistance to, gender integration and are often used as expressions of interschool rivalry. BYU coed jokes were once perhaps the best-developed and most enduring of all coed joke cycles. Coed jokes are ripe for psychological interpretation, especially because their popularity on the BYU campus may have exceeded their popularity at other schools. For collected stories about BYU coeds, see WAWFA, FA9, 3.2.3.1.3.1–3.2.3.1.3.1, L. Tom Perry Special Collections; see also Siporin, "For Time and All Eternity."

5. Student, male, Provo, Utah, 2000, collected by Brooke Anglesey in 2000 (WAWFA: FA9, 3.2.2.1.1.37). This story, although sometimes attributed to J. Golden Kimball, seems to fit better with the president of the church as the protagonist and is told more often this way. The other two religious leaders are at the pinnacle of their professions, and the level of holiness associated with walking on water conforms more to Mormons' popular image of the prophet than it does to J. Golden Kimball.

6. Lavell Edwards was Brigham Young University's successful coach for much of the latter half of the twentieth century, Merill Bateman was the university's president from 1996 to 2003, and Mike Leavitt was the governor of Utah from 1992 to 2003.

7. Student, female, West Jordan, Utah, 1997, collected by Amy Ward in 1997 (WAWFA: FA9, 3.2.3.9.10.3). The implication is that only God is worthy to be chauffeured by President Hinckley.

8. Student, male, Provo, Utah, 1987, collected by Eugene Ingram in 1987 (WAWFA: FA9, 3.2.3.8.12.1).

9. Roofer, male, Provo, Utah, 1972, collected by Dina Giles in 1972 (WAWFA: FA9, 3.2.3.8.4.2).

10. Student, male, Sandy, Utah, 2000, collected by Mark Nielson in 2000 (WAWFA: FA1, project 2132).

11. A similar story is often told about a priest and a rabbi. The rabbi in the story, like the Mormon named Heber, must convince the priest that he should not destroy or banish his people. Moreover, like the Mormon named Heber, the rabbi, without talking, discusses the matter with the priest. Of course the irony of the story is that each man interprets the exchange of signs and hand gestures differently. Where the priest claims that "because he answered the questions of the gospel, I am letting the Jews live," the Jew believes that he and the priest exchanged several obscene gestures, lunched, and then parted ways. For more on this joke see Cray, "The Rabbi Trickster," 331–45. Because, as Cray explains, "the story of the discussion between a priest and a rabbi has a worldwide distribution" (342), it is probable that the Mormon Named Heber story has Jewish origins. Certainly, at least, there is similarity between the words *Heber* and *Hebrew*; "Heber" is not the name of any particular character in Mormon folk humor except as he appears in this joke.

12. Student, female, Fresno, Calif., 2001, collected by April Lambert in 2001 (WAWFA: FA9, 3.2.1.1.15.1).

13. Student, female, Hunnington, Ind., 1987, collected by Rita Myers in 1987 (WAWFA: FA9, 3.2.2.1.12.3).

14. Retired professor, male, Provo, Utah, 2002, told by Richard Cracroft, collected by Angie Margetts, Provo, Utah, Dec. 18, 2002.

15. Student, female, Ontario, Ore., 1998, collected by Rebecca Kent (WAWFA: FA1, project 1642). This joke—a riddle, really—references J. Golden Kimball's nephew, church president Spencer W. Kimball, who promoted the motto "do it" long before a shoe company urged consumers to "just do it." Another familiar favorite saying of Spencer W. Kimball, "lengthen your stride and quicken your pace," would also work nicely as a slogan for an athletic shoe company. The riddle was attributed to Spencer W. Kimball's counselor N. Eldon Tanner by playwright James Arrington, who spoke with Tanner while researching his one-man play on J. Golden Kimball.

16. Attorney, male, Atlanta, Ga., 1998; anonymous e-mail collection provided by (presumably) an attorney, Sept. 12, 2001. Cleon Skousen's "Thousand Years" books (*The First Two Thousand Years*, *The Third Thousand Years*, and *The Fourth Thousand Years*) are regarded by many as forceful presentations of speculation as doctrine, and the joke might delight those uncomfortable with Skousen's works. For Lee's role in correlating church materials and doctrine (a change in church policy designed in part to prevent people from presenting speculation as doctrine), see Lee, "The Plan of Coordination Explained," 34–37; and Lee, "Report from the Correlation Committee," 936–41; see also Allen and Leonard, *The Story of the Latter-day Saints*, 593–623.

17. Member of the Presidency of the Seventy, male, Salt Lake City, 1998; see also Marlin K. Jensen, interview with the *Salt Lake Tribune*. On the historical context for this story, see chapter 2, note 24.

18. Health-care executive, male, Kingston, N.Y., 1997; Alan Burgess, to author, e-mail, Nov. 15, 1997. Part of the duty of every devout man in the church is home teaching—a once-a-month visit with a companion to several individuals or families. Ideally, home teachers visit once a month in the person's home and present a pre-

pared gospel message following a set appointment. Because statistics are gathered for each month, however, and it is human nature to be slothful, many Mormons are familiar with pop-in visits at the end of the month by well-meaning but procrastinating home teachers—hence the reference to holidays that fall on the thirty-first day of the month and conflict with what sometimes becomes the last day for home teaching.

19. Professor, male, Provo, Utah, 1995.

20. Kent Larsen II to author, e-mail, Dec. 29, 1998. See chapter 7, note 10 for a discussion of Mormons and horns.

21. Student, male, Taylor, Ariz., 1999, collected by Justin Maner in 1999 (WAWFA: FA9, 3.2.1.1.13.7).

22. Graduate student, female, Seattle, Wash., 1975, collected by Joan Boyce in 1975 (WAWFA FA9, 3.2.1.1.4.5). Jokes like this one appear in many combinations juxtaposing many different religions. In communities with both Catholics and Mormons, such as Salt Lake City, Catholics will tell the same joke, but in their version the prophet calls his flock together to announce a call from the Vatican. Occasionally, people will tell the joke in such a way that the religion not their own comes out on top. For the most part, however, triumphalism trumps self-depreciation in inter-religious joke telling.

CHAPTER 11: REPEATING

1. Richards, *J. Golden Kimball*, 112–32.

2. Bell, *In the Strength of the Lord*, 85–86. Jim Bell has explained that in the story originally told by Elder Faust, President Brown had said, "St. Peter will look at me and look at the rug and tell me to go to hell."

3. Kimball and Kimball, *Spencer W. Kimball*, 183–84.

4. Wirthlin, "Live in Thanksgiving Daily," 3–4.

5. Packer, *Teach Ye Diligently*, 287.

6. Kimball, *Conference Reports*, April 1975, 168.

7. Kimball, *The Teachings of Spencer W. Kimball*, 520.

8. Nibley, *Conference Reports*, Oct. 1924, 97. For another story on the difficulty of paying tithing see "Tithing" (chapter 1).

9. Grant, *Gospel Standards*, 354.

10. Brown, "An Address," 2.

11. Ivins, *Conference Reports*, Oct. 1931, 93.

12. McKay, *Conference Reports*, April 1953, 22. For other versions of this story see "Sustaining Leaders: 1 and 2" (chapter 1). Perhaps it is significant that McKay presents a more smooth and less harsh, but no less trickster-like, ending to this story than the other versions (chapter 1).

13. Lee, *Conference Reports*, April 1963, 84.

14. Richards, *Conference Reports*, April 1969, 20. For a slightly different version of this story see "Tithing" (chapter 1).

15. Kent S. Larsen II to author, e-mail, Aug. 10, 1998.

Bibliography

All citations from the Bible refer to the Authorized (King James) Version. "Doctrine and Covenants" refers to the Doctrine and Covenants of the Church of Jesus Christ of Latter-day Saints. Other books, such as Alma and 2 Nephi, are located in the Book of Mormon.

Aarne, Antti, and Stith Thompson. *The Types of the Folktale: A Classification and Bibliography.* Helsinki: Academia Scientarum Fennica, 1961.

Abrahams, Roger D. *The Man-of-Words in the West Indies.* Baltimore: Johns Hopkins University Press, 1983.

———. "Some Varieties of Heroes in America." *Journal of the Folklore Institute* 3 (1966): 341–62, as quoted in William A. Wilson, "The Paradox of Mormon Folklore." *Brigham Young University Studies* 17 (1976): 40–58.

———, and Alan Dundes. "On Elephantasy and Elephanticide." *Psychoanalytic Review* 56 (1969): 225–41.

Alexander, Thomas G. *Grace and Grandeur: A History of Salt Lake City.* Carlsbad, Calif.: Heritage Media, 2001.

———. *Mormonism in Transition: A History of the Latter-day Saints 1890–1930.* Chicago: University of Illinois Press, 1986.

———. *Utah, the Right Place: The Official Centennial History.* Rev. ed. Salt Lake City: Gibbs Smith, 1996.

Allen, James B., and Glen M. Leonard. *The Story of the Latter-day Saints.* 2d ed. Salt Lake City: Deseret Book Co., 1992.

Allred, David. "J. Golden Kimball Stories (a Report)." Unpublished manuscript in author's possession.

Alter, J. Cecil. *Jim Bridger.* Norman: University of Oklahoma Press, 1962.

Arrington, James. *J. Golden.* Starring Bruce Ackerman and Dalin Christianson. Video by Kevin Mitchell. Videocassette. Orem, Utah: James Arrington Productions, 1992.

———. "On Being Wrongly Accused." In *J. Golden.* Starring Bruce Ackerman. Contributing research compiled by James N. Kimball. Compact disk. Salt Lake City: Covenant Communications, 1997 (originally released 1988).

Arrington, Leonard J. "The Provo Woolen Mills: Utah's First Large Manufacturing Establishment." *Utah Historical Quarterly* 21 (1953): 97–116.

———, Feramorz Y. Fox, and Dean L. May. *Building the City of God: Community and Cooperation among the Mormons.* Salt Lake City: Deseret Book Co., 1976.

Bagley, Will. "No 'Flip' or 'Frick': The Early Utahans Knew How to Cuss a Blue Streak." *Salt Lake Tribune,* Sept. 29, 2002, B2.

Baker, Margaret P. "Humor." In *The Encyclopedia of Mormonism,* edited by Daniel H. Ludlow, 2: 664. 5 vols. New York: Macmillan, 1992.

Basgöz, Ilhan. "More about Politics and Folklore in Turkey." *Journal of American Folklore* 111 (Fall 1998): 413–15.

Basso, Keith H. *Portraits of the Whiteman: Linguistic Play and Cultural Symbols among the Western Apache*. New York: Cambridge University Press, 1979.

Bauman, Richard, ed. *Folklore, Cultural Performances, and Popular Entertainments: A Communications-Centered Handbook*. New York: Oxford University Press, 1992.

———. *Story, Performance, and Event: Contextual Studies of Oral Narrative*. New York: Cambridge University Press, 1986.

Bay, Andrew, and Eric A. Eliason. *Culturegram 2000: Utah*. Orem: MSTAR.NET and Brigham Young University, 2000.

Baym, Nina, ed. *The Norton Anthology of American Literature*. New York: W. W. Norton, 1999.

Bell, Elouise. "When Nice Ain't So Nice." In *Only When I Laugh*. Salt Lake City: Signature Books, 1990.

Bell, James P. *In the Strength of the Lord: The Life and Teachings of James E. Faust*. Salt Lake City: Deseret Book Co., 1999.

Ben-Amos, Dan. "Folktale." In *Folklore, Cultural Performances, and Popular Entertainments: A Communications-Centered Handbook*, edited by Richard Bauman. New York: Oxford University Press, 1992.

Bendix, Regina. *In Search of Authenticity: The Formation of Folklore Studies*. Madison: University of Wisconsin Press, 1997.

Bergson, Henri. *Laughter*, translated by Cloudesley Brereton. New York: Macmillan, 1928.

Berry, George Ricker. *Higher Criticism and the Old Testament*. Hamilton, N.Y.: Republican Press, 1937.

Bitton, Davis. "Brigham Henry Roberts." In *Utah History Encyclopedia* at http://www.media.utah.edu/UHE/r/ROBERTS%2CBRIGHAM.html. Accessed Nov. 22, 2006.

Boatright, Mody C. "More about 'Hell in Texas.'" In *From Hell to Breakfast*. Austin: Texas Folk-Lore Society, 1944.

Boer, Harry R. *The Bible & Higher Criticism*. Grand Rapids, Mich.: William B. Eerdmans, 1981.

Bosco, Joseph A. "China's French Connection." *Washington Post*, July 10, 2001, at http://www.taiwandc.org/wp-2001-10.htm. Accessed March 1, 2006.

Bradley, Martha Sonntag. *Kidnapped from That Land: The Government Raids on the Short Creek Polygamists*. Salt Lake City: University of Utah Press, 1993.

Briggs, Charles L. *Competence in Performance: The Creativity of Tradition in Mexicano Verbal Art*. Philadelphia: University of Pennsylvania Press, 1988.

Bronner, Simon J. *American Folklore Studies: An Intellectual History*. Lawrence: University of Kansas Press, 1986.

Brown, Carolyn S. *The Tall Tale in American Folklore and Literature*. Knoxville: University of Tennessee Press, 1987.

Brown, Hugh B. *The Abundant Life*. Salt Lake City: Bookcraft, 1965.

———. Address given Feb. 20, 1968. In *Eternal Values Night—Ricks College*, 2. Rexburg, Idaho: Ricks College.

Brunvand, Jan Harold. *The Study of American Folklore: An Introduction.* 4th ed. New York: W. W. Norton, 1998.

Bunker, Gary L., and Davis Bitton. *The Mormon Graphic Image, 1834–1914: Cartoons, Caricatures, and Illustrations.* Salt Lake City: University of Utah Press, 1983.

Burnham, John C. *Bad Habits: Drinking, Smoking, Taking Drug, Gambling, Sexual Misbehavior, and Swearing in American History.* New York: New York University Press, 1994.

Burton, Richard F. *The City of the Saints and Across the Rocky Mountains to California.* New York: Alfred A. Knopf, 1963.

Cannon, George Q. *Gospel Truth.* Salt Lake City: Zion's Book Store, 1974.

Carne-Ross, D. S. *Pindar.* New Haven: Yale University Press, 1985.

Cheney, Thomas E. *The Golden Legacy: A Folk History of J. Golden Kimball.* Santa Barbara: Peregrine Smith, 1974.

Conference Reports. Salt Lake City: Church of Jesus Christ of Latter-day Saints, 1880–present.

Conrad, JoAnn. "The Political Face of Folklore: A Call for Debate." *Journal of American Folklore* 111 (Fall 1998): 409–13.

Cook, Lyndon. *The Revelations of the Prophet Joseph Smith.* Provo, Utah: Seventy's Mission Book Store, 1981.

Cray, Ed. "The Rabbi Trickster." *Journal of American Folklore* 77 (1964): 331–45.

Danielson, Larry. "The Dialect Trickster among the Kansas Swedes." *Indiana Folklore* 8 (1975): 39–59.

———. "Religious Folklore." In *Folk Groups and Folklore Genres: An Introduction,* edited by Elliot Oring, 45–70. Logan: Utah State University Press, 1986.

Darnton, Robert. *The Great Cat Massacre and Other Episodes in French Cultural History.* New York: Vintage Books, 1985.

Davies, Christie. *Jokes and Their Relation to Society.* New York: Mouton de Gruyter, 1998.

Dégh, Linda. "Politics Alive in Turkish Folklore." *Journal of American Folklore* 112 (Fall 1998): 527–29.

Deseret News 2003 Church Almanac. Salt Lake City: Deseret News, 2002.

Dorson, Richard M. *American Folklore.* Chicago: University of Chicago Press, 1959.

———. *American Negro Folktales.* Bloomington: Indiana University Press, 1958.

———. *Buying the Wind: Regional Folklore in the United States.* Chicago: University of Chicago Press, 1964.

———. "Davy Crockett and the Heroic Age." *Southern Folklore Quarterly* 6 (1942): 95–102.

———. *Folklore and Fakelore: Essays toward a Discipline of Folk Studies.* Cambridge: Harvard University Press, 1976.

———, ed. *Handbook of American Folklore.* Bloomington: Indiana University Press, 1983.

———. "Maine Master-Narrator." *Southern Folklore Quarterly* 8 (March 1944): 279–85.

———. "The Rise of Native Folk Humor." In *American Folklore,* 39–73. Chicago: University of Chicago Press, 1959.

Downing, Charles. *Tales of the Hodja.* New York: Henry Z. Walck, 1965.

Dundes, Alan. "African Tales among the North American Indians." *Southern Folklore Quarterly* 29 (1965): 207–19.

———. "Metafolklore and Oral Literary Criticism." *The Monist* 50, no. 4 (1966): 505–16.

———. "A Study of Ethnic Slurs: The Jew and the Polack in the United States." *Journal of American Folklore* 84, no. 332 (1971): 186–203.

Eliason, Eric A. "Curious Gentiles and Representational Authority in the City of the Saints." *Religion and American Culture: A Journal of Interpretation* 11 (2001): 155–90.

———. "Jim Bridger." In *American Folklore: An Encyclopedia*, edited by Jan Harold Brunvand, 103. New York: Garland Publishing, 1996.

———. "Joe Hill." In *American Folklore: An Encyclopedia*, edited by Jan Harold Brunvand, 369. New York: Garland Publishing, 1996.

———. "Mormons." In *The Encyclopedia of Civil Rights in America*, edited by Shelley Fisher Fishkin and David Bradley, 612–16. New York: Salem Press, 1997.

———. "Nameways in Latter-day Saint History, Custom, and Folklore." In *Names in Mormon Belief and Practice*, edited by William G. Eggington, Dallin D. Oaks, and Paul Baltes. New York: Edwin Mellen Press, in press.

Epperson, Steven. "Some Problems with Supersessionism in Mormon Thought." Review of *Our Destiny: The Call and Election of the House of Israel* by Robert L. Millet and Joseph Fielding McConkie. *BYU Studies* 34, no. 4 (1994–95): 125–36.

Eyring, Henry. "Religion in a Changing World: Fifteenth Annual Joseph Smith Memorial Sermon." In *Joseph Smith Memorial Sermons at the Logan Institute of Religion: The Annual Joseph Smith Memorial Sermons.* Logan, Utah: Institute of Religion, Church of Jesus Christ of Latter-day Saints Logan, 1966.

Faust, James E. "The Need for Balance in Our Lives." *Ensign* 30 (March 2000): 2–6.

Fife, Austin, and Alta Fife. Fife Mormon Collection 1, Fife Folklore Archives, Utah State University, Logan.

———. *Saints of Sage and Saddle: Folklore among the Mormons.* Bloomington: Indiana University Press, 1956.

Finnegan, Ruth. *Oral Traditions and the Verbal Arts.* New York: Routledge, 1992.

Flexner, Stuart. *Listening to America.* New York: Simon and Schuster, 1982.

Freud, Sigmund. *Jokes and Their Relation to the Unconscious,* translated by James Strachey. 1905. Reprint. New York: W. W. Norton, 1960.

Fritz Wetherbee's Speak N'Hampsha Like a Native: A Short Course in the Language and Them That Speak It Ayuh. Sound cassette. Acworth, N.H.: Fritz Wetherbee Talent and Productions, 2001.

Gardner, John. *J Golden Kimball Stories* at http://home.clara.net/wabei/golden.htm.

Georges, Robert A., and Michael Owens Jones. *Folkloristics: An Introduction.* Bloomington: Indiana University Press, 1995.

Gibbons, Francis M. *Ezra Taft Benson: Statesman, Patriot, Prophet of God.* Salt Lake City: Deseret Book Co., 1996.

Gilmore, David G. *Manhood in the Making: Cultural Concepts of Masculinity.* New Haven: Yale University Press, 1990.

Givens, Terryl L. *By the Hand of Mormon: The American Scripture That Launched a New World Religion.* New York: Oxford University Press, 2002.

———. *The Viper on the Hearth: Mormons, Myths, and the Construction of Heresy.* New York: Oxford University Press, 1997.

Gottlieb, Robert, and Peter Wiley. *America's Saints: The Rise of Mormon Power.* San Diego: Harcourt Brace Javanovich, 1986.

Grant, Heber J. *Gospel Standards.* 7th ed. Salt Lake City: The Improvement Era, 1943.

Green, Rayna. "Folk Is a Four-Letter Word: Dealing with Traditional **** in Fieldwork Analysis and Presentation." In *Handbook of American Folklore,* edited by Richard M. Dorson, 525–32. Bloomington: Indiana University Press, 1983.

Güldiz, Mehemet. *Nasreddin Hodja.* Istanbul: Revak, 1997.

Gundry, Linda Ririe, Jay A. Parry, and Jack M. Lyon. *Best-Loved Humor of the LDS People.* Salt Lake City: Deseret Book Co., 1999.

Hamblin, Jacob, and James A. Little. *Jacob Hamblin: His Life in His Own Words.* 1881. Reprint. New York: Paramount Books, 1995.

Hartley, William G. "The Seventies in the 1880s: Revelations and Reorganizing." *Dialogue: A Journal of Mormon Thought* 16 (Spring 1983): 62–88.

Hilton, Hope A. *"Wild Bill" Hickman and the Mormon Frontier.* Salt Lake City: Signature Books, 1988.

Holland, Jeffrey R. *Of Souls, Symbols, and Sacraments.* Salt Lake City: Deseret Book Co., 2001.

Jackson, Bruce. *Fieldwork.* Urbana: University of Illinois Press, 1987.

Jansen, William Hugh. "The Esoteric-Exoteric Factor in Folklore." *Fabula: Zeitdchrift feur Erzèahlforschung* 2 (1959): 205–11.

Jensen, Marlin K. Interview with *Salt Lake Tribune,* May 3, 1998, A1.

Jenson, Edgar M. *Sanpete Tales: Humorous Folklore from Central Utah.* Salt Lake City: Signature Books, 1999.

Jones, Loyal. *The Preacher Joke Book.* Little Rock: August House, 1989.

Joyner, Charles. *Down by the Riverside: A South Carolina Slave Community.* Urbana: University of Illinois Press, 1984.

Juda, L. *The Wise Old Man: Turkish Tales of Nasreddin Hodja.* Edinburgh: Thomas Nelson and Sons, 1963.

Kenney, Scott G. "Mormons, Genesis and Higher Criticism." *Sunstone* 3 (Nov.–Dec. 1977): 8–12.

Kimball, Edward L., and Andrew E. Kimball Jr. *Spencer W. Kimball: Twelfth President of the Church of Jesus Christ of Latter-day Saints.* Salt Lake City: Bookcraft, 1980.

Kimball, James N. "J. Golden Kimball: Private Life of a Public Figure." *Journal of Mormon History* 24 (Fall 1998): 55–84.

———. "Remembering Uncle Golden." N.p., n.d.

Kimball, Jim. *On the Road with J. Golden Kimball.* Videocassette. Salt Lake City: KUED Television, 1998.

Kimball, Spencer W. *The Miracle of Forgiveness.* Salt Lake City: Bookcraft, 1969.

———. *The Teachings of Spencer W. Kimball*. Salt Lake City: Bookcraft, 1982.

Kimball, Stanley B. *Heber C. Kimball: Mormon Patriarch and Pioneer*. Urbana: University of Illinois Press, 1981.

Kirby, Robert. "LDS Authority's Words Were Not Always Golden." *Salt Lake Tribune*, Dec. 3, 1998, C1.

Kushner, Howard I. *A Cursing Brain? The Histories of Tourette Syndrome*. Cambridge: Harvard University Press, 1999.

Lamb, Stephen E., and Douglas E. Brinley. *Between Husband and Wife: Gospel Perspectives on Marital Intimacy*. Salt Lake City: Covenant Communications, 2000.

Lankford, George E. "Trickster." In *American Folklore: An Encyclopedia*, edited by Jan Harold Brunvand, 716–17. New York: Garland Publishing, 1996.

Larson, Gustive O. "Orrin Porter Rockwell—the Modern Samson." In *Lore of Faith and Folly*, edited by Thomas E. Cheney. Salt Lake City: University of Utah Press, 1971.

Lawless, Elaine. *Holy Women, Wholly Women: Sharing Ministries through Life Stories and Reciprocal Ethnography*. Philadelphia: University of Pennsylvania Press, 1993.

Leach, Maria, and Jerome Fried, eds. *Funk and Wagnall's Standard Dictionary of Folklore, Mythology, and Legend*. 1949. Reprint. New York: HarperSanFrancisco, 1972.

Lee, Harold B. "The Plan of Coordination Explained." *Improvement Era* 65 (Jan. 1962): 34–37.

———. "Report from the Correlation Committee." *Improvement Era* 65 (Dec. 1962): 936–41.

Lee, Hector. *Folk Humor of the Mormon Country as told by Hector Lee*. Sharon, Conn.: Folk-Legacy Records. Vinyl release, 1964; cassette release, 1993.

Lillie, Diane DeFord. "The Utah Dialect Survey." M.A. thesis, Brigham Young University, 1998.

Limerick, Patricia Nelson. *The Legacy of Conquest: The Unbroken Past of the American West*. New York: W. W. Norton, 1987.

Lofgren, Mikal. *Wheat: Humor and Wisdom of J. Golden Kimball*. Salt Lake City: Moth House Publications, 1980.

Long, Eleanor R. "Ballad Singers, Ballad Makers, and Ballad Etiology." *Western Folklore* 32 (Oct. 1973): 225–36.

Ludlow, Daniel H., ed. *Encyclopedia of Mormonism*. Vol. 4 of 5 vols. New York: Macmillan, 1992.

Lundquist, Susanne Evertsen. *The Trickster: A Transformation Archetype*. San Francisco: Mellen Research University Press, 1991.

Madsen, Susan Arrington. *The Lord Needed a Prophet*. Salt Lake City: Deseret Book Co., 1996.

Madsen, Truman G. *Defender of the Faith: The B. H. Roberts Story*. Salt Lake City: Bookcraft, 1980.

Marzolph, Ulrich, and I. Baldauf. "Hodscha Nesreddin." In *Enzyklopädie des Märchens*. Vol. 6, 1127–51. Berlin: De Gruyter, 1990.

Mauss, Armand I. *All Abraham's Children: Changing Mormon Concepts of Race and Lineage*. Urbana: University of Illinois Press, 2003.

May, Dean. "Mormons." In *Harvard Encyclopedia of American Ethnic Groups*, edited by Stephen Thernstrom, 720–31. Cambridge: Harvard University Press, 1980.

———. *Utah: A People's History*. Salt Lake City: University of Utah Press, 1987.

Mayfield, James B. "Electoral Patterns, 1895–1980." In *Atlas of Utah*, edited by Wayne L. Whalquist, 169–77. Provo, Utah: Brigham Young University Press, 1981.

McConkie, Bruce R. "Understanding the Book of Revelation." *Ensign* 5 (Sept. 1975): 85–89.

McDermott, Gerald R. *One Holy and Happy Society: The Public Theology of Jonathan Edwards*. University Park: Pennsylvania State University Press, 1992.

McNamee, Gregory. *Gila: The Life and Death of an American River*. New York: Orion Books, 1994.

Merrill, Milton R. *Reed Smoot: Apostle in Politics*. Logan: Utah State University Press, 1990.

Millet, Robert J., and Joseph Fielding McConkie. *Our Destiny: The Call and Election of the House of Israel*. Salt Lake City: Bookcraft, 1993.

Morgan, Dale. *The State of Deseret*. Logan: Utah State University Press with Utah State Historical Society, 1987.

Mosser, Carl, and Paul Owen. "Mormon Scholarship, Apologetics, and Evangelical Neglect: Losing the Battle and Not Knowing It?" *Trinity Journal* 19 (Fall 1998): 179–205.

Muallimoglu, Nejat. *The Wit and Wisdom of Nasraddin Hodja*. New York: Cynthia Parzych Publishing, 1986.

"The Official Internet Site of the Church of Jesus Christ of Latter-day Saints." The Church of Jesus Christ of Latter-day Saints. http://www.lds.org.

Oring, Elliot, ed. *Folk Groups and Folklore Genres: An Introduction*. Logan: Utah State University Press, 1986.

———. *Jokes and Their Relations*. Lexington: University Press of Kentucky, 1992.

Olrik, Axel. "Epic Laws of Folk Narrative." In *The Study of Folklore*, edited by Alan Dundes, 129–41. Englewood Cliffs: Prentice-Hall, 1965.

Ostling, Richard N. *Mormon America: The Power and the Promise*. San Francisco: HarperSanFrancisco, 1999.

Packer, Boyd K. *The Holy Temple*. Salt Lake City: Bookcraft, 1980.

———. *Teach Ye Diligently*. Salt Lake City: Deseret Book Co., 1975.

Palmer, Susan. "No Sects, Please—We're French." *Montreal Gazette*, Sept. 4, 2001.

Paredes, Américo. *With His Pistol in His Hand: A Border Ballad and Its Hero*. Austin: University of Texas Press, 1958.

Piddington, Ralph. *The Psychology of Laughter: A Study in Social Adaptation*. London: Figurehead, 1933.

Powell, Allan Kent. "J. Golden Kimball." In *Utah History Encyclopedia*, edited by Allan Kent Powell. Salt Lake City: University of Utah Press, 1994.

Primiano, Leonard Norman. "Vernacular Religion and the Search for Method in Religious Folklife." *Western Folklore* 54, no. 1 (1995): 37–56.

Radin, Paul. *The Trickster*. New York: Schocken Books, 1956.

Raglan, Lord. *The Hero: A Study in Tradition, Myth, and Drama*. Westport: Greenwood Press, 1975.

Ramazani, Muhammad. *Six Hundred Mulla Nasreddin Tales* (Silsilah-I Tajdid Chap-I Mutun-I Mashhur-I Farsi). Bethesda: Ibex Publishing, 1997.

Randolf, Vance. *Hot Springs and Hell and Other Folk Jests and Anecdotes from the Ozarks*. Hatboro, Penn.: Folklore Associates, 1965.

Redfield, Robert. *The Little Community: Peasant Society and Culture*. Chicago: University of Chicago Press, 1960.

———. "The Natural History of the Folk Society." *Social Forces* 31 (1953): 224–28.

Remembering Uncle Golden. Produced and edited by Elizabeth Searles. Narrated by H. E. D. Redford. Videocassette. Salt Lake City: KUED Television, 1996.

Reventlow, Henning Graf, and William Farmer, eds. *Biblical Studies and the Shifting of Paradigms, 1850–1914*. Sheffield, Eng.: Sheffield Academic Press, 1995.

Reynolds, Noel B., ed. *Book of Mormon Authorship Revisited: The Evidence for Ancient Origins*. Provo, Utah: Foundation for Ancient Research and Mormon Studies, 1997.

———. "The Coming Forth of the Book of Mormon in the Twentieth Century." *BYU Studies* 38, no. 2 (1999): 6–47.

Richards, Claude. *J. Golden Kimball: The Story of a Unique Personality*. 1934. Reprint. Salt Lake City: Deseret News Press, 1966.

Roberts, B. H. *The Autobiography of B. H. Roberts*. 1933. Reprint. Salt Lake City: Signature Books, 1990.

Rosaldo, Renato. *Culture and Truth: The Remaking of Social Analysis*. Boston: Beacon Press, 1993.

Rose, H. J. "Hero-Cult." In *Oxford Classical Dictionary*, edited by N. G. L. Hammond and H. H. Scullard. 2d ed., 506. New York: Oxford University Press, 1970.

Schoemaker, George. "Made in Heaven: Marriage Confirmation Narratives Among Mormons." *Northwest Folklore* 7 (1989): 38–53.

Shah, Idries. *The Exploits of the Incomparable Mulla Nasrudin: The Subtleties of the Inimitable Mulla Nasrudin*. London: Octogan Press, 1989.

———. *The World of Nasrudin*. London: Octagon Press, 2003.

Shepherd, Gary, and Gordon Shepherd. *Mormon Passage: A Missionary Chronicle*. Urbana: University of Illinois Press, 1998.

Shields, Steven L. *Divergent Paths of the Restoration*. Los Angeles: Restoration Research, 1990.

Siporin, Steve. "For Time and All Eternity: BYU Coed Jokes and the Complexity of Mormon Humor." Unpublished paper, copy in author's possession.

Skousen, Cleon W. *The First Two Thousand Years*. 1953. Reprint. Salt Lake City: Bookcraft, 1973.

———. *The Fourth Thousand Years*. Salt Lake City: Bookcraft, 1966.

———. *The Third Thousand Years*. 1964. Reprint. Salt Lake City: Bookcraft, 1974.

Smith, George Albert. "Tribute to Richard Ballantyne." *The Instructor* (Nov. 1946): 502–6.

Smith, Gibbs M. *Joe Hill*. Salt Lake City: Peregrine Smith, 1984.

Smith, Joseph Fielding. *Doctrines of Salvation*. Salt Lake City: Bookcraft, 1955.

————, ed. *Teachings of the Prophet Joseph Smith*. Salt Lake City: Deseret Book Co., 1979.

Smith, Joseph, Jr. *History of the Church of Jesus Christ of Latter-day Saints*. 7 vols. 1948–50. Reprint. Salt Lake City: Deseret Book Co., 1980.

Smith, Joseph. *Teachings of the Prophet Joseph Smith*. Edited by Joseph Fielding Smith. Salt Lake City: Deseret Book Co., 1979.

Steeples, Douglas, and David O. Whitten. *Democracy in Desperation: The Depression of 1893*. Westport: Greenwood Press, 1998.

Stegner, Wallace. *Mormon Country*. New York: Duell, Sloan, and Pearce, 1942.

Stehl, Jean Sebastian. "Utah and the World Press." Interview by Doug Fabrizio. *Radio West*. KUER Utah Public Radio, Feb 7, 2002.

Stephens, Evan. "A 'Mormon' Boy." In *Aaronic Priesthood Choruses*, compiled by the Presiding Bishopric of the Church of Jesus Christ of Latter-day Saints. 2d ed., 90–91. Salt Lake City: Pioneer Music Press, 1946.

Stocking, George W., Jr. *Victorian Anthropology*. New York: Free Press, 1991.

Swensen, Russel. "Mormons at the University of Chicago Divinity School: A Personal Reminiscence." *Dialogue: Journal of Mormon Thought* 7 (Summer 1972): 37–47.

"Symposium on Obscenity." *Journal of American Folklore* 75, no. 297 (1962): 189–282.

Tatar, Maria. "Born Yesterday: Heroes in the Grimms' Fairy Tales." In *Fairy Tales and Society: Illusion, Allusion, and Paradigm*, edited by Ruth B. Bottingheimer, 95–114. Philadelphia: University of Pennsylvania Press, 1987.

Terry, Jill. "Exploring Belief and Custom: The Study of Mormon Folklore." *Utah Folklife Newsletter* 23 (Winter 1989): 1–4.

Thompson, Stith. *Motif-Index of Folk Literature*. 6 vols. Bloomington: Indiana University Press, 1966.

————. "The Trickster Cycle." In *The Folktale*, 319–28. New York: Holt, Rinehart, and Winston, 1946.

Titon, Jeff Todd. *Powerhouse for God: Speech, Chant, and Song in an Appalachian Baptist Church*. Austin: University of Texas Press, 1988.

Toelken, Barre. *The Dynamics of Folklore*. Logan: Utah State University Press, 1996.

————. "The 'Pretty Languages' of Yellowman: Genre, Mode, and Texture in Navaho Coyote Narratives." In *Folklore Genres*, edited by Dan Ben-Amos, 145–70. Austin: University of Texas Press, 1976.

Vansina, Jan. *Oral Tradition as History*. Madison: University of Wisconsin Press, 1985.

Van Wagoner, Richard S., and Steven C. Walker. *A Book of Mormons*. Salt Lake City: Signature Books, 1982.

Vestal, Stanley. *Jim Bridger, Mountain Man: A Biography*. New York: William Morrow, 1946.

Watts, Jill. *Mae West: An Icon in Black and White*. New York: Oxford University Press, 2000.

Welsch, Roger L. "Enter Laughing." *Natural History* 105 (July 1996): 64–65.

White, Richard. *"It's Your Misfortune and None of My Own": A New History of the American West*, 236–97. Norman: University of Oklahoma Press, 1991.

William A. Wilson Folklore Archive (WAWFA). L. Tom Perry Special Collections, Harold B. Lee Library, Brigham Young University, Provo, Utah.

Wilson, William A. "A Bibliography of Studies in Mormon Folklore." *Utah Historical Quarterly* 44 (1976): 389–94.

———. "Folklore a Mirror for What? Reflections of a Mormon Folklorist." *Western Folklore* 54 (1995): 13–21.

———. "Folklore." In *Encyclopedia of Mormonism*, edited by Daniel H. Ludlow, 4: 1477–78. 5 vols. New York: Macmillan, 1992.

———. "Mormon Folklore." In *Mormon Americana: A Guide to Sources and Collections in the United States*, edited by David Whittaker, 437–54. Provo, Utah: BYU Studies, 1995.

———. "Mormon Folklore: Cut from the Marrow of Everyday Experience." *BYU Studies* 3 (1993): 521–40.

———. "Mormon Folklore—Faith or Folly?" *Brigham Young Magazine* 49 (May 1995): 47–54.

———. "The Paradox of Mormon Folklore." In *Essays on the American West, 1974–1975*, series 6, Charles Redd Monographs in Western History, edited by Thomas G. Alexander, 127–47. Provo, Utah: Brigham Young University Press, 1976. Reprint. *Brigham Young University Studies* 17, no. 1 (1976): 40–58; and *Idaho Folklife: Homesteads to Headstones*, edited by Louie W. Attebery, 58–67. Salt Lake City: Univeristy of Utah Press, 1985.

———. "Personal Narratives: The Family Novel." *Western Folklore* 50 (April 1991): 127–49.

———. "A Sense of Place of a Sense of Self." *Southern Folklore* 57, no. 1 (2000): 3–11.

———. "The Seriousness of Mormon Humor." *Sunstone* 10 (Jan. 1985): 6–13.

———. "The Study of Mormon Folklore: An Uncertain Mirror for Truth." *Dialogue: A Journal of Mormon Thought* 22 (Winter 1989): 95–110.

———. "Trickster Tales and the Location of Cultural Boundaries: A Mormon Example." *Journal of Folklore Research* 20 (May 1983): 55–66.

Wirthlin, Joseph B. "Live in Thanksgiving Daily." In *Brigham Young University 2000–2001 Speeches*, 115–22. Provo, Utah: Brigham Young University Publications and Graphics, 2001.

Wixom, Hartt. *Hamblin: A Modern Look at the Frontier Life and Legend of Jacob Hamblin*. Springville, Utah: Cedar Fort Books, 1996.

Wolfenstein, Martha. *Children's Humor: A Psychological Analysis*. Glencoe, Ill.: Free Press, 1954.

Yarbrough, Stephen R., and John C. Adams. *Delightful Conviction: Jonathan Edwards and the Rhetoric of Conversion*. Westport: Greenwood Press, 1993.

Young, Karl E. "Why Mormons Were Said to Wear Horns." In *Lore of Faith and Folly*, edited by Thomas E. Cheney with Austin E. Fife and Juanita Brooks, 111–12. Salt Lake City: University of Utah Press, 1974.

Zall, P. M., ed. *Abe Lincoln Laughing*. Berkley: University of California Press, 1982.

Zumwalt, Rosemary Lévy. *American Folklore Scholarship: A Dialogue of Dissent.* Bloomington: Indiana University Press, 1988.

Zwerling, Israel. "The Favorite Joke in Diagnostic and Therapeutic Interviewing." *Psychoanalytic Quarterly* 24 (1955): 104–14.

Index

ERIC A. ELIASON is an associate
professor of English
at Brigham Young University.

The University of Illinois Press
is a founding member of the
Association of American University Presses.

_____

University of Illinois Press
1325 South Oak Street
Champaign, IL 61820-6903
www.press.uillinois.edu